Cultural Residues

Cultural Studies of the Americas

GEORGE YÚDICE, JEAN FRANCO, AND JUAN FLORES, SERIES EDITORS

Cultural Residues
Chile in Transition

NELLY RICHARD

Translated by Alan West-Durán
and Theodore Quester

Foreword by Jean Franco

University of Minnesota Press
Minneapolis • London

Published by the University of Minnesota Press
111 Third Avenue South, Suite 290
Minneapolis, MN 55401-2520
http://www.upress.umn.edu

Library of Congress Cataloging-in-Publication Data

Richard, Nelly.
  [Residuos y metáforas. English]
  Cultural residues : Chile in transition / Nelly Richard ;
translated by Alan West-Durán and Theodore Quester ; foreword by Jean
Franco.
     p. cm.—(Cultural studies of the Americas ; v. 18)
  Includes bibliographical references.
  ISBN 0-8166-3641-9 (hc : alk. paper)—ISBN 0-8166-3642-7 (pb : alk.
paper)
    1. Chile—Intellectual life—20th century. 2. Chile—
History—1988– I. Title. II. Series.
F3100.R52313 2004
983.06′4—DC22

2004012753

Printed in the United States of America on acid-free paper

The University of Minnesota is an equal-opportunity educator and employer.

12 11 10 09 08 07 06 05 04   10 9 8 7 6 5 4 3 2 1

Contents

Foreword

JEAN FRANCO

Nelly Richard is a critic and the founder-editor of the *Revista de Crítica Cultural*, a journal that, for more than a decade, has fostered incisive critical thinking. A Chilean citizen who was born in France and educated at the Sorbonne, she became well known for her judicious assessments of the art auctions that took place during the repressive government of Pinochet, a government that profoundly altered Chile's political and cultural climate. Writing and researching usually without institutional support, she has since published a series of books, *La insubordinación de los signos* (1994), *Masculine/femenino* (1993), and *Residuos y metáforas* (1998), and many articles that monitor and comment on the postdictatorship cultural scene.

Nineteen seventy-three, the year that Salvador Allende was ousted by a military coup, marked a watershed in a country that up to that date was a functioning democracy with a strong trade union movement and an equally strong tradition of left activism. The military, under the leadership of General Pinochet, not only overthrew a democratically elected government but brutally crushed and terrorized former Allende supporters. The military justified the seizure of power on the grounds that the coup had rescued the country from chaos; once secured in power, it restructured the economy according to neoliberal principles, guided and encouraged by the U.S.-based economists known as "the Chicago boys." The Pinochet government was not so much overthrown as replaced in 1982 by a transitional government that took over its economic policies while restoring electoral government. The present government, like that of Blair's Britain, is nominally social democratic, but the restructuring of the economy on

neoliberal principles has made the market the arbiter of value and promoted a business class that is impatient of reminders of the past and
guided by pragmatism. Nowadays, Chile is often held up in the United
States as the exemplary Latin American country, thanks to the privatization of the social security system and its successful negotiation of trade
agreements unimpeded by the Left that was decimated under the military
regime. Fear of a return of the military has persuaded many people to
forgo harsher questions and to acquiesce to a national accord.

Richard charges that the postdictatorship governments have secured
a consensus by "neutralizing different counterpoints, antagonistic and
polemical stances . . . by means of an institutional pluralism that forced
diversity to become noncontradictory." At the same time, the fact that
Pinochet received a triumphant welcome from his many supporters when
he returned to Chile after his house arrest in London on charges of crimes
against humanity revealed the deep divisions within the nation. Those
divisions, the scars of past violence, and the channeling of desires into safe
outlets are the focus of much of Richard's cultural criticism, which also
monitors the violence of modernization that has altered language, affected
all manner of representation, and profoundly changed the way people live
their lives.

The dampening down of controversy and hence of real differences is, of
course, a general problem of our time. Although the United States has
been spared the drastic experience of a dictatorship that worked through
overt threats and visible symbols of repression—the army uniform, the
gun-toting military—and terrified the population with the deadly message of disappearance, the situation after 9/11, when patriotism became
the binding force that overcoded older antagonisms and differences, has
created a somewhat similar consensus effect to that of Chile. Thus, though
firmly grounded in Chilean reality, Richard's analysis has more than a
little relevance to our own situation.

What happened to the remnants of the militant and the democratic
Left in the postdictatorship? Returning from exile or emerging from clandestinity, they found themselves in a different world. Older systems of
meaning were eroded, and old loyalties and principles had become irrele-
vant. In a striking passage, Richard talks of "subjects without scripts"
whose roles now seem incoherent, yet who search "for something believable, since the codes of honor and morality have failed." The traditional
Left, especially those who belonged to the Chilean Communist Party, a
genuinely popular party with a long and respected tradition of political

participation, faced a dual crisis as survivors both of repression and of
the collapse of the Soviet Union. It is not surprising that many withdrew
into silence or inaction, "neither recognizing a version of a past of heroic
resistance nor a present of Madison Avenue confetti." Those whose relatives were among the disappeared would find their efforts to discover their
fate frustrated while demands for accountability were lost in the babble of
the marketplace. The bland, unexceptional narrative of redemocratization
disallows what Richard refers to as "the torments of memory, violence,
and injustice." Worse, as she shows in her discussion of the recorded testimony of a homeless schizophrenic taped by the writer Diamela Eltit,
what has occurred in the past decades is a veritable "debacle of sense," so
that the dislocated and fragmented speech of the schizophrenic is symp-
tomatic of a whole society. In this depoliticized society governed by market values, "what language can be counted on, what tongue can we trust?"
Richard asks.

But language is only one symptom of the dislocations of modernization. The military government transformed the old republican city,
building showcase shopping malls and overseeing the expansion of television into the poorest homes. Rapid induction into the technological age
contributed to the interment of a past that many did not want to revisit.
Not surprisingly, Richard is deeply concerned with the production of
amnesia; in the chapter titled "Torments and Obscenities," she offers
some notorious examples of the way both print and visual media tamper
with the past and recycle events. One of these "obscenities" is the published "confessions" of women who, after being tortured, crossed over to
the side of the dictatorship and became agents of the secret police. Despite
their sensational material, the books and confessional video published
after redemocratization aroused no public debate. The sensational stories
of capture, betrayal, and reconciliation are subsumed into a metanarrative
of redemption in which the sinner is welcomed back into the nuclear
family, into the family of the nation and into that of the church. Perhaps
what is most striking about these confessions is their valorization of adapt-
ability over loyalty, which, in turn, is absorbed into a metanarrative of
conversion and salvation. Richard underscores the apparently odd combination of religious fundamentalism with the flexible subjects of postmodernism that is also reflected in other contemporary Latin American
societies, not to mention the United States, where family values and faith-
based organizations coexist with the free-floating slogan that "you can be
all you want to be."

In Chile a strong Catholic lobby, empowered, as Richard points out, by the influence garnered by the church because of its defense of human rights during the dictatorship, has successfully blocked the rights of women to choose and upheld traditional values, at a time when advertising and the market economy are modifying those values. The church strongly resists the liberalization of morals that the market encourages, so that, in the words of another Chilean critic, Kemy Oyarzún, market fundamentalism exists side by side with a fundamentalism of moral values. The incompatibility of these bedfellows goes largely unnoticed by most writers on postmodernism and globalization. But in Chile, as Richard points out, it became an issue in 1995 just before the Beijing conference on women when the Chilean Senate actually debated the use of the term "gender" in a ministerial report. Some of the senators condemned the term as a foreign import alien to Chilean customs, thus closing off any further discussion.

Even more of an obscenity was the televised reporting of the illness of General Contreras, who, after being condemned for his role in the state terror of the Pinochet regime, was declared too sick to be imprisoned. The television public were treated to an inside look at the x-ray examination and the screening of the general's supine body, which took on the aspect of a torture victim at a time when the families of the tortured and disappeared were trying to put an end to the impunity of the torturers. The guilty general assumed the posture of the tortured, blurring the distinction between himself and his victims. Yet because of a number of factors— the rapid turnover of the marketplace in the case of the confessions of the women traitors—and because of the "live" reporting of television (its truth), Richard underscores that what should be regarded as obscene, as offensive, is neither really "seen" by the majority nor properly understood.

Richard has a sharp eye when it comes to visual culture. In "The Congealment of the Pose and Urban Velocities," she contrasts the contemporary scene in the Plaza Italia in Santiago with some carefully posed photographs originally taken by a street photographer in the Plaza Italia in the 1970s and collected by the artist Eugenio Dittborn. The old photographs respected "the vertical and the central, hierarchies and symmetries," while the contemporary scene is one of "compulsive flows of speed and spatial displacement" that "thrust popular bodies into a city dominated by the erasure of useful memories (formerly accumulated in corners and localities), thanks to the hysterical multiplication of signs and imported logos that encrust their metropolitan look onto the daily life of peripheral bodies, that are called on every month to remember their local debt to globalized capital because of their debt to the shopping mall." The old photographs recall the leisurely customs of the Sunday stroll and the day of rest from work when the working-class girls had themselves photographed in front of the monuments, waging without knowing it "a battle of the individual against the standardized format of the collective" (that is, their unique features caught in the standardized pose). Far from being nostalgic, Richard is looking for what is missing in the picture. And what is missing, perhaps, is true democracy, which is present neither in the class-based society of the 1970s nor in the speeded-up modern city where people are shackled to the global economy.

In the present regime of representation, what might formerly have been considered propaganda (in Spanish, "propaganda" translates both the sense of the word in English and advertisement) becomes transparent, as if there were no hidden agenda. Richard's compelling example is the iceberg that was towed to Spain in 1992 and put on display at the World's Fair as the symbol of the new postdictatorship Chile. As she points out, the whiteness, purity, and transparency of this glittering trophy underscored the need of the organizers to distance and differentiate Chileans from the "dark" Latin Americans, whom Spaniards disrespectfully term *sudacas*, and to foreground a transparency that in current political jargon separates the good nations of globalization from the bad or the imperfect.

Given these examples, Richard's cultural criticism might seem reminiscent of the ideological critiques of the 1970s except for her attention to what she calls the "residual zones"—"deposits and symbolic and cultural sedimentations of torn significations that tended to be omitted or set aside by social reason." This resembles Judith Butler's notion of "cultural intelligibility," which refers to the often overlooked armature of the status quo—the organization of everyday life, the unquestioned rules of behavior as well as the formal requirements of institutions such as the academy, the press, and the media. Like Butler, Richard privileges whatever—politically, culturally, or aesthetically—upsets and dislocates the frame. Hence the broad scope of a criticism that embraces art, photography, literary texts, fashion, everyday life, transvestism, and knowledge outside the academy. Hers is not a superstructure/infrastructure argument; rather, politics, culture, and aesthetics each constitute signifying systems that may converge, interact, or rub against one another. Her approach is best understood in her discussion of different instances in which routinization and habits, instilled in all kinds of ways—the disposition of urban space, visual overkill,

academic institutions, and language—are opened up to questioning and
interrogation, to suspicion of all that is too neatly sewn together. Crucial
to her argument are the spatial structures that contain both common sense
as well as academic discourses and urban arrangements subtly dictated by
the disposition of margins and divisions and transgressed by the oblique,
the lateral, the tear and cut. Although she shares many of these concept
metaphors with much poststructuralist writing (for instance, that of Gilles
Deleuze and Félix Guattari), Richard's focus is on the "unofficial fragments," "the slight gaps," and the "falling apart of sense" that occur on the
"periphery." And while she uses terms—First and Third World, center and
periphery—that were introduced by social scientists in the 1950s and
1960s, they are often (though not entirely) used in a cultural rather than a
sociological or economic sense. Thus, in a discussion of secondhand clothing, the "secondhand" becomes a concept metaphor for the hybridization
that characterized Third World culture. Secondhand clothing, first sold
among the poorer sectors of the Chilean population and then adopted
by the middle and upper classes, gave people the opportunity to mix and
create their own styles. As a "corpus of citations," secondhand clothing
can also be read as a metaphor for a peripheral identity fashioned out of
disconnected languages. Poor transvestites would recognize the satirical
potential of secondhand clothing, which they used to exaggerate the disparity between the peripheral copy and the metropolitan original. Recognizing the possibilities of the metaphor, a group known as the Art Action
Collective organized an installation called *American Residues* (1983), which
brought together used clothing from the United States with the tape-
recorded sounds of an operation on the brain of an indigenous person. In
Richard's view, the installation not only underscored an economic im-
balance between First and Third Worlds but could be understood as a
commentary on the "secondhand" that had long defined Latin America's
cultural relationship with the metropolis, which the art installation both
satirized and made explicit.

Richard cites myriad seepages of dissent and disparity, whether in street
life, fashion, or events that capture the imagination and throw off meanings far in excess of their obvious political impact. One such event was
the escape from a maximum security prison in 1966 by members of the
Manuel Rodríguez Patriotic Front, which had attempted during the final
years of the dictatorship to ambush General Pinochet. Not only did the
meticulous planning of the successful escape, in which a helicopter touched
down in the prison yard and then took off with high-level prisoners, defy

the efficiency of the prison system, but a series of publications and events connected to the flight caught the imagination of the public and inverted the government's distinction between their own "transparency" and the dark forces that threatened them. Richard draws a parallel between the prison break and the baroque style of the writing, which "escaped from the denotative-referential prison of the univocal message, throwing off the search for linear meaning and objective information through which the intelligence services control information about the progress of the antisubversive war machine." Although the escape involved what would these days be labeled a terrorist group, Richard shifts the focus to the symbolic aspect of the flight, a liberation that also liberates buried utopian sentiments and the uncontrollable flight of metaphor in a highly controlled society.

In the discussions of secondhand clothing and of the prison escape, Richard extends the idea of the aesthetic far beyond high culture. This in turn raises the question of where literature and art stand, given that their role and influence have been eclipsed by the overwhelming domination of pop culture and "lite" literature especially, and that "the new," once claimed by the avant-garde, is now appropriated by the marketplace. In the 1980s, some Chilean writers and artists had still been able to deploy, in a limited way, avant-garde actions in their attempt to awaken a dormant population to the methods of dictatorship, actions that Richard herself documented in *La insubordinación de los signos* (*The Insubordination of Signs* [1994]). With the multiplication of cultural practices and the expansion of the media, neither art nor literature has the dominant role each formerly held as placeholders of national and Latin American identity and as gateways to the globalized community of "civilized" nations. Aesthetics, in Richard's view, is not only the "will to form" but a transgressive energizing not only of art and literature but of many other cultural practices. She offers two striking examples of what she has elsewhere termed a refractory aesthetic. The first is the case of Juan Dávila, an artist who mailed postcard reproductions of the Latin American independence hero Simón Bolívar, portrayed as a prostituted transvestite. Although this was part of a project financed by the Chilean Ministry of Education through the Foundation for the Development of Art and Culture, the postcard caused a diplomatic crisis when Venezuela registered its outrage at the "travesty." It was widely criticized as offensive to "good taste," thus revealing an aesthetic criterion that "contemplates the artistic as a sublime and transcendent expression of the idealization of Beauty." The postcard depicted the

Liberator as racially mixed, with the body of a woman and riding a horse that was part realistic, part abstract, thus directly attacking the patriarchal and illusionist vision of Latin American history, along with its obfuscation of racial difference and its rigid demarcation of gender difference. As Richard also points out, the very parodic techniques that caused a scandal in 1994 won praise in 1996 when Dávila showed his series on a well-known Chilean stereotype, the *roto*, that he presented as feminine, as the *rota*. A possible explanation may well be that while Bolívar has acquired iconic status (in Venezuela, his bust is in every park), the low-class Chilean stereotype is not an ideal type. Thus, conditions of reception and the limits of cultural intelligibility constantly change, so that transgression itself is never fixed.

Richard has unreserved admiration for an unclassifiable book, *Infarto del alma* (*The Heart Attack of the Soul*), which includes a series of photographs of loving couples by Paz Errazuriz taken in the mental asylum of Putuendo, along with commentaries and reflections by the writer Diamela Eltit. The photographs of these doubly marginalized people put them in the center of the frame, "thereby correcting the asymmetries and inequalities that normally victimize these inhabits of third and fourth worlds." The written commentary, a meditation on love and madness, underscores the gratuitous nature of desire outside all accountability and normalcy. In this case, the aesthetic "will for form" enhances hitherto degraded and marginalized subjects.

Although Richard has taught at the private Arcis University, most of her work has been done outside the constraints of the academy, of whose formalism she is sharply critical. During the dictatorship, there was a division between the knowledge authorized by academic institutions and the unauthorized knowledge that took refuge in alternative institutions. At this time, the media and alternative groups of scholars (sometimes funded by foreign organizations) began to focus on popular culture and the media. After the dictatorship, the Internet and the media multiplied sources of knowledge, a development that should have brought about changes in the universities to accommodate new cultural practices. Yet, Richard points out, when the *Annals of the University of Chile* invited a broad discussion of the reorganization of the university, the journal insisted that contributors follow academic guidelines, thus controlling the errant and unorthodox by subjecting them to disciplinary rigor. This failure to examine the norming of constraints is also at the heart of Richard's criticism of cultural studies, which embraced all kinds of knowledges outside the canon but stopped short of disrupting the forms of academic knowledge. Cultural criticism, on the other hand, as Richard defines it, involves not only a reflection on new topics (democracy, feminism, globalization, citizenship, postcolonialism) but also a criticism of the theoretical bases and the enunciatory positions that authorize them.

The essays included in *Cultural Residues* illustrate the importance of cultural practices guided by healthy suspicion and careful reading of the multiplicity of representations that we confront on a daily basis. The value of Richard's critique extends beyond the Chile of the transition to our own realities.

Acknowledgments

Certain parts of this book were published in magazines, journals, and anthologies before their reinsertion and transformation into this new body of work. Chapter 2, "Torments and Obscenities," first appeared as "Lo impúdico de lo público," *Revista de Crítica Cultural* (Santiago) 11 (November 1995). Chapter 3, "Neobaroque Debris: Scabs and Decorations," revisits, transforms, and amplifies the text "Bordes, diseminación, postmodernismo: Una metáfora latinoamericana de fin de siglo" (Borders, dissemination, postmodernism: An end-of-century Latin American metaphor), which I presented at Yale University in April 1994 before its publication in *Las culturas de fin de siglo en América Latina,* compiled by Josefina Ludmer (Rosario: Beatriz Viterbo Editora, 1994). Chapter 5, "Dismantlings of Identity, Perversions of Codes," is a rewrite of "La ropa usada y su estética de segunda mano" (Used clothing and its secondhand aesthetic), *Revista de Crítica Cultural* 9 (November 1994). A first version of chapter 6, "The Academic Citation and Its Others," was published as "El modelo académico del saber universitario y su crítica" (The academic model of knowing and its critique), *Anales de la Universidad de Chile* (Santiago), 6th ser., no. 1 (September 1995). Chapter 7, "Antidiscipline, Transdiscipline, and the Redisciplining of Knowledge," reworks parts of "Intersectando Latinoamérica con el latinoamericanismo" (Intersecting Latin America with Latin Americanism), *Revista Iberoamericana* (Pittsburgh) 180 (July 1997).

Other sections of this book were read as papers at conferences (in the Second Colloquium of Latin American Cultural Studies at the Universidad

Nacional de Colombia, July 1997, and at "New Perspectives from/on Latin America: The Challenge of Cultural Studies" at the University of Pittsburgh in March 1998) or were presented as talks (at Princeton University and the University of California–Berkeley in February 1998). I also worked with material in this book during my seminars at Stanford University (November 1996) and New York University (February 1998).

I am grateful for these invitations because I was able to share stimulating reflections with students, professors, and friends. I appreciate the confidence placed in my work by the people who made my visits possible: Josefina Ludmer, Mary Louise Pratt, Jesús Martín Barbero and Luz Gabriela Arango, Arcadio Díaz-Quiñones, Julio Ramos, Sylvia Molloy, Mabel Moraña, and John Beverley. A special thanks to those "partners in crime" and their conversation across wide geographies: Francine Masiello, Alberto Moreiras, Jean Franco, and George Yúdice.

Here in Chile, the Cultural Critique Seminar at the Universidad Arcis has created a milieu more than propitious for the extensive discussion of topics that are pervasive throughout this book. I express thanks to members of the group in general and to Sergio Villalobos in particular for the quality of their contributions. Finally, I give thanks to those who regularly come across my critical work (including *Revista de Crítica Cultural*), accompanying it with friendship and intellectual dialogue: to Diamela Eltit for the years of closeness and many shared histories, and to Carlos Pérez V. and Willy Thayer for their demanding dialogue on issues of criticism, politics, and writing.

Special thanks to the John Simon Guggenheim Foundation for the grant in 1996 that allowed me to write this book.

Cultural Residues

Introduction

An introduction constitutes the last time one speaks in a text, and also, disturbingly, the first time in which one commences to perceive the distance that separates you from the text.

—SYLVIA MOLLOY

Aesthetics, culture, and politics: these are the lines of force—and desire—through which this book seeks to analyze certain zones of tension and conflict in Chile under the democratic transition process. These zones are more or less residual, pointing to unstable formations of symbolic and cultural deposits and sedimentations, where shredded meanings that for social reasons have been omitted or discarded come together. At times the book deals with discursive fragments judged insubstantial by the strong categorizations of discipline-driven knowledge; with details (forms, styles) considered superfluous and derivative in relation to the central predominance of content and representation; with intermediary formulations that convert what is tenuous and floating into its preferred framework for conceptual exploration; with symbols and metaphors whose referential ambiguities raise suspicions about objective knowledge. The "residual" as a critical hypothesis connotes the way in which the secondary and the nonintegrated are capable of displacing the force of signification toward borders less favored by the scale of social and cultural values, in order to question their discursive hierarchies from lateral positions and hybrid decenterings.

In saying "aesthetic," I speak of the figurative gestures and the expressive markings that distinguish signifying practices. In saying "culture," I mean symbolic figurations in whose theater social practice and its subjects display interpretive variants that open up the real to plural slippages. By saying "politics," I mean the codifications of power, the struggles and antagonisms surrounding the definition of the social, be they violent or contractual. In saying "aesthetics," "culture," and "politics," I am speaking not of isolated series, or separate regions that the ebb and flow of an inclusive reflection could eventually bring together to broaden the framework of readings, but instead of an incessant—and conflictive—play of mutual attractions and refractions between these discursive planes.

The chapters that follow refer to postdictatorial Chile and seek to bring special attention to traces of sense that social science research would discriminate against and overlook, since they do not speak in a language sufficiently clear to warrant systematization within large explanatory frameworks. The text moves between certain references—quite intermittent—to the official traces drawn by the horizon of the Transition (modernization, consensus, market, pluralism, etc.) and to the fragmentary detail of sign constructions that make what is *minor* its reason for being, its manner of speaking. To give value to the theoretical benefits of its furtive details, what is minor and off the track needs that small incision made by cultural analysis on the surface of utterances, which only then permits us to see—obliquely—its underside: the almost hidden textures formed by that which has no precise definition, sure explanation, or stable classification. To look beneath and between the principal codifications, to pursue lateral meanings and sinuosities of sense, allows us to see what has been set aside by the narratives of authority and its hegemonic tales (what has been reduced, devalued, underrepresented by them) to throw into relief the loose and disparate fragments of ongoing experiences: fragments that lack a formal translation in the communicative language that dominates current sociology, and that would remain on the sidelines had certain readings not decided to incorporate the diffuse and precarious into their thought.

In saying "the Chile of the Transition," I designate both the social and cultural landscape of the analysis, as well as the zone of theoretical problems to which any text referring to a current context has to face: how to work with (or on) the Chile of the Transition (and how to renounce that reference if we seek to intervene critically in the discourses of the present) without having to subordinate the voice to its composition, to its symmetries of planes, to its serial orderings? How to pry loose from the obviousness of the (already) present that intends to suture all the intervals of nonidentity (reserve, deferral, malaise) that resist the automatisms of signs of a preassigned reality?

On the one hand—especially if we are speaking of "cultural criticism"—one would have to insist on a lively dialogue with the context and its ongoing productions, with the contingencies of local practices and the social heterogeneity of its sign-forming dynamics that open themselves to the inconclusive formulations of the new. But on the other hand, one would have to extricate oneself from those all-too-common networks of naming and designating, trivialized by the dominant language of the now and the standardized communication of the mass media, sociology, the market, and cultural policy. This dialogue would be a matter, then, of criticizing the design of the present (its logics and rhetorics) by not practicing simple inversions of meaning within its same predrawn map of rationality and arguments but exploring the diagonals that look toward the irregular or unsought-out zones, the disconcerting areas. This implies constructing certain *representational maladjustments* that break the functional equilibrium of predefined categories. But certain verbal disaffiliations are also needed, certain idiomatic ruptures, so that the dissonances of the "how" (strangeness, rarities) can introduce their critical signs of alteration and nonconformity into the routines of speech that live too confidently in the normality of their way of saying things. In this vein, this book tries to highlight the artifices of representation, the figurative mediations that give discursive practice their maximum formal density and all of its expressive resonances. It seems to me that these oblique qualities of language not only intensify the play of signs in a powerfully complex way, with its intriguing zigzag of recurrence to symbols and metaphors. I also think it is necessary to defend the secret of its opacity and refractions against the linguistic tyranny of the simple, of what is direct and transparent, today exercised by social communication that has left language without the mythic and poetic resources that revel in duplicities and ambiguities of sense. Practical reason, direct language, and useful knowledge are nowadays the leading partners in this campaign of transparency (denotative realism, referential explicitness) through which powerful bureaucracies and technocracies of meaning conspire daily to erase any critical-reflexive interval that seeks to complicate communicative transactions with any suspended or dilated mode of interpretation. To defend the artifices of meaning (theatricalities, stagings) not only challenges the supposed poverty and simplicity of language to which the politics of the object fact condemns us, which solely believes in a monoreferential concept of truth. It also opens up reality to a multidimensional and changing play of forms and stratifications of language through which the unfinished, the fluctuating, can slip.

Politics, art, and deconstructions; articulation of signs and figurative montages; rhetorical and institutional mediations; ideological plots; representational folds; semantic cuts and ruptures: all weave a braid of motives and operations that I would like to use inexhaustibly to bind certain fragments of social discourse, of cultural imaginaries and aesthetic symbolizations that float in the Chilean Transition landscape, and from its patchwork of cuttings and pastings make a certain critical look emerge, a look that is not always recognizable by organized academic disciplines.

Part I, "Policies and Politics of Memory, Techniques of Forgetting," starts by evoking the emotional tone of the postdictatorial climate and the difficulties in elaborating languages that can resignify the historical citation of violence (fragments, residues: broken narratives) in a sufficiently allegorical mode so as to break off the sedimented indifference that constructs the mediated erasures of a present heavily engaged in suppressing all the codes of equivalent meanings between what has been damaged and the social networks of memory transference. If "giving an account" of what happened means not betraying the memory of what the present leaves behind as pain and affliction in words that carry no scars (not to subject the memory of the victims to the humiliation of seeing their past narrated in the unscathed language of the triumphant narrative of actuality), then the question about memory is concerned with the nexus between memory, language, and fissures of representation. But memory needs surfaces of inscription to record itself so that the lived relationship between mark, texture, and event can liberate new capabilities of meaning. But where to find these surfaces of inscription if Chile of the Transition has left the broken sequences of histories without narrative; if the ethical rigor of the demand for justice contained in the black-and-white portraits of the detained-disappeared is condemned daily by the barrage of advertising, openly hostile to its drama of meaning?

The tracks of the past today suffer from repeated erasures, and not only political and institutional ones. There are erasures dressed in a televised seductiveness, of commercial pleasure. An end-of-century globalization that moves to the same furtive rhythm of the commodity without having the time or the wherewithal to ask itself about what each novelty leaves in its wake, a globalization that dissipates the value of historicity painfully ciphered in the experience of the dictatorship, making of what we thought unerasable ever more blurred. The endless theoretical agendas that decide the relevance of academic and international topics in end-of-century conferences also contribute to this evaporation of memory. The postdictatorship ended up being one of those "posts" that form the list of prefixes charged with enumerating epochal crises, without letting anything too brusque contained in these prefixes (neither torments nor desperation) disturb the calculations that support the turn-of-the-century syntheses. To insist on the residualness of the dictatorship's traces in order to give them a value-laden thickness is a way of inscribing an enunciative commitment that emphasizes my own critical positionality. I only hope that words like "positionality" and "critical" printed here, whatever their eventual passage through university libraries in the future, can conserve their local trace as an intellectual exercise difficult to translate into standard academic and metropolitan recapitulations whose diagnoses of disasters and catastrophes (for example, "dictatorship") rigorously leave their control of knowledge safe and untouched.

Part II, "The Popular and the Urban: Scenic Fragments" collects materials and significations (leftovers and discards) that the productivist language of social modernization leaves out of the balance sheet of its progress. There are various Latin American leftovers and remnants that find themselves marginalized in the utilitarian tally of capitalist integration and recycling, deprived of a language capable of making the discordant resonate beyond the homogenization of mass culture and production. One of these remnants is the "popular." Thanks to the new orientations in Latin American cultural theory, the popular has broken with a strongly essentialist folkloric version that assimilated it to the autochthonous and to the myth of an unchanging purity of origin, and has launched into the adventure of new hybrid mixings—between the hegemonic and the subaltern, the global and the local, the oral and telecommunications—that now impurely redefine it. But the cultural and theoretical redefinitions of the popular worked on by sociological discourse and mass communications have, above all, privileged consumption as an example of the resemanticizations that illustrate the plasticity of the local with which a peripheral receptor transforms the circulating grammar emitted by dominant messages. I tried to extricate the urban and the popular from the sociological box (which treats them as an object of interest, but not necessarily of attraction) and transfer it to three microscenes where it not only articulates social resignifications but also aesthetic transgressions. The first of these is a testimonial poetics (*El padre mío*, by Diamela Eltit) that records a diseased orality and disseminates its baroque outbursts of madness in a landscape that brings together the street vagrancy of social marginality and the wandering, fugitive names of literature. The second is photographic memory (as collected by Eugenio Dittborn), whose freezing of the pose allows a reading—by way of contrast—of the vertiginous changes experienced in the relationship between body and city under the chaotic and dispersive effect of the new urban symbols of Santiago that would erase any lapse of incongruity between the premodern and the postmodern, susceptible to revealing asynchronies, dissonances, and stuttered speech. The third is used clothes, whose secondhand aesthetic repackages styles that create peripheral identities with the disassembled scraps of international modernity, putting together excentric combinations between use and context thanks to its discontinuity of styles and references. The urban-popular is one of those holdover dialects that the compulsive modernization of the Chilean Transition seeks to make uniform at all costs, so that its heterogeneous encrustations and transplants of stirred-up memories should not spoil the shiny geometry that urbanizes the city in such a way that, between shop windows and neon signs, there is nothing without brilliance or sparkle, nothing that is shamefully dirty, nothing disastrously poor.

Part III, "Academic Borders and Hybrid Knowledges," departs from the images of the Transition to reflect on cultural criticism open to analysis, and on the relations between traditional academic knowledge and the critical production that overflows the borders of university-led specialization, with its irregular trajectories across living contexts. This production has a local antecedent that was articulated around issues of art and literature in Chile during the 1980s: the "Avanzada" scene, removed from any academic formality that involved risky conceptual operations that were meant to reflect an abrupt sundering in communication and the ruptures in memory and identity, along with a dismantling of frameworks of specialized knowledge; a scene that refers us to a work of "cultural criticism" in which disarrayed knowledges and border theorizations shape a reading of practices and their surroundings that intensified transgenre mixings. This part of the book retrieves this antecedent in order to situate cultural criticism within a relationship of dialogue and questioning that pertains to certain transdisciplinary projects (for example, cultural studies) whose intersection of knowledges has begun to stimulate a discussion in some Chilean universities about fields of study and disciplines, rules of specialization and disciplinary paths, academic and political criticism of intellectual work, writing stances and stylistic variations.

If it is true that the abuses of academic-literary deconstruction made it necessary to defetishize the text because it had erased the materiality of social conflict, it seems to me that it is now equally necessary to return to the text (but not self-referentially) to defend critical textuality against the reductionism of the scholarly paper industry and the academic bureaucratization of knowledge. The technical realism of the practical knowledge that dominates research on social communication and cultural sociology increasingly suppresses the value of uncertainty in thinking conceived as a reflective interlacing of subject, language, and knowing, whose wanderings on conceptual shores question, from their own provisional situation, the normalized system of academic criticism.

Three public debates that were widely covered in the press serve as the basis for the fourth part of the book, "Polemics and Transvestisms," in order to revise definite lines of hegemonic articulation drawn by official discourse, and also the confrontation zones between voices that dispute certain margins of critical pluralism made by normative consensus. Beyond the particular cases already mentioned, it is worth noting the media saturation that periodically captures events and situations in the redundancy of the news as one of the strategies designed by the continuous present of the Transition to hide its true lack of substance; to gloss over its empty historical significance with the smoke screen of a feverish hustle and bustle, as if this fake multiplicity of fleetingly newsy signifiers that simulate a hyperactivity of information could cover up the lack of thinking about a present stripped of experiential complexity or density of meaning.

The first public debate in this section surfaced with the modernization theme in relation to "Chile Expo–Seville 1992." Seen retrospectively, the performance of identity enacted in Seville—its advertising extrovertedness—condensed several of the official meanings that mapped out the lines of force of the Transition's "discourse of change." The surface effects (appeal) of the commercial graphics style, whose flattened languages represented Chile in Seville, was perhaps one of the first operations destined to illustrate a denarrativization of memory orchestrated by voiding its historical reference.

The other two politico-cultural debates commented on in this part of the book (the Simón Bolívar case and the Senate polemics concerning the Fourth International Women's Conference in Beijing) refer to two types of critical interventions that destabilize the repertoire of official symbols that are strongly clustered around the defense of sexual morality. The double censure enacted by political officialdom and forces of traditional morality over these gender dissidences that attacked canonical views manifested the contradictions that shake up a neoliberal democracy. This democracy is divided, on the one hand, by the exacerbated rhythms of capitalist globalization, whose promiscuous regime of commercialization dissolves hierarchies of values and transcendent meanings, and, on the other hand, by the moral conservatism of sectors that need to oppose, in the cultural sphere, this dissolving force of the same market that they so dearly uphold economically, seeking a value-based refuge against the mercantile desacralization in a retrograde defense of the purity and integrity of national traditions. In the case of both polemics, what unleashed the conflict was the signifying overload of words and images that did not want to adhere to the repressive hypothesis of a "true" proper identity. In both cases, it was transvestism, with its unstable play of sexual sides of the coin that made the essentialist faith in an original truth waver, sowing confusion in the marrow of these supposedly natural categories defended by conservative morality. In both cases, parodic reconversions and simulations of identity led cross-dressing to emphasize the undressings of representation so that the multiplicity of meaning could dangerously filter through; as well as the paradoxes and ambivalences of double meanings that seek to repress the monological voice of absolute meaning.

The fifth and last part of the book, "Points of Flight and Lines of Escape," deals with two scenes in which the fugitive (through ruptures and imaginary leaps; deviations and overturning of meanings; breakdowns in reason and disarrays of passion) breaks through the grammar of consensual and market uniformity, defying its chains of moderation and resignation. The first scene concerns the news item of an "out of an action movie" rescue (four prisoners from the Manuel Rodríguez Patriotic Front flee from a maximum security prison in December 1996), making a spectacle that was both a high-flying deed and a soaring act of imagination, challenging the seriousness of democratic realism through the disruptive force of the unexpected. Beyond the political and contextual content of the news item, what interests is its poetics of the event: the mode in which this space odyssey generated a symbolic revision of the utopian thanks to the narrative ability of transforming a news item into an unimaginable cinematographic story that introduced the suspense of adventure into our mechanically programmed times, envisioned as a reality without risk or uncertainty. By showing how a symbolic action was able virtually to uncoordinate the rules of the power game (fissuring a subset of the whole controlled by a political logic whose blocks of signs and reasons seemed untransgressable), the narrative of flight suggested, in passing, that there is no normativity of order whose surveillance screen does not offer certain relaxed or distracted zones through which the nomadic expressivity of a desire for nonclosure can be liberated. In the case of the fugitives, they used the tactics of poetic fiction and literary metaphor to throw off their pursuers, enabling them to escape—figuratively speaking—from the sad dungeon of realism.

The second scene that pertains to this last part of the book also speaks of the breaks that undermine the oppressive linearity of sense, only in this case the focus is on love's extravagances. Finally, I linger in a world of love and madness (*El infarto del alma*; [The Heart Attack of the Soul], by D. Eltit and P. Errázuriz), a world that loses itself in the meandering flow of enigmatic concepts and emotions to sketch out risky complicities with the despair of marginal subjectivities, whose profoundly broken psyches furrow with fear and shame the shaping of identities under the Transition. In dealing with lovers of fugitive passions that inhabit the body of inmates who obstinately wait for something that will break the infinity of their enclosure, the semiotic affectivity of *El infarto del alma* is also allied with the imaginary of flight, as it rebels against the confining framework of rigid identifications. The book expresses its disobedience of the norms of the publishing world by exceeding and confusing the typology of the testimonial genre, by expressing a reserve of something "less" and an uncontainable "more" that symbolize fantasies of irreverence found in savage biographies or in a poetics of rebelliousness. The aberrations of signs committed by this work on the borders of subjectivity are faithful to the mental ramblings and sentimental digressions of their protagonists, exiled from the legality of common sense. It shares with them the unconditional aspect of an absolute desire to love, a mad love, the work of art's passion. That insistence on "loving" as something personally untransferable because it is structured by its own laws (to love, yes; for no good reason) is what most radically opposes—as metaphor for a passionate enigma, of a secret carrying out of desire—the indifference of a regime of total economic interchangeability in which the capitalist marketplace makes each sign of value exchangeable for another without anything disturbing making a difference between one sign and another.

The intransitive mark of a desire outside-the-contract that exalts itself in the fascination of desiring ("today my dazzling desire will be art") perhaps represents what is most removed from the pluralism of indifference with which the market and the consensus fabricate passive agreements between signs reconciled by force and uninterested in one another. To disturb this neutral reconciliation of the sum by reintroducing demarcations and antagonisms of sense—thereby activating "the conflict as a moral state of difference" (Barthes)—could be one of the tasks of cultural criticism: a task that would consist of exalting the contradictory plurality of meaning and disordering the planes and surfaces of representation that ideologies intend to keep smooth, without the marks of the interpretive wars that are continuously unleashed around the hierarchies, arbitrariness, and censorship of codes of symbolic and political legitimation.

Cultural criticism—at least as I understand it—would not only try to raise the reader's suspicion against the supposed false innocence of the forms and transparencies of language that hides the self-interested conventions that tacitly bind together value, meaning, and power. Additionally, it would try to excite the critical imagination concerning the fissures between reality and its others that art suggestively maintains open, so that the reader is motivated to break the mold of prefabricated meaning with an unmaking and remaking of a free subjectivity that lets itself be attracted by the categorical unknown and wandering words.

Thus, in saying "aesthetic," I speak of forms and materials that take on all their full expressiveness by working with the ambiguities, indefinition, and paradoxes that maintain sense and identity in suspense, slippery and unfinished. In saying "culture," I speak of the symbolic transfigurations with which social reality theatricalizes its enigmas and conflicts of representation. And in saying "a political gaze," I speak of empowering the minority coefficient of certain deviations or ruptures of signification virtually capable of removing the satisfied smile of complacency through which reality is permanently reconciled with itself, to the point where it erases any malaise, blunders, or unsuitableness from its surface, as if they were suspicious signs from a slippage that eludes conformity. From this complacent position, the stable commonplace of democratic realism formulates its crude schemes of comprehension, its trivial and mean-spirited arrangement of signs; and this to balance the ledgers of the Transition with an economy of the reasonable that must leave out of its utilitarian tallies both the failures and excesses of symbolic imaginaries. Aesthetic dislocation and the political gaze of cultural criticism dwell on these failures and excesses in order to fictionalize around the way that unorthodox pulsations of change are mobilized, thereby taking syntax, representations, and genres to the limits of maximum tumultuousness and oppositionality.

PART ONE

Policies and Politics of Memory, Techniques of Forgetting

In an extreme paradox, thought during the postdictatorship is more suffering than celebratory. Marked by the loss of object, it thinks from a depressed point of view; moreover, it even thinks depression itself. As the dictatorial symbol dilutes its hard edge and encrypts itself in the mere administration of the loss of meaning within the framework of late capitalism, the situation of symbolic loss and libidinal retraction tends to maximally increase. The most extreme possibility is that this libidinal impasse will lead mourning to conditions of radical melancholy. In contemporary postdictatorships, cultural struggle is not so much between opposed ideological meanings, but a struggle for the establishment or reestablishment of the possibility of meaning making.

—ALBERTO MOREIRAS

We live transitionally under the effect of an informational policy (politics) of remembering. Every mark from the past, anything evoked can circulate, can be vociferated in the mass media, can walk around in the street or the university like a body or burnt face, like a psyche flogged and wounded, like a murderer. Anything can circulate, but as information, not as an irreducible life experience, tense, nonfestive, in mourning.

—WILLY THAYER

What "overtook" us was the new scene where an intellectual consciousness withdrew, distanced itself, or became extinct. A consciousness, a reflective subjectivity that could give an account on the scale of politics, values, aesthetics, of that profound breakdown of languages (of ethics and the memory contained in them) that led history to one of its forms of ruin: of forgetting that it had forgotten.

—NICOLÁS CASULLO

CHAPTER ONE

ॐ

Cites/Sites of Violence: Convulsions of Sense and Official Routines

Not to be able to count on history, to recount its passage, or to count on memory—this is exactly our malaise in a democracy. . . . That which has been dislocated and divided is the relationship between politics and sensibility, because a politics of malaise, I think, doesn't exist.

—SERGIO ROJAS

The consensual model of a "democracy of agreements" formulated by the Chilean government of the Transition (1989) marked a passage from politics as antagonism (the dramatization of conflict governed by a mechanism of confrontation under dictatorship) to a politics of transaction (the formula of a pact and its techniques of negotiation). The "democracy of agreements" made consensus its normative guarantee, its operational key, its de-ideologizing ideology, its institutionalized rite, and its discursive trophy.

What overflows did the consensus try to limit, in attempting to force a unanimity of voices and conduct related to the formal and technical rationalization of the agreement? An overflowing of names (the dangerous revolt of words that disseminate their heterodox meanings in order to name what is hidden-repressed outside the official networks of designation); an overflowing of bodies and experiences (the discordant ways in which social subjectivities break the ranks of identity normalized by the political script or the publicity spot with its zigzagging imaginary lines of escape); an overflowing of memories (the tumultuous reinterpretations of the past that maintain the memory of history open to an incessant struggle of readings and meanings).

Memory and Disaffection

The Chilean slogan of recuperation and normalization of a democratic order sought to exorcise the ghost of multiple fissures and dislocations of signs produced during the dictatorship, making the formula of the consensus responsible for neutralizing differentiating counterpoints, antagonistic stances, and polemical demarcations of contrary meanings through an institutional pluralism that obliged diversity to become "noncontradictory."[1] This passive chain of differences is juxtaposed indifferently, one alongside the other, without confronting their values so as not to upset the neutral axis of reconciliation of the totality. Pluralism and consensus were the issues called on to interpret a new social multiplicity whose ebbs and flows of opinion should, supposedly, express the diverse, but whose diversity had to be, at the same time, regulated by certain pacts, understandings, and negotiations that would contain its excesses so as not to revive the collision of ideological forces that divided us in the past.

The paradigm of political normality and legitimacy that the consensus established to control the heterogeneous plurality of the social made it necessary to rein in antagonisms and confrontations, placing limits designed to protect the agreement from everything capable of overflowing the formality of its construction.[2] The consensus excluded from its signed protocol the memory of the dispute between the reasons and passions that had been struggling within the elaborative process of its discursive pact. The Oneness of the consensus made official by the Transition now resists accepting not only that all social objectivity "necessarily presupposes the repression of that which its instantiation excludes"[3] but also that the negative forces of what had been removed and excluded would continue to upset the limits of political normalization in order to impede the trace of official identity from sacrificing the memory of its "others," as well as erasing from its ultimate normative definition the plural trace of struggles for validation and legitimacy between identity, difference, and alterity.

The official consensus of the Transition discarded that private memory of the disagreements (that memory previous to the formalization of the agreement) which would have rendered an account of the polemical and controversial vitality of its internal mechanisms of constitution. But also, and above all, it eliminated historical memory from the sociopolitical consensus, that is, the memory of a past judged inconvenient by the interpretive wars it continues to unleash between truths and unsettled positions in conflict.

Memory is an open process of reinterpretation that unties and reties its knots so that events and understandings can again be undertaken. Memory stirs up the static fact of the past with new unclosed meanings that put its recollections to work, causing both beginnings and endings to rewrite new hypotheses and conjectures and thereby dismantle the explanatory closures of totalities that are too sure of themselves. And it is the laboriousness of that unsatisfied memory that never admits defeat, that perturbs the official burial of that memory seen simply as a fixed deposit of inactive meanings.

"Consensus is the highest stage of forgetting,"[4] says Tomás Moulian, alluding to the whitewashing, which in the Chilean Transition scene began clarifying the contradictions surrounding the historical value of the past and also of the disagreements of a present in which "politics no longer exists as a struggle between alternative visions, as historicity," but as a "history of small variations, adjustments, changes in aspects that don't call into question the global dynamics."[5] Small variations, adjustments, and changes that only proclaim a prereconciled future: a future unburdened of all expectation, freed of the weight of uncertainty, whose merit lies in leaving open the realm of decisions and wagers that surround what is still undetermined, keeping it politically tense and vibrant.

The Transition entrusted the official administrators of the consensus with the task of attenuating all the scars of violence that remained clinging to the shapes of words that named the contentiousness of recollection, in order to euphemistically reduce the gravity of meaning contained in the drama of memory and to ensure that nothing intolerable, nothing insufferable, would spoil the official celebrations of the bearable. The inoffensive names, the banal permissiveness, avail themselves of words drained of emotion or commotion in order to transmit political meaning that has become routine by the monotonous locutions of the media. It seems, then, that the political consensus is only capable of "referring to" memory (evoking it as a topic, processing it as information), but neither of practicing it nor of expressing its torments. "To practice" memory implies making available conceptual and interpretative instruments needed to investigate the symbolic density of the narratives; to "express its torments" supposes relying on figurative language (symbols, metaphors, allegories) sufficiently moving so that they enter into a relationship of solidarity with the emotions unleashed by memory. The consensus that represses that emotional unleashing of memory only names the past with words exempt from the convulsions of sense, so as not to alter the minute and calculated formularization of political and mediated exchanges.

The consensus's official scenario has made memory into a double citation, respectful and almost painless. Tribunals, commissions, and monuments to human rights regularly quote memory (they mention her) but leave aside from their diligent wording all the wounded substance of remembrance: the psychic density, the magnitude of the experience, the emotional wake, the scarring of something unforgettable that resists being submissively molded into the perfunctory forms of judicial procedure or inscription on an institutional plaque.[6] Moreover, the consensus summons us all, regardless; it convenes us and brings us together around the cited memory, inviting us to share the simple value of taking note of something—expurgated of all personal reckoning—with which public discourse formally settles its debts with the past without too much grief, without ever dealing with the aversions, supplications, hostilities, and resentments that tear apart real human beings. The word "memory," like many that insipidly circulate, without weight or gravity, through the communicative channels of the mediating politics of television, has erased from its public voice the untreatable, unsociable recollection of the nightmare that tortured and tormented its subjects in the past. Memory, dislodged even from the words that name it,[7] now suffers from an emptiness with a lack of affective context that daily cancels its horrible past, increasingly separating and distancing the historical memory from an emotional network that previously resonated collectively.[8] It would seem that the word "memory," thus recited by the mechanized discourse of the consensus, subjects the memory of its victims to a new offense: making the memory insignificant by letting it be spoken in words weakened by official routines, which work carefully to put the names at a safe distance from any kind of biographical investigation dealing with the convulsive and fractured elements of lived experience. Words reduced to the unfeeling language of objective certification—the political report, sociological analysis—which tells us something, in the best of cases, of what the past "was," but without any reference to that "having been" of indignity, of having to see its expressive conventions overturned by the insufferable violence that makes up memory. That is, without a trace of the consensus formula being stirred up by the raising of voices that may reveal the paroxysms of fury and desperation.

Biographical Shatterings, Narrative Disarticulations

The experience of the postdictatorship welds together individual and collective memory around figures of absence, loss, suppression, and disappearance.

All these figures are surrounded by the shadows of a grieving process in suspense, unfinished, tension filled, that leaves subject and object in a state of heavy sorrow and uncertainty, wandering endlessly without peace around the unfound body, and of the missing and needed truth.

Absence, loss, suppression, and disappearance evoke the body of the detained-disappeared in the most brutally sacrificial dimension of violence, but they also connote the symbolic death of a mobilizing force of a social historicity no longer recoverable in its utopian dimension. The force of that historicity was lived by the cultural sphere during the military regime as an urgent struggle for meaning, to defend a meaning both urged and urgent. Undoubtedly, the heroic task of having to reinvent languages and syntaxes to survive the catastrophe of the dictatorship that submerged bodies and experiences in the dismembering violence of multiple shocks and shatterings of identity, and to have to face expressive codes as if the battle for meaning were a life-and-death matter given the danger of naming, subjected cultural practice and social biographies to overwhelming demands of rigor and truthfulness that ended up exhausting them. Many subjectivities today, wearied from the heroic disciplining of this maximalist combativeness that until recently governed their behavior, prefer to please themselves with the small satisfactions of a neoindividualistic flight to the personal and daily, to the subjective, as partial tactics of retraction and distractions that create the illusion of a certain "relative autonomy regarding the structures of the system" when it is no longer reasonably possible to believe in its imminent collapse.[9]

But furthermore, the democratic Transition and its normalizing networks of order deactivated the exceptionality of character with which the adventure of meaning was imbued when it came to combating the horror and terror from zones of thought under a constant state of emergency. This value of the extreme, previously summoned by the rebellious passion of defending irreplaceable (absolute) truths, passed over to form part of a regime of plain replaceability of signs that today de-emphasizes wills and passions that favor change in the name of a relativism of values.[10]

Whatever the painful motive of this renunciation, the postdictatorial condition is expressed as a "loss of the object" in a definite situation of "mourning":[11] psychic blocks, libidinal retreats, affective paralysis, inhibitions of the will and desire faced with the sensation of loss of something that can no longer be made whole (body, truth, ideology, representation). Postdictatorial thought is, as Alberto Moreiras has pointed out, "more suffering than celebratory": "just like grief which fundamentally must assimilate

Photographs from the documentary video *La memoria obstinada* (1966), by Patricio Guzmán.

and expel at the same time, thought tries to assimilate the past looking to reconstitute itself, reform itself, following lines of identity with its own past; but it also tries to expel its dead body, extrude its tortured corruption."[12] The melancholic dilemma between "assimilating" (remembering) and "expelling" (forgetting) traverses the postdictatorial horizon, producing narratives divided between a muteness—the lack of speech linked to the stupor of a series of changes that, given their velocity and magnitude, cannot be assimilated to the continuity of a subject's experience—and overstimulation: compulsive gestures that artificially exaggerate the rhythm and signs to combat depressive tendencies with their artificial mobility. On the one hand, we have biographies trapped in the sadness of an unmoving memory in its fixed morbidity. On the other, we have "lite" narratives that hysterically precipitate themselves into an ephemeral overabundance, celebrating this flightiness with the trivial wink of advertising novelty. From muteness to overstimulation, from dumbfounded ailment to chatty simulation, the answers offered—consciously or unconsciously—regarding the memory of tragedy speak of a problematics of historical memory in postdictatorial times: a memory tussled about between a petrified nostalgia of yesteryear in its repetition of the same and the advertising choreography of the new, which exhausts itself in the futile variations of the series-market.

The replacement of history, as body and event, with the plain surface of an administered consensus and its mechanisms of stripping all passion of meaning generated in certain social actors a retrospective effect of a nostalgic intensification of memory for the antidictatorship period, with its metasignifying epic. The mythologization of the historical past, as an emblem of uncontaminated and pure political ideals, led to a sanctification of the victims used to remedy the lack of heroic exemplariness of a present that had surrendered to a mere pragmatism of action bereft of any moral rebelliousness. The radical overturning of that universe so clearly defined under the dictatorship through such categorical oppositions between official and dissident forces, accompanied by the pathos of such a monumental battle, produced disastrous effects of utopian exhaustion. Hence the melancholic-depressive symptom that affects the postdictatorial subject, leaving him or her sadly submerged in discouragement, in the retreat of silence or inaction, because he or she is "incapable of guaranteeing sufficient self-stimulation to initiate certain responses" faced with a world so confusingly reordered.[13]

The loss of a macroreferentiality of sense and the fragmentation of a relativity of values in the "post" horizon were, perhaps, experienced by some as something liberating, since it allowed them to break away from an oppressive hierarchy of absolute meanings, which committed one to total truths in the doctrinaire times of ideological credos. But these dismantlings of horizons and perspectives were above all lived as panic and disorientation by militants faced with a shattering of interpretive frameworks that had previously ordered their world outlooks according to the univocal outline of definitive centralities and homogenizing totalities and now deprived them of all certainty of belonging and identification. The Transition landscape filled up with diffuse centralities and runny margins whose mechanisms of control have become ubiquitous in reason and power, segmented by an oscillating scale of values that are not ethically confronted among themselves, to the point where they form a map of opportunist conversions where one does not have to be committed to anything, because biographies and identities mutate according to the same rhythm of rapid permutation of services and commodities, in superficial harmony with a logic of change that obeys only the stimuli of consumer taste.

But moreover, the utopian horizon of the former pitched battle—a horizon that is betrayed daily by the adaptive conformism of the new social actors enrolled in the ranks of political power and economic success— reveals traumatic fractures that inhibit the recollections of memory; inhibitions that censor the connections between past and present, making the moral or psychic breach unspeakable, a breach that splinters the life project of actors converted by history.[14] Faced with the multiple estrangements between past and present that technologies of forgetting fabricate as experts in suppressing the biographical and historical articulations of chronological sequences, perhaps we should activate a proliferation of narratives capable of multiplying schemes of narrativity that put into motion advancements and retrospections so that the temporality of history folds back on itself at every intersection of event and meaning, thereby exploding the falsifying image of a "now" severed from all antecedents and official calculation.[15]

The Transition's present takes advantage of this social discomfort of memory and of the self-censorship with which its protagonists cut the strings that bind "before" and "after" and protect its "now" from historical comparison, divorcing it from any precedent from which it could claim fidelity or sanction incoherencies. The current scene of the Chilean Transition avails itself of that thinly sliced "now" briefly cut up—bereft of historical links—in order to saturate the present with evanescent moments devoid of commitment that suffuse the momentary with rhythms and virtues so

that history will become definitively forgetful. Moreover, instantaneous-
ness and momentariness are frivolous resources with which the novelty
of the Transition disguises its ambivalent game of masks between present
(the democratic reopening) and past (dictatorship). In effect, the government of the consensus began marking its distance and breaking away from
the antagonistic world of the dictatorship, whereas neoliberal democracy
needed to reinforce the complicit hegemony of the market to guarantee the
"reproducibility" of modernization policies of the military dictatorship.[16]
That is, the present of the consensus had to defend its politico-democratic
"novelty"—its "discourse of change"—by silencing the economic continuity of the inherited past, and hiding this perversion of temporal schemes
that mixes continuity and rupture under the guise of an incessant self-
affirmation as actuality, thanks to the exhibitionist pose of a present created
by legerdemain.

The Presence of the Memory of Absence

To rake over, undermine, and unearth the footprints of the past are the
actions undertaken by human rights groups, defying the sinister audacity
of a power that had erased the proofs—the remains—of its criminality in
order to have acts safely removed from any kind of concrete verification.
To rake over, undermine, and unearth are signs of a will to make body
parts and truth appear so as to join together (re-member) a proof that
completes what the judiciary left incomplete.

The remains of the disappeared—the remains of a disappeared past—
must first be discovered (uncovered) and later assimilated: that is, rein-
serted into a biographical and historical narrative that is admission of
proof and is able to weave around its narrative a coexistence of meanings.
To unblock the remembrance of the past that pain and guilt encrypted in
a sealed temporality, diverse interpretations of memory and history must
be freed up and made capable of assuming conflicting narratives; and
starting from the multiple and disconnected fractions of a contradictory
temporality, new versions and rewritings of what has happened that translate the event to unexplored networks of historical intelligibility must be
attempted.[17] It's not a matter, then, of turning one's gaze to the dictatorial past to engrave the contemplative image of what has been suffered and
resisted onto the present, in which that image becomes mythically encrusted as memory, but instead a matter of opening up fissures in the
blocks of signification that history closes off as being past and finished, in

order to break up its unilateral truths using the folds and creases of critical questioning.

Where memory of the past is most dramatically displayed is in the crisscrossed narratives of the detained-disappeared and of their relatives who struggle against the disappearance of the body, always having incessantly to produce the social appearance of the memory of its disappearance. "The commitment to their memory is the true key to the symbolic elaborations of the victim's family,"[18] who, faced with the absence of the body, must prolong the memory of its image in order to keep alive the memory of the absent person and not make him or her "disappear" a second time through the act of forgetting. "The suffering of memory is used to give life to death":[19] the obsessive fixity of memory can't stop repeating itself because by vanishing it would duplicate the violence of the first erasure of identity executed by the disappearance, making both definitive accomplices of a total suppression (in space and in time) of the vestiges (traces) of the subject. What endures in the memory of the victims' relatives is then a "life-or-death" matter. That explains the inexhaustible remembrance of the traumatic event that reiterates the loss, which marks it again, thus contradicting the lack of evidence with which the social and political mechanism executed the physical suppression of bodies. That is why there is a multiplication of symbolic acts of remembrance that redefine memory against the indefinition of death without certainty. That is why there is a will to actualize memory against the forgetfulness of the present through a litany "infinitely reiterated like a monotonous chant," which in its repetitiveness seeks to "exorcize the invoked name from oblivion."[20]

But in what language can the desperation of memory and its irrepressible demand for actualization be heard in a context where both memory and the immediate are banalized by dehistoricizing techniques of a media-saturated present that has severed all links between "politics" and "sensibility"?

There are various techniques of forgetting that beckon us to slough off the past: to turn the page of what's happened and lose one's head in the transitory effects in which the Transition parodically involves itself, thereby disguising its "stationary and intransitive reality,"[21] allowing it to look at infinity, to a limitless end-of-century capitalism as a backdrop to a powerful machinery of ingenious devices, barters, and humiliations. Among the various techniques of forgetfulness, there is the consensus with its postulates of order and social reintegration that counsel leaving out of their watchful limit of similarity brandished by their tranquilizing "we" the dissimilar and bothersome "them": those who embody the past, those who wear their stigmata raw on the skin without wanting to apply the makeup of the general welfare and its modes of entertainment. There are the policies of institutional obliteration of guilt that through nonpunishing laws (pardons and amnesties) separate truth from justice and distance both—by decree—from an ethical claim that those identified as guilty don't come out winning (again) in their perverse operation of nonidentification. And weaving secret associations between both networks of convenience and deal making are the dissipated forms of forgetting that the mass media fashion daily, so that not even the memory or its suppression is noticed in the middle of such fine and invisible censorships that restrict and anesthetize the field of vision ("one enjoys the soap opera, the soccer game, and in the narrative flash one loses without a sense of dignity. . . . Meanwhile repression increases in novel and merciless ways").[22]

The relatives of the victims know about the difficulty of keeping the memory of the past alive and of putting memory into practice, when all the consumer rituals are geared to distract it, to strip memory of meaning or focus. That's why one sees the endless list of declarations, facts, and news regularly published by the Association of the Families of the Detained-Disappeared in their "news summary" each year. That explains the hyper-documentation of tasks and events neurotically proliferating around the suffering of loss, which reconstructs a semblance of a daily normality anxious to produce signs and messages whose objective accounting of fact fills up—in substitution—the subjective void left by absence. The will to remember and commemorate the loss that the victims' relatives try to keep alive collides with the passive universe of sedimented indifference that today conjures up machinations and spontaneities, calculations and automatisms, impositions and inclinations, all enmeshed at the moment where they jointly produce an exhaustion of the meaning of acts and words that were previously charged with rigor and emotion. The question "Where are they?" has no place in which to lodge itself in this current Chilean landscape without intense narrative or dramatic voices. Concerning this dismantling of drama, Germán Bravo reflected on the testimonies of the Association of the Families of the Detained-Disappeared and the difficulty of being able to inscribe their problematics of memory in a Transition Chile that only hears their lament as if it were some "boring chant, a song that had lost its melody, its ability to change tone, a name . . . facing the statue of time with the sole force of its repetition. The infinite repetition of an insufferable name, of a name become inexpressible and inaudible."[23]

"Justice is not negotiable," says the Association of the Families of the Detained-Disappeared; that is, "the suffering of each one and of all is not quantifiable."[24] The experience of suffering would then be what is unquantifiable: what the bereaved families wanted is irreducible to the exchange laws of the market expert in leveling qualities and properties in order to more easily convert them to a regime of neutral equivalencies that assume the contours of the form-commodity and the form-sign.[25] But how to manifest the value of the experience (the lived materiality of what is unique, singular, and contingent, of what can be made testimony)[26] if the consensus's and market's lines of force have standardized subjectivities and technologized speech, making its expressions monochord, so that it is increasingly harder for the irreducible uniqueness of the personal event to dislocate the passive uniformity of the series? Where to record the most frightening part of memory if there are hardly any sensitive surfaces of reinscription of memory left? Where can this recollection be moved to save it from the (c)rudeness, mean-spiritedness, and indolence of ordinary communication?

Tremors of Representation

To speak of sensitive surfaces of memory reinscription means to address a scene of production of languages, of the expressive means to restore the faculty of enunciating sense (meaning) and denouncing the performance enacted by signs of violence, placing horror at a distance thanks to a conceptual or figurative mediation capable of partially debrutalizing the lived immediacy of events. Only a scene of language production allows one both to break the traumatic silence of a complicit nonword of oblivion and to be saved from the manic-obsessive repetition of memory, imbuing it with the intellectual tools of decipherment and interpretation and modifying the lived texture and psychic consistency of the drama. Images and words, forms and concepts, help to transfer the resignification of the experience to planes of legibility where the lived materiality will become part of an understanding of the events capable of unveiling the knots of violence that existed previously as a figure without a face or expression.

But what language can be relied on to claim that the past be given moral attention as interpellation of a still-relevant social narrative, if almost all the languages that survived the crisis have gone on recycling their lexicons in passive conformity with the uncaring tone—"disaffected"—of the mass media, and if the mass media only administer the "poverty of experience"

(Benjamin) of a technological actuality without compassion for the fragility of the remnants of a wounded memory?[27]

Indeed, what language can be counted on, what tongue can we trust? In Chile the dilemma of language arises from the need to recuperate the word after the upheavals of the dictatorship, which almost deprived experience of the names available to communicate the violence of its mutilation. That dilemma disturbed—and still disturbs—certain critical writings of the postdictatorship, sufficiently honest and delicate to confess their malaise; meanwhile academic traditions of knowledge preferred defensively to hide the depth of the fracture that made it untenable to employ the same discourse as if nothing had happened, that is, as if the linguistic tools that made up their knowledge were not also part of the crisis of signification that obliged them to revise their assumptions. Sociological discourse, for example, should have been willing "to rethink the social after the collapse of the social."[28] The extreme limit of experience lives in the course of certain sociological research on human rights that processed the testimonies of the victims using what were merely techniques for collecting and organizing data (techniques whose objective was to put together the quantifiable information that the statistics on violence were seeking), and this experience showed that these techniques were not capable of "sharing a common situation of ethical and intellectual torment with those who were 'the object of their investigation.'"[29] Faced with identities that had lost shape or unity of meaning, the professional narrative of sociological research continued abusing its technical rationality and its methodological efficacy as barometers of knowledge at a distance that blocked the question asked by T. Moulian: "how to describe those infernos, how to transmit emotions that allow 'comprehension' using the circumspect, frozen, grave, falsely objective language of the 'human sciences'?"[30]

Faced with this situation of derailed meaning, there were two principal Chilean responses that attempted to overcome its violence: on the one hand, the reactivation of scientific discourse, and, on the other, an active pursuit of poetic textuality. The first response was organized from within sociology to comprehend the social transformations during the dictatorial paradigm—"repression" and "modernization"—that functionalized the social and the political through analyses that had adjusted to these changes. Meanwhile, the second response erupted—in maladjusted fashion—on the Chilean art and literary scenes of the eighties from emergency practices that joined fragments of obliterated and abandoned languages to allegorically narrate the ruins of meaning.[31] The discourse of the alternative social sciences analyzed this crisis of meaning of dictatorial Chile but did so relying on the disciplinary outlook of an institutionalized knowledge that was careful not to experiment—in its own corpus and language—with the dislocation of objective reason that the monumental crisis of system and truth might have unleashed from within their professional networks of knowledge.[32] The discourse of the social sciences organized the symptoms of the crisis using a language that restored processes and subjects: a language, therefore, incompatible—in its will to rebuild a normativity—with what had been broken, separated, a landscape of divided social and cultural subjectivities. Meanwhile critical texts on art and literature that were contemporaneous to these technical analyses being undertaken by alternative sociology sought to create equivalent expressions that were in tune with the correlation of signs clustered about the categorical disaster of the system of social representation with a language made up of incomplete sentences, errant vocabularies, and unraveling syntax. Instead of wanting to suture the gaps left by the representational voids with a discourse of reunifying sense (like the technical and operational discursiveness of the social sciences), these "poetics of the crisis" devised by Chilean art and literature of the eighties preferred to restylize cuts and fissures, discontinuities and eruptions. By revisiting the historical particularity of those two forms of rebuilding signification, one can see that each one (the sociological that rearticulates and explains, and the aesthetic-critical that dearticulates) foreshadowed two ways of relating to memory and recollection. While sociology worked, professionally, in favor of a technical version of the consensus that had to eliminate all superfluous or recalcitrant opacity from its administrative machine of order, art and literature of the "new scene" explored the zones of conflict through which "forgotten figures, unwilling images, and the detritus of memory retake the road toward theory,"[33] by means of a "knowledge of the precarious"[34] that speaks a language sufficiently splintered so as not to again mortify what has been wounded with new categorical totalizations. And, I believe, it is these zones of conflict, negativity, and refraction—these zones in which the darkest elements are condensed into a counterscene still filled with latencies and interrupted virtualities—that keep, in their tense, filigreed secret, a critical knowledge of the emergency and the rescue resonating with the most fragile aspects of the memory of disaster.

CHAPTER TWO

❧

Torments and Obscenities

One of the tactical moments of the Transition is dissimulation: to pretend you do not have what you have. To remain silent about the bodies that float in the memory of death, and by doing so, allow the present to construct a discourse where closure is impossible. Politics editorializes its cruelties and through testimonies it apologizes for the bodies exiled by speech.

—CARLOS J. OSSA

Between memory and history, there is a difficult meshing of signs that deal with the critical operation of memory production. Woven into the diffuse folds of twisted meanings, this tangle of signs escapes from the principal narrative toward secondary narrations.

What should be revisited from memory's past so that critical thought can delineate a history sensitive to details or nooks and crannies? How to reveal the small incisions and dispersals of sense, the microtextures of lived histories where the most insidious symbols of violence filter through? Perhaps the unofficial fragments of the most entangled narratives are the ones we must reread with an eye to the hidden, so that memory and remembrance confess the muddle of their guilt, torment, and obscenity.

In the thick of a Transition government, two autobiographies were published, authored by Luz Arce and Marcia Alejandra Merino,[1] which tell the stories of women who were left-wing militants during the Popular Unity Government (1970–1973) and were later detained by the secret police of the military regime (DINA), who imprisoned and tortured them until they both worked as informers and collaborators of the DINA for more than ten years.

The narratives were assembled at the intersection of various lines of conflict (ideological, political, moral, ethical) whose confused and troubled nature no doubt contributed to the silence of the Chilean media, which feigned complete ignorance of the publications, even though the information on human rights violators contained in each book directly addressed Transition politics. These testimonies, which overflow—in public scope and magnitude—the editorial limit of simple life stories, took the form of two autobiographies of women caught between the verbal compulsion of wanting to say more and more ("women don't know how to shut up") and the complete silence with which the sociomasculine norm of political reason punished their disobedient excess of words.[2] But contrary to what the cliché expresses about women who can't stop talking and don't say anything, the narratives by Arce and Merino say more than they tell. They do so by mixing the rhetoric of sincerity that guides their autobiographical writing with the artifices of self being recomposed in a scenario that simultaneously plays with the codes of simulation and dissimulation of democratic change.

The Blackmail of Truth: Bodies and Names

M. A. Merino starts her autobiographical narrative by saying the following: "in the middle of my nakedness, the shrieks produced by electroshock, the humiliation, the blows, I screamed without being able to control my first name: María Angélica Andreoli. I felt that everything had finished for me. I had betrayed what I most loved up to that moment."[3]

From the moment of their initial detention and incarceration, Merino and Arce were forced by coercive measures to tell the truth. To tell the truth, to confess what they knew, was the condition for the body to be saved from torture, in exchange for a few names. Nowadays, in the context of the publication and rereading of these autobiographies, it seems that bodies and names again become objects of a sinister extortion. In order to know about the bodies of the disappeared and yank them from the violence of anonymity, of being "N.N." (nonidentifiable body), one would have to make the agents of that violence anonymous, in spite of knowing who they are. To tell or be silent, to reveal or hide, are the verbs of blackmail that divide the machinery of knowledge into an absolute search for the total truth about the destiny of those bodies, on the one hand, and the intermediate formulas of transaction of an always-partial information, on the other. This division between the total and the partial, the absolute and the relative, accusingly points to the drama of the impossibility of creating a balance between damage and compensation so that in the name of justice and truth, one could measure something intrinsically incalculable: the pain of the loss.

The autobiographical confession of La Flaca (Skinny) Alejandra not only seeks forgiveness for having handed over certain names. It wants to name again: "to now give the names of those responsible and hand over a history of their misdeeds that will unmask them."[4] The book ends with an appendix where the disappeared-detained and functionaries of the DINA are named, which re-creates the primal scene of guilt from its reverse: repentance. La Flaca Alejandra pays for the betrayal of her first denunciation with a new one, enacted so that the author can pay her moral debt to society, thanks to a restitutive supplement of counterinformation.

The book closes with a depressing and endless enumeration of people that mechanically repeats the act of "spilling out names" under torture, putting together a compulsive list that alternates between victim and victimizer, recorded in an ambiguous shared zone of informant-confession-accusation. But these names of victims and victimizers, made to seem equal by the use of capital letters, resonated very unequally in the national context when they were published. General Contreras—ex-chief of the DINA and the most important figure of the accused—filled up the front pages of the papers for months (between June and December 1995) with the illegitimate excuse of illness that was orchestrated to defer his being sent to jail. Meanwhile the unresolved tension of the legitimate wanting to know "Where are they?" (the detained-disappeared) kept being relegated to a triple marginalization of national malaise: without a documented answer as to their being alive or dead, without the narrative dramatizations of the horror of their mutilated truth, without any symbolic elaboration of the loss that obsessively accompanies mourning.

In contrast to General Contreras, who protagonized current events by making the delay an episode of a work-in-progress, the detained-disappeared already knew the sad denouement of being filed away as simple cases in the common grave of official lists prepared by commissions and tribunals. The comedy of deferral because of the ailments of General Contreras held public attention with the hypertelevised "When?" of going to jail, which again sacrificed the "Where?" of the bodies that were still undocumented: a double national suspense from the same plot in a continuous present, with its strings secretly tied at some silenced point by the Reconciliation's logic. By pulling only one thread, the whole web unravels, since the points of convergence of when to know and be silent, when to disguise and hide, when to confess and lie, are all invisibly intertwined among themselves by the complicity of silence that surrounds the dark background of guarded secrets and hidden deals.

Obscenity I

During his stay in the military hospital of Talcahuano, General Contreras was taken to different medical centers to have tests performed that would confirm the illnesses that would delay his going to jail. At various times, televised images of General Contreras would show him reduced to a patient being examined, placed in the inconceivable relationships of formal analogy to bodies that were tortured: bodies transferred from place to place, stripped naked, placed in obligatory positions, becoming the object of the fragmentary actions of machines, being corporeally investigated in the search of a truth.

General Contreras theatrically performing his ailments necessarily exhibited the regrettable flip side of a body that had exercised terror from an erect or vertical position within a chain of command: now he was a body laid flat like a patient, at the mercy of the camera's examining eye, which anatomically cut him off (and down), in order to bring secret information to light.

General Contreras was parodically condemned by TV to also be a victim of certain corporal technologies of truth (to be submitted to observation, to be the focus of medical questioning, to be watched by examining equipment and subjected to objectification—reduced to an object—in a public ceremony of physical debasement), but only under the scandalous protection of the media and the political system.

The shots of General Contreras being x-rayed and the results being screened to show the organic and visceral details of tissue invaded by the disease elevated the sickness to an inquisitive transparency of a close-up of his crannies, of his morbid interiors and depths, zones of the body that were somewhat unconfessable and obscenely penetrated by the news media. The sick body was televisually submitted to a whole array of semantic associations that link the imaginary of tumor-linked diseases to pathological figures of people who are suspicious and malignant,[5] making those associations shift and move inevitably from the body (as the scene of abnormal proliferation) to the mind (as creator of indignities). The echo, diabolically resonant, of the expression "contra natura" that was applied to the intestinal movements of the patient and repeated in all the national press, thus communicated a latent subtext of an expectant moral trial on the inhumanity of the sick patient, which was at last named by a single word: "degeneration." A word that unofficially elevated the corporal symptom to the figurative realm of a denunciatory metaphor.

Perpetual Betrayal

In their two autobiographies, M. A. Merino and L. Arce designate themselves as "Skinny Alejandra the collaborator" and "Luz Arce, the informer, the traitor." Each tale tells us that the first act of betrayal is committed by giving up information under torture, or from the fear of being tortured. There would be a dividing line, traced out by the "first name" given, which separates the loyalty zone where a person remains *whole* from a betrayal zone in which the person finishes by informing on her comrades because her integrity (moral, psychic) has been *broken*: loyalty and uprightness, betrayal and brokenness, assimilate a moral principle of the firmness of an ideal of rectitude that is betrayed by the first name. But as we move into their autobiographies, this dividing line between a "before" (pure) and an "after" (impure) of that first error also "breaks": it doubles up and twists; it ramifies and splits off ambiguously. What are the first renunciations and surrenders that make L. Arce and M. A. Merino traitors: giving up the first name under torture, or later becoming DINA officers in exchange for their freedom, or their subsequent repeated and complicit efforts to finally be accepted and recognized by the power of the military hierarchy? The forms that point to or obscure the profile of betrayal are themselves treacherous.[6] We never know exactly where the limit of reliability of their repentant words lies, or in which unjudgeable margins of the narrative the testimonial truth of repentance disintegrates. The emblem of betrayal by which the authors of these testimonies recognize themselves is not univocal but instead overflows boundaries that are erased and redrawn in tortuous regions of consciousness and judgment, contaminating us with their uncertainties. If we forgive the treason, are we not betraying those who died by being informed on by these now-confessed authors? Can we definitively trust that this now-published truth is the whole truth if they themselves have admitted to have confessed many times to "half-truths" in order to "safeguard implicated third parties," and if now the clandestinity of the names of the guilty continues to need, more than ever, strategies of secrecy disguised as judicial prudence? Furthermore, are we sure that the autobiographical versions of Merino and Arce, which call out for forgiveness by confessing to deceit, do not distract from the weight of the truth of other, less-publicized betrayals that are perhaps more collectively mute, and more nationally insidious?

From these two autobiographies, the symbol of betrayal extends to present-day Chile to double back on itself in suspiciously similar figures that multiply disbelief and lack of confidence.[7] The reiteration of suspicion creates the general effect of living under the menacing signs of a perpetual betrayal put in place by false reasoning and fake proofs. If it is true that the Transition's official slogan was transparency (proceedings, languages, and actions invoked to hide nothing, to uncover and discover all), there is a growing feeling that the division between private (what is secret) and public (what can be confessed) has shifted its bearings to continue functioning in disguise from within democratic officialdom, filling its corridors with secret orders, with classified materials, of clandestine deals, of indirect power.

While the Transition government officially declares its commitment to truth, accusations, lies, and denials daily sow the panic of deceit in the words uttered under oath on the parliamentary stage. From falsity to concealment, from disloyalty to perjury, the figures of deceit and betrayal speak of the multiple internal breakdowns of the hidden pact that ties certain names of the Transition to the unconfessable nature of its secrets. Shadows of doubt continue to fall over the appeals to the "transparency" of its policies that hide their accommodating infidelities among ridiculed positions behind smoke screens.

Obscenity II

In the video made by Carmen Castillo on "Skinny Alejandra" (1994), there is a woman character who resolves not to play the game of truth as confessed by the protagonist; a woman who ridicules the pathos of the confession with which M. A. Merino justifies herself, her moral superiority endorsed by the pain of having known "hell." She is the only character in the video who doesn't believe the story, and she exhibits a derisive laugh faced with the dramatic tone of the conversation between M. A. Merino and C. Castillo, both submerged in the dilemmas of memory and forgiveness. The off-camera voice that comments on the entry of this new character tells us that she is a woman, in disguise, who disguises herself every Saturday "to act out the artifice of the country that dissimulates, lies, and deceives." She is a comic figure who resorts onstage to disguise, to place herself at a frivolous distance and thereby break the psychological dramatization of guilt, taking it to the realm of carnivalesque interplay of masks and disguises. A figure, then, who converts artifice and disguise into metaphoric keys of the behavorial transvestism that identifies the Chilean society of the Transition.

Lies, deceit, and betrayal, artifice and disguise, simulations and dissimulations: all a game of costuming and transvestisms acted out by characters who opportunistically change discourses and justify themselves by invoking a "politics of change," without any complications that might involve judgment or conscience that could interfere with these flighty rites of identity conversion. Between ruins and celebration, between the funeral procession and the carnival masquerade, various characters of the postdictatorship have dressed up their grief with the garments of entertainment. The parade shows the aleatory combination of incoherent roles that wander outside the script, searching for something believable, since the codes of honor and morality have failed.

The scene fills up with a collection of uninserted acting roles, of false poses, of vocal impostures, of discursive mimicry, of mendacious phrases: all a game of appearances meant to compensate for a breakdown of meaning (historical, political) with an exhibitionist proliferation of flashy signifiers. The Transition parodically conjoins the theme of disappearing, in the grave register of those who mourn, with that of appearing—in the frivolous register of market styles and commercialized posing.

The Conversion

The autobiographies of Marcia Alejandra Merino and Luz Arce take the form of a confession in which guilt and repentance apportion the framework of narrative atonement. Both autobiographical tales display the progressive continuity of life's passage(s), signified by the mnemonics of remembrance that orders the past in a reasoned sequence of facts and explanations. Both autobiographical tales open with a preliminary text signed by the authors announcing and summarizing the content of their confessional narrative, superimposing the point of arrival—the chronological end of the life trajectory that the book re-creates—with the starting point: the beginning of our reading. This superimposition of beginning and end—so dear to autobiographical writing—makes the recapitulation of the events contained in the book appear signed by the subject-author as coinciding with herself, and she is thereby finally reintegrated into the core (womb) of her identity. Said effect of *reintegrative identity* avails itself of the circularity of a story that narratively goes around the "I" in order to fill in the potholes of inconsistency with a line of continuity, as if the surviving word that narrates torture required that kind of editorial closure to suture the wounds of memory and meaning.

But both autobiographies are confessions, and also conversions: they describe the moral transformation experienced by their protagonists, starting from their reencounter with God, which taught them to gain consciousness of their errors and gave them "the courage to tell the truth" in search of forgiveness.

The general rule of performativity of confession-conversion discourse tells us that its word acts out the experience it describes without any further proof of truth (that it *says* the truth) than what is revealed in the subjective testimony of the person who speaks. It is a inner consciousness that dictates the private truth of the confessions-conversions, and that truth does not have a verifiable referent outside the biographical intimacy of the personal narrative that puts it into words. There is always something morally disturbing in the unverifiability of confessions. The moral disturbance that arises from not being able to authenticate confessional narratives has been regulated and controlled symbolically, in the two autobiographies at hand, by a religious guarantee (God, the church), a further guarantee of the sincerity of the repentance. In the case of *El infierno* (hell), the prologue written by a priest gives faith to the L. Arce conversion to the faith and also gives the merciful example of Christian forgiveness in order to anticipate and commit us, from the beginning of the book, to our future forgiveness as readers. The undecidability of the truth content that habitually characterizes confessional narratives has here been annulled by deciding on a prologue text. Such a prologue serves as a way of relieving the readers of making a judgment, by situating the adjudication of sense (which should be undertaken freely in the reading) under the subordinating authority of the ecclesiastical voice that predestines us to receive the text as a model of Christian exemplariness. The Chilean church of the Transition insists on dictating the norms of behavior to be followed, meddling in the editorial secrets of these political confessions.

The converts' dignifying reencounters with God narrated by these two books explains various other moralizing reencounters. For example, the conversion described in *El infierno* leads Luz Arce from a code of political militancy to the rite of observance, from political dogma to religious creed, from party discipline to Christian obedience. The imperative of duty has changed signs between the first and second part of the book, but it is always a matter of rigid fidelity to a superior truth that subjects identity to a severe framework of invocations and prescriptions ("so many times unfaithful, the Luz who felt miserable began wanting to say yes to the Lord").[8] The reiteration of the figure of obedience to a system of doctrines and mandates that goes from the political to the religious throughout the books of both these women only reinforces the ideological convention of a submissive femininity, loyal and docile. This convention is formalized by readapting the sign of "woman" to the traditional roles laid out by social morality ("Father Gerardo . . . showed me God in this world. To him I owe learning how to value family, being a mother, commitments, etc.").[9] The value of religious conversion through faith that saves the political traitor from the burden of her guilt by calling her conscience to a reencounter with the Truth also has her undergo another symbolic tribute of another necessary reencounter—this time sexual—with her nature as a woman, ideologically summed up in the vocation of wife and mother. This double reconciliation combines the happy ending of the return to the straight and narrow path of good conduct in which these women had betrayed their political ideals with the idealization of feminine roles along with their party-affiliated deviations,[10] their return to the truths, to the fixed and consecrated essences of a normative feminity, sanctioned by the family. The reintegration of the traitors to the convention of an identity sealed by their autobiographical narratives is hereby channeled by a family and domestic reprogramming of the nature of femininity that leads both of them back to the primordial roles of mother and wife. How else could it be in the Chile under Transition, where the voice of the church and Catholic traditionalism lords over social discourses and sanctions a body politic?

The moralizing reconversion of both traitors atones for the guilt of their betrayal of the preestablished sexual roles of the normal Christian family. Without that sexual and ideological atonement, the trajectory of the remorse realized in these political autobiographies would be imperfect in the eyes of the church. Only the remorse of the bodies that have witnessed their conversion of faith makes it possible for that feminine trajectory to be read as a healthy and constructive examplar of identity and gender reinsertion in the Chilean society of Transition.

Silence, the Scream, and the Printed Word

The stories narrated by M. A. Merino and Luz Arce again and again pass through questions of naming, voice, and identity, traversing a stigmatizing sequence of diminutions, confiscations, and annulments of the self, which seeks ultimate compensation in the unerasable finality of the printed word.

First, their past as political militants led both women to experience clandestinity and noms de guerre in order to hide and mask a dangerous identity. Later, during their confinement, they were stripped of their "legal existence" and reduced to being "a simple number" in the military prisons. Afterward their links to the DINA-CNI demanded that they change their names many times to erase any proof and confuse any possible clues that would identify them. Identities suppressed or distorted leave a hollow sense of alienation and lack in the subject, which derives from the dual story in which the subject perceives herself as a "not-I," another self: someone with a "usurped name" and "an existence without an identity."[11] The material consistency of that "someone" has also endured the physical travail of torture that undid her or reduced her to "something" that has been tossed around, of being used to the ultimate paroxysm of disarticulation.

Silence (the tenacious refusal to utter sounds) and the scream (the physical crushing of the locutory form of the word) are two manifestations linked to the situation of torture that transgress the law of phonetic articulation of meaning. Silence and the scream are what precede or exceed the formulation of the "first name," which in being handed over under torture temporarily suspends the punishment meted out on the body of the tortured captive. Silence and the scream are two forms of nonspeech: of an unusable word whose negativity—controlled or savage—must be forcefully converted by the torturer into some meaning that can be useful.[12] The spoken confession is the victorious trophy wrenched from the clash between a damaged and useless body and the mechanism of cruelty that ends up extracting a finally useful word.[13] The physical violence of torture literally disjoints, breaks the world into pieces. It fractures the corporeal unity of the person, dislocating members and detonating the nucleus of conscious reasoning. If torture reduces the body to the prelinguistic state of silence or scream, to verbalize the story of a subject who has managed to trespass such a destructive limit is to transform it into an act by which the damaged subject will exact revenge on his or her past when she or he was condemned to the subhuman state of the scream, naming what had been unnameable.[14]

The narrative of L. Arce repeatedly associates the reason for the blocking of identity with the trauma of the loss of speech: "it is as if one's own voice stopped making sound; as if one ceased to exist."[15] The lack of voice (of the voice as expressive vehicle of a speaking subjectivity) somaticizes the destruction of the person already incapable of producing sound, of being able to witness oneself as a source of meaning. After so many deteriorations

of the faculty of speech, to write a book, to draw on the eloquence of playing with the art of word making, is a superlative way of recovering one's
voice.

Before publishing these two autobiographies, Merino and Arce had broken the silence that had burdened their pasts as informants and collaborators of the DINA. Both had made declarations before the tribunals to
clear up the truth on human rights violations by means of their confessions. These autobiographies show the posterior condition—added on—
of being a textual "supplement": why the need of this written supplement,
of this autobiographical supplementation of a truth already given as testimony, that had already fulfilled its social function of public usefulness?

It seems as if the press interviews and the court declarations hadn't been
enough for M. A. Merino and L. Arce to reclaim their long-captured and
kidnapped identities at the hands of repressive blackmail. It was as if both
needed an autobiography to completely repossess themselves, remembering the shattered "self" of the stories of their lives through a telling able to
confer on them retrospectively a narrative continuity.

The autobiographical pact formally guarantees the confluence of narra-
tor, author, and character, sealing the issue of identity under the reaffirming
mark of an "I" (self) triply asserted. And this reaffirmation-confirmation
of identity projects the illusion of being able to repair the multiple anni-
hilations of the "self" suffered all along these successive types of violence
(violations). By supposing the referential continuity of a subject endowed
with a psychological narrative of flesh and blood, the testimony and its
autobiographical conventions fill in the vacuums left by the suppressions
and alienations of identity. Furthermore, the criteria of veracity that upholds
the definition of testimony based on the rules of documentary authenticity and the commercial success derived from this genre would contribute to
a double proof of reality that converges to turn around that insistent "fear
of not being believed" manifested by both authors throughout their stories.

The narrative recomposition of the "I" of testimony that supports both
autobiographies is guided by a will to reclaim one's name: *El infierno* begins
with "My name is Luz Arce, and it has cost me a lot to redeem that name,"
while *Mi verdad* ends with "I, Marcia Alejandra Merino . . ." The names
of both women were obliterated and distorted so many times that now
they must be pronounced publicly and openly and be written in capital
letters to banish the ghosts of identity disfiguration that inhabit their
clandestine past. The capital letters lift up the shame of guilt and give a
public rendering of a reconstructed identity that finally dares to say "I,"

patenting its truth under the legitimizing authority of the printed publication.[16] In fact, *El infierno* describes how Luz Arce moves from the
"usurped name" to the legitimate and legitimated name by way of a
double circuit of recognition, both moral (the church) and political (the
Transition government).

If the signature is a sign that identifies a person according to what is
proper to him or her; if the history of Luz Arce is a story of nonappropri-
ations of the I, what better than the author's signature to consecrate the
reappropriation of the name in full caps as trophy of an identity clearly
justified and distinguishable?

The signature of the author—an editorial marking of the propriety of
meaning—is the emblem of an identity that owns its own brand, which
puts her name into circulation as a nameable, referable, and quotable sign
in the cultural marketplace of names. The name written in capitals on the
cover of a book published by Planeta in the prestigious place of the author
concludes that process of reappropriation of the "I" (self) of the autobiographical narrative of L. Arce ("I knew that living in Chile had a price.
And that price was to say publicly my name is Luz Arce").[17] In this case
the registered signature of the name materializes the symbolic economy of
the reconciliation of the subject with her identity in the Chile of the Transition, thanks to the legitimation, the bestowal of worth, by a publishing
house that makes her name something valuable after so much unworthy
treatment, that finally her name would have worth in the market of social
representation. But whom does the "I" of these books address? Who will
pick up the currency that circulates this editorial worth if the voices of past
tortures collected in these narratives are systematically denied by our current oblivion and forgetfulness?

Obscenity III

*The disappearance of memory and the apparitions of remembrance. How and
where to maintain (free of confiscations and evasions) the transformed traces
of the narrative of historical violence so that they can be used as sources for critical reflection?*

*For memory in mourning, it is key to be able to count on the testimonial
sign of an "image memory": an image that the force of a look could reanimate
so that once again it can supply the evidence that the nonresignation of shame,
pain, or anger permanently needs to resuscitate a living reality. In the landscape
of photographic documentation that composes our inventory of mortality, the*

portraits of the detained-disappeared condense the meanings of greatest dramatic intensity through the painfully interminable imprint of the absence of a body whose death-life continues to be indeterminate. But the portraits of the detained-disappeared, just like the rest of the photographic documents of the dictatorship, have been relegated by mass-media policy to an invisibility outside the frame.

By severing all links of responsibility with the effect of memory by erasing all iconic and visually figurative marks of the narrative biography of violence, the politico-communicative scenario of Chilean TV has left memory struck down, wounded from blows, without faces or bodies as a reference point, and has deprived its actors and agents of the possibility of recognizing themselves as subjects of history or as subjects with (hi)stories. Today, portraits of the detained-disappeared don't link up with anything amid a televisual festivity whose advertising aesthetic demands only smooth presences without the stigmata of deterioration. Those fixed portraits, congealed in a continuing present of a suspended death, are out of sync with the changing velocity of television's flows and electronic erasures. It is as if the poor technical quality of the photocopied portraits of the detained-disappeared and their black-and-white ethical rigor were betraying, in the face of the mass-mediated contemporary, the visual pastness of a shameful incompetence of language that thus ends by rendering ineffectual its own inherent drama.

Memory and Market

Published in 1993, these two books, which combine biographical confessions and politico-social testimony, were not commented on or analyzed until a text was published that dared to follow the obscure meanderings of the books' conformist truths following the torturous script of guilt and repentance.[18]

Even though both books are memoirs and recall the time of the dictatorship, unearthing controversial images of the past, nothing happened at the time of their publication. The finely printed pages of *The Inferno*, sold at the commercial stand at the Chilean Book Fair, right in the middle of Santiago, did not elicit a reaction from anyone. It is as if the provocative truth witnessed by L. Arce in her book was a truth among other truths, worthy or unworthy of attention as any other truth. All of them appear to be reconcilable truths—regardless of how divergent they are—because they fit into a pluralism that applauds, in each version of history, the particularity of a narrative absolved of the general responsibility of a collective understanding, in order to avoid revisiting and confronting the tactics of meaning through which each narration differs or opposes others.

Remembering is much more than evoking a prior event: it is an elaborative knot that conjugates residues of historical signification with ongoing narratives. The memories of the dictatorship's past need to build meaningful links that reinsert them into interpretive plots so that this past can retrospectively say what previously it had silenced or been unaware of. What place exists for the reflexive and analytical density of memory, for these conflictive knots of interrupted but not entirely severed memories, whose meanings, wills, styles, passions, and calculations remain undebated because our present fears the perturbing tensions of its divisive substance?

El infierno edits a fragment of the dictatorship's past that the Transition's marketplace puts into circulation through one of the registered trademarks of its culture industry: Planeta Publishing. That fragment enters into the parade of trademarks and logos of the democratic market, whose continuing regularity of undifferentiated images and levels does not allow itself to be interrupted by any accident in the passage of time, obliging one to historicize the nexus between present and memory: "every commodity incorporates the past exclusively as antiquated totality that summons a smooth substitution, without residues. . . . Market memory tries to think of the past as a substitutive operation without lingering remains."[19]

The speed of designer and logo commodity flows rests on their transitory nature, since signs must continuously be replaced and exchanged one for another so that the rhythm of novelty can be stimulated by the substitutive logic of exchange and renovation. The memory of the dictatorship that circulates along the pathways of the market joins the play of signs speedily recycled, a market that can't be bothered to make of history anything more than a brief and passing comment: a briefly interposed reference that should not upset the light rhythm of variations and diversions of media aesthetics with the inopportune demand for material whose gravity calls for ethical judgment on issues of conscience. Market and TV have expelled from their accelerated rhythms of consumption anything that requires delaying attention to—and thought of—anything incompatible with its simultaneity of purely visual effects.

Obscenity IV

The image of "Guatón Romo" (Porky Romo), interviewed on Chilean TV in June 1995 to comment on the dark details of state terrorism, was obscene in

*various ways. He abused the delicate state of emotional resistance by brutal-
izing souls that were still affected, dealing blows to a still-scarred and far-too-
wounded past, mistreating the shattered affectivity of irreparably damaged
lives. Nonetheless the interview did not produce the slightest resurgence or
reawakening of political debate. No one publicly complained about the untenable violation of remembrance that unpunished evil had inflicted, that we as
spectators were obligated to watch. There was no critical and reflexive pause
that detained the rhythm of the flurry of images in order to interrupt the televisual sequence and ask about the porous frontier of our ethical gatekeeping
that exposed us to the worst: not only the disappearance of the victims' memory, but also the shameless reappearance of cruelty in the tale of the victimizer,
who, while enjoying the indignant privilege of being interviewed, usurped the
public voice of those affected.*

*What made Romo's interview obscene was not the story but the fact that
something so ethically shocking did not disrupt the smooth and polished surface
of the information-advertising-entertainment visual effects of Chilean television. The limit between what can be shown or not shown has been abolished
by a neutral, permissive indifference that absorbs everything in its uninterrupted sequence of shots, skillfully emptied of any semantic value.*

*It's not that the interview revealed unknown horrors but that Guatón Romo's
depraved exhibitionism, which defied the camera by naming those horrors in
such a malignant fashion, personalized the sinister dimensions of impunity by
means of a body scandalously placed in a position directly inverse to those occupied by the bodies he victimized: a monstrously uninjured body, protected from
any physical sanction by the abstract, incorporeal media-ted distance of an
image that was also safe, because it was justified by his successful newsworthi-
ness in the TV ratings.*

In the same week, Chilean TV had run the program Mea Culpa, *which
re-created a crime committed during the military regime. This program
generated more polemics than the Romo interview. It was as if the reality
of the Romo interview was less "spectacular" than that offered by a reality
show, whose success consists in being able to confuse—melodramatically—the
limits between reality, realism, and simulation, in order to hyperactivate that
confusing or blurring of limits enacted by the TV journalist's performance:
a murky sentimentality, and syrupy pathos of a "drama of conscience" translated to a serial story style. Seen from the tricks-of-the-trade perspective of
"remaking the scene" on which testimonies like* Mea Culpa *base their success, it seems as though the contents of the Romo interview lacked the deceitful supplement of a doubling effect characteristic of a "re-creation." Only*

in this fashion would they have been treated by Chilean TV as a drama of horror.

What makes Mea Culpa *obscene is the repulsive pathos of the moralizing commentary that masks the truculent gains of TV's trade in the simulacra of emotions. The obscenity of Romo's screen appearance was the absence of a commentary capable of questioning the scandal of how the rules of modesty-truth-morality that govern our daily condition as TV watchers are made to censor even minor transgressions—and commercialize the censorship from the standpoint of its inoffensive sexual margin—in order to systematically divert our attention from the truly offensive and indecent political mise-en-scènes (Contreras, Romo, and others).*

PART TWO

The Popular and the Urban: Scenic Fragments

We can't renounce speaking about what is above and beyond technical and practical languages, otherwise the way these languages might transform themselves would be inconceivable. We should recognize the resistances that the politician does not understand: its "remains," the "discards" that end up by imposing a radical transformation of the very rules of the political. The remains are precisely what challenge our certainties. Their incompleteness is the structure of critical knowledge.

—FRANCISCO RELLA

Imagine another kind of economy that says not everything that is untimely in relationship to modernity is pure anachronism. It could be the nonintegrated residue of a still living utopia.

—JESÚS MARTÍN-BARBERO

The "remains" are a contingent form of existence. They are there even if no one calls for them, but nonetheless they call out for a time that has been trampled on by hasty fashion and suspicious enthusiasms.

The politicization of what remains configures the style, and if we accept this we must also accept that embedded in the improper appropriation of the defeated physiognomies of the fashion world there is a way of facing the obvious that has been hidden, and it is a form of thought that thinks about what is in its place.

—FEDERICO GALENDE

 osv

Neobaroque Debris:
Scabs and Decorations

In Chile, I thought. Chile whole and in pieces . . . tatters of diaries, fragments of extermination, syllables of death, pauses that lie, commercial phrasing, names of the dead. It is a deep crisis of language, an infection of memory, a disarticulation of all ideologies.

—DIAMELA ELTIT

Modernity is expert at multiplying eviction notices against anything that disobeys the slogan of temporal rupture that "the new" uses to coldly dismiss the old and toss in the garbage whatever is left behind by the velocity of commodity production. However, "modernity sees growing all around it the uncomfortable proximity of wastes, the unexpected accumulation of objects in disuse and spirits without domestic utility who resist being cashiered and who threaten to burst into the present and redeem the memory of a captive temporality."[1] Garbage, remains, leftovers, dregs: everything that shows signs of physical unusefulness or vital deterioration; everything that remains like a ruined fragment of discarded totality, of a broken totality of thought or existence.

Remains are also imprints and vestiges of a shattered cultural symbolization, of a landscape torn by a dimension of catastrophe that must move those truths toward more disaggregated, darker edges of knowing and experience. The Benjaminian allegorization of ruins that mixes the desolation of memory with the strength to survive, deposited in minor events and episodic shards of history threatened with extinction, configures the images of an "after" that postdictatorial social and historical temporalities retain and summon as key notions of self-understanding of their dismantled (hi)stories, their broken narratives, their disturbed speech.

The crossroads between memory as *remains* and the *narratability of remembrance* raises strategic questions about the critical treatment of the fragmentary and the residual:[2] minor settings that drift apart, remains waiting for some micronarrative that will take charge of its errant partiality in order to help us understand—from the vantage point of the unbound, the fleeting, and the interstitial—the ruptured stories that wound the trademark of the "post" (dictatorship).

But remains and vestiges are also what the system of rationalized thinking does not know how to integrate into its analytical frameworks because they consider that those remnants lack firmness and consistency. They exceed and overflow the explanatory synthesis that tries to patch up the (w)holes in the unintelligible or the unrepresentable with its operational languages, as if the crisis of full meaning did not invalidate on its own the pretensions of controlling knowledge still guided by a reconstructive end. And there, where the disciplinary framework of philosophy and sociology fails, where knowledges bump up against the diffuse significations of material that is too imprecise, thereby resisting generalization, there frequently art and literature are the areas that take up the challenge of converting the disunity, the disconnected, and the vagrant nature of the remains into a "poetics of memory." These labyrinthine zones of memory, explored by art and literature with their knowledge of discontinuity and fragmentation, do not appeal to a will to know that nostalgically reconciles these shards with a damaged totality, or to the suturing of what has been cut short in order to reintegrate what has been fractured to a new plenitude of origin. Artists insist on breaking up the series, on breaking down those huge bodies of knowledge now divided into parts that can't be put back together again under the protection of a harmonious totality. Many of these remainders only want to have the opportunity to resonate in the baroque discontinuities of the fold, remnants traversed by a desire for hypersignification that seeks to restylize its disfigured material to extract from it new and brilliant conceptual and rhetorical flourishes. Remainders wrapped in an overabundance of artifice destined to repair the contents *of lessness* (enduring lack, enduring violence) with the luxury of a form *of more*: supplementary and exaggerated, that is, aesthetically charged with a proliferating and mobile diversity of creative signifiers.

Vagaries of Identity, Errant Names

I want to linger on a Chilean fictionalization of *memory as residue* that employs an allegorical mode and hybrid symbols to give testimony of the dictatorship's and the postdictatorship's fissured horizons.

If it is true that postdictatorial aesthetics tend to become obsessed with "geohistoric fragments and urban ruins,"[3] the world of the city opens up a privileged dimension that visually imprints an image of a decomposing landscape, reduced to a trash heap of memories, corpses, rubble, vestiges of experience, to which must be added a series of cultural discards composed of lost illusions, obsolete narratives, bygone styles, lapsed traditions. The urban environment from which the voice in *El padre mío* (My Father) by Diamela Eltit emerges infuses its vagabond scenes with psychic fragmentation and social deterioration in order to speak to us of a disease of evil and madness that lies astride the end of one decade and the beginning of another.[4] The time covered in *El padre mío*—which goes from 1983 (when the first testimony was taped) to 1989, when the book was published—allows for both the voice of the protagonist and Eltit's editorial gesture to be crisscrossed by the beginning of the "post." That is, the fragmentary and schizoid constellation of metaphorical meanings that surround, in *El padre mío*, the hallucinatory evocations of power (authoritarian saturation, social regimentation, bureaucratic totality, economic conspiracy, etc.) is marked by a historical date that impels the book to carry its symptoms from one period to another, extending its memory of the contagion and disseminating the vestiges of insanity, showing how these vestiges continue to infect our capacity to reason with its suppurating consciences and its purulent forms of speech.

El padre mío is a book produced at the margin of the narrative system that has made Diamela Eltit the most singular woman writer of the Chilean eighties and nineties. *El padre mío* is a story at the margin, and of the margins; it makes a publishing gesture not foreseen by the official literary establishment and has been shunned by academic critics who have been disoriented by its testimonial poetics.[5] I say "testimonial poetics" because the discursive material presented in the book is a testimony (the faithful transcription and edition "of a person's speech discourse in the city" that identifies a real, existing vagabond), and because at the same time the turns of phrase that affect the material and its presentation constitute an antinaturalism that makes up and adorns the vagabond's crises of speech with the cultural metaphors of a complete ruin of meaning, which extends itself trans-symbolically to a turn-of-the-century landscape ("It's culture, I thought. Sculptures disseminated at the edge . . . facades after a cataclysm").[6]

We know that testimony is called on to play a strategic role within contexts of social violence and destruction, of historical struggles, because its convention of objectivity vouches for a truth of the facts; its direct and provable referentiality serves as document to the founding of a story's veracity, becoming an unobjectionable claim to the "having been" of a reality that can be denounced on behalf of its victims. *El padre mío* is structured on the basis of a testimony that could have fulfilled such a function of social accusation and denunciation, amply validated by sociology and literary criticism, which see the in first-person documentary of life stories an efficient means to pierce the academic boundaries of cultural institutions, piecing together political solidarities from within and without the literary realm.[7]

The protagonist of Diamela Eltit's *El padre mío* is an urban vagabond who belongs to a popular milieu, situated in that human and social configuration of the marginal and dispossessed that grants the testimony a counterhegemonic value, endowed with a format that can bring together and reinforce the voices of subalternity. The figures obsessively reiterated by the testimonial voice of the Chilean vagabond are those of power (state, religious, family, etc.), and even the name of Pinochet appears in the account, bringing to the fore the crude realism of the dictatorship, the social framework within which the speaker makes his plea as a witness: "but I am the one who should be witness."[8]

However, the book frustrates the denunciatory mission this marginal voice might warrant. The testimonial function is deliberately complicated by what a certain politics of the genre would expect to see fulfilled in orthodox fashion. *El padre mío* mixes up the documentary axiom of transparent speech that is merely presentational with an unusual metaphorical theater that displaces the naturalism of the recorded voice into a surprising display of literary artifice.

First, the recorded and transcribed testimony of the vagabond in *El padre mío* is the story of a schizophrenic free fall into verbal incoherence. This labyrinth of words doesn't lead to revealing a social "truth"—subordinated to criteria of referential authenticity—since the delirium of persecution shatters all limits between true and false. In addition, *El padre mío* exhibits the erratic consciousness of a subject whose words flee through various significatory voids, without "an experiential content" that can be derived from the testimony and transmitted as a social model of struggle or resistance. Nor does the victim's dispossessed situation appeal to redemption by means of a compensatory discourse that tries to fill up the holes of his identity and lack with a "profound" message of humanism. The sculptural modeling of "figures in the abyss emptied of all interiority,"[9] celebrated by the baroque criticism of the introduction signed by D. Eltit, does not coincide with the principles of identity formation that the politico-ethical will of testimony writers usually seek to collectivize in order to nourish new types of social subjectivity.

El padre mío, a text suffused with the courage of its antiliteral and overloaded speech, exceeds and confuses the norm of the testimonial genre. It not only works with a schizoid delirium that shatters the borders between the imaginary and the real but exalts their confusion to the point that it ambiguously and parodically converts it into the figurative "truth" of a crisis of truth and thought that drags judgment and consciousness into the vertigo of irrationality. *El padre mío* stages the destructuring form of a rudderless verbosity that breaks the traditional framework of the testimony function destined to exemplify a social truth, according to the model of "a personal voice that seeks to insert itself into a collective space of meaning . . . and create a perspective for an interpretation of the events,"[10] a consciousness-raising voice that guides the individual "I" toward a community-based "we" capable of involving its readers out of solidarity and in vital commitment to judgment and historical participation. In the case of *El padre mío*, the only nonsocializable "truth" exhibited by the story evoking the sick Chilean world of the dictatorship is its hyperbolic parade of false identifications, disconnected references, disintegrating phrases, erratic pronouncements, and crazy interpellations.

In the tale told by the vagabond, *El padre mío* designates the figure "who doles out illegal orders in the country": a metaphor of the dictator (Pinochet) who fraudulently exercises power. But the figure of "my father" is doubled and multiplied in an endless array of names that are repeated, superimposed, or changed (Mr. Luengo, King George, the soccer player William Marín de Audax Italiano, Mr. Colvin, Argentino Ledesma, etc.), to which other names are added (Mr. Frei, Mr. Alessandri, Mr. Allende, etc.), overpopulating the mind in a complete state of verbal delirium with ranks, identities, names, and representations where "what is shattered are the different names of power": "different areas of administration and social power both national and international, from the Alliance for Progress, the Abdel Nasser Organization, commitments to Peru, Argentina, and Central

America; from banking, food distribution and hospital management; to the granting of medicines, contact with King and Queen of Spain, political parties, etc."[11] The debunked names of power are crazily disseminated to contaminate a dislocated subjectivity that the legal-bureaucratic machinery saturates with orders, contracts, reports, and jurisdictions, thereby forming a concentrated and regimented world of the I (self), which ends up breaking up this asphyxiating closure thanks to the psychotic flight of the vagabond. *El padre mío* takes the representation of testimony out of a frame that seeks to "give voice to those without a voice,"[12] using the errant words of a subjectivity adrift—without logical support, without conceptual caution, without a clear and firm enunciation, without elocutionary coherence—which, even though it accuses those in power (thus fulfilling the denunciatory requirement of testimonial ethics), does so without guidance from a sociopolitical referent of action.

The book's critical gesture produces an interlacing of the speech delirium of "my father" (which is unmoored from any degree of verisimilitude) with the Chile to which his monologue alludes as an image of a delirious country, monstrously uprooted from the regular order of normal citizenship. Both the mental incoherencies and the aberrations of power shatter the social structures of order with their pulverized discursivities that conjoin multiple dimensions of the emptiness and annihilation of meaning: from the flee(t)ing dimension of unreality that disconnected the vagabond's mind from any social convention to the noninteriorization of bodies who are perpetual vagabonds in a city that forces their encrustation into the facades as discards deprived of everything and abandoned by everyone. What remains are the names spinning on themselves in a vertiginous trance of words fired off in a chaotic and disintegrative succession of enunciations without referential underpinning. The eccentricity of meanings displayed by the circular repetition of the maniacal and obsessive delirium of *El padre mío* is what the author compiles, edits, and publishes, like a double metaphor that functions both to point out the arbitrariness of power and to exhibit the insurrectionary acts of speech with which marginality breaks through the siege of normative speech.

Gender/Genre Rebellions

The narrative interchange between the crazy man and the author ("united by the desire of discourse")[13] simulates a relationship of father/daughter, whose fictitious roles are displaced and redistributed editorially in order to

jointly question the same vertical order of hierarchies and centralizing functions: power, canon, authority, institution, law, totalitarian totalities.

The vagabond's story in *El padre mío* designates the figure of Pinochet,
but in the introduction to the book, D. Eltit designates the vagabond as
such ("the man I call My Father"),[14] subverting the reference of the first
designation with this ambiguous barrage of possessive pronouns that leave
the sequence of identifications open to indefinite rotations of identity.
The writer rambles through the city, drawing from the wasteland of adversity, distilling the oral tale of the vagabond, saving him from the elements,
gathering the word of an indigent person within the literary bosom of the
written text. She is the "mother" who protects the destitute from social
adversity, giving him refuge and institutional worth. But she is a mother
who later poses as a "daughter" by placing herself on the book cover, under
the authority of My Father, who in the title is above her: a father from
whose symbolic transgression she has derived the creative energy to fashion a poetic-testimonial remaking of his popular orality. The figurative
father is not a supreme figure of power but instead a crazed victim of a
patriarchal-dictatorial symbolic realm that hounds and disintegrates him:
and he thereby shares the same space as the daughter, whose minority
poetics battles against the canon and its cultural hierarchies. The figures
of father and daughter are not divided here by the conflicts of authority of
the masculine Logos, but instead they alternate and both witness the spectacle of its ruins, united by the effects of the same debacle of meaning.[15]
Social marginality, mental fragmentation, and rebellion of genders/genres
lead father and daughter to defy authoritarian control, from the vantage
point of precariousness and dissidence of the underside of the established
order. Both multiply diverse points of communicative rupture in the chain
of power's enunciation, in order to wildly yank the story away from its
public investiture. These points of rupture disseminated in the text are
intertwined thanks to the aesthetic-literary design of the "presentation"
(preface) signed by the author: a presentation that combines and infuses
the intensive charges of various nonconforming voices and postures that
locate both author and character at the edge of their respective places of
belonging. The noncentrality of voices and genres editorially designed as
a representational framework, that is, as a border, is what produces the
contortion between documentary (testimony) and literature (poetics) that
puts the language of *El padre mío* in a disturbing place that is *out of joint*,
in an oscillating limit situated between reality and metaphor, that indicates
a threshold of border genres, made to unsettle the propriety of meaning.

The question "How to situate this book . . . from where can we capture this speech?" that the author asks herself displays a complex stratification that intersects the wasteland (social marginality) with the format of the book (testimonial marginality with regard to literature, literary marginality in relation to testimony).[16] Such a question passes through different ambiguities of signification that lead the book and its preface to cross the line of discursive conventions that institutionalize genre references, here handled by the clandestine traffic of strange displacements and indefinite meanings. The literary signature of D. Eltit creates a "framework," so that the vagabond's fringelike speech forms a tension with, and is propelled by, the poetic fantasy of a cultural imaginary that borders on these genres (drifting along the shores of its conventions) at the same time that it overflows the borders of identity representation, normatively defined by the centrality of a dominant voice and subject. The framework of the presentation "frames" the liminal position that leads subject, identity, and language to creatively disorganize its center, that is, to refute plurally the hierarchical position that, in the interior of every universe of signs, tends to codify values and interpretations according to the predominance of a sole and binary regime. The literary border of the presentation signed by the author is what destabilizes the presentational rhetoric of the testimony to be framed—by questioning the value of the linguistic critical moment unleashed in the margins of the communicative system. And this eccentric literary valorization of nonsense dramatizes the opposition and resistance of an unframed subjectivity that uses drift to flow and flee equally from identities, and nomenclatures fixed by the rigid socializing mechanism of the self-identical I, as well as from the fixed domiciles and obligatory residences of genre-driven writing.

The urban vagabondage of *El padre mío* becomes a metaphor of certain critical forms "remaining as a residue that passively transgresses the institutional vocation,"[17] and the delirious speech of its protagonist on the margins becomes a subversive vector of the carnivalization of power that consumes itself in verbal abandon. In both counterofficial scenarios, that of the city and that of literature, there is an opulence of facades and redressing of signs that adorn materials and surfaces with an excessive overlay of decorative markings. And it is this same forceful aesthetic that converts the *residue* (social) into *surplus* (literary and critical), that is, something that subverts the orthodoxy of economic rationality, accustomed to punishing the rejects, because of their nonutility and perverse insistence in being accumulative and derivative "leftovers," in the excess realm of brand names that betray a whimsical taste for the exaggerated lack of formal symmetry.

The "baroque" character of what is discarded would in this case have to do with the metamorphosis of bodies that attract the rhetorical effects of a creative dissemination of plural significations over their antisocial textures. Baroque would be the jumbled, chaotic will to form, scandalously counterposed to a reductionist system that views the marginal as a mere symptom of social disintegration that must passively be reintegrated into power's control, as well as the uniform programming of knowledge that denies these subjects from the margins the right to their diverse and exuberantly singular fantasies. Baroque would be this "lumpen political aesthetic" (N. Perlongher) that shifts the social and popular residue to scenarios that grant them the power to symbolize—in fragmented fashion—the uprisings of desire, with its insurrection of murky marginal voices.

El padre mío works on an aesthetic relationship with the margins that puts into action a political overflow of borders and illuminates identities that are habitually encased in darkness and in clandestineness, the least favored zones of the system. In being able to do so, the story inverts the direction taken by the market and institutional culture, which project their hierarchical beams of light; the story changes "center" for "periphery" as a new cherished territoriality of circulation of those critical energies that pretend to undermine the predominance of fixed perspectives and true representation. This inversion is a ubiquitous periphery—deterritorializing—which changes its place, image, and representation, thanks to the artifices that art tactically elaborates in order to redesign the visual field of the social from new breakdowns in perspective and the contortion of angles.

But *El padre mío* doesn't just invert the stigma of existential dispossession in an accumulation of nomadic and actively proliferating signs that make an urban critique of the poverty of language under which the existing order obligates the inhabitants of the city to live by submitting to the law of wage labor. In addition, its aesthetic productivity transports the problematic of the residue from a sociology of marginality (which only knows how to diagnose lack and alienation in relation to a schematic order of needs) toward a new symbolic-metaphoric mode of overflowing forms that liberate a plurality of expressive material and analogical flows. Aesthetic creativity composes the potency of a story that carries the social narrative beyond the borders guarded by normative thinking, which only seeks to redirect the flare-ups of the aberrant (symptoms and metaphors) to an axis of analytical control that reinserts its contents into the explicative and disciplinarian reticulum of science.[18]

El padre mío's perspective on the residues of social marginality avails itself of the creative and imaginary distances (fictional) that its poetic marginality interposes against the recuperative will that the system uses to appeal to the unadapted and unadaptable so that they readapt themselves to the map of functional identities. The novel brandishes a poetic inscription in the text that it is "not trying to overturn anything or cure anyone" but instead proposes to "install that moving effect of speech and an aesthetic relationship of words emptied of meaning, of any logic, except the anguish of syllabic persecution of syllables, the echo from the enjambment of its rhymes, the vitality of the subject who speaks, the rigorously real existence of the city's margins."[19]

The baroque nature of this politico-aesthetic reading of the margins is due to the contortions created by the madness of the marginal character and by the crazy utterances of a poetic dissidence. Both simultaneously exalt their irreducible transgressiveness to the social order (given the urban drift of a body radically alien to its normal productivity) and to sociology (because of the antitestimonial aspect of a wandering speech that perverts the explicit demand for objective reality in testimonial works). *El padre mío*'s performance of these contortions had to exercise a significant displacement that was capable of exchanging the *names of power* (the dictator and his other incarnations) for *the power to play with names*: that is, for the power of using the "truth" of testimony to fictionalize the voice in a baroque register that intensifies disparity and eccentricity as traits of fragmentation (social, psychic, and verbal) of identity representation, but now bereft of any valid, unifying synthesis. Such a displacement between power and literature passes through a meltdown of names and a metaphorization of the residue, that is, by means of an intensifying criticism of social and cultural residualness undertaken by the aesthetic metaphor.[20] By dressing up the scabs with adornments in order to cross-dress the social figure of the vagabond with the luminescence of linguistic particles that do not yield to the dogma of the representational, *El padre mío* conjoins residue and metaphor as a double parasitical mark of errancy and deviation (of meaning's nonlinearity), but also that of excess and contagion: a mark impure not only in its stylistic modes of contaminating the present with the suppurating wounds of the past with unclear borders, but also by virtue of being left over—contrary to neoliberal realities that are technically oriented toward a sole economic capitalization of that which is "useful."

CHAPTER FOUR

The Congealment of the Pose
and Urban Velocities

There is no center here. . . . I have sought it out attentively, with
determination and focus. I have situated the beginning of these events in
different areas, trying to move from them: Mapocho Station, Plaza de Armas,
Barrio Cívico, Paseo Ahumada, la Quinta Normal, Plaza Italia. All refer to a
date of failure, to that which robs them of existence. They implore me to
question another monument, to be left in peace. None have the mark, the
inscription.

—GUADALUPE SANTA CRUZ

Ever since I became familiar with these photos collected over the years
by Chilean artist Eugenio Dittborn,[1] they have been hovering around me,
without my knowing whether they were so powerfully captivating because
of the images themselves (the seriality of the bodies, the obsessional mark
of an invariable repetition of manners and postures), or because of the
obsessive decision to join all these images to create this unique collection
of stereotypes and thereby satisfy a strange mania for systems.

For years, I maintained a latent interest in these photographs, suddenly
reactivated by the contrast of looks between past and present, nowadays
implicated in their condition as images brutally divided between a photographic freezing of time and the new scenario of urban precipitations and
accelerations in Santiago. The intersecting lines of the subway that daily
transports multitudes of semiperipheral bodies to the Baquedano station,
going underneath the imperial tower of the Chilean Telecommunications

Company (CTC)—bodies being transported to a "center" whose physical and communicative density no longer belongs to them, since message flows are exchanged via satellite by the long-distance commerce of transnationals—are simply one of the innovations that have redesigned the crossing of Plaza Italia according to the increasing speed of transformation of the city, which none of the women in these images could have dreamed remotely possible.

As I look at the anteriority of these poses still unaware of the modernizing shock awaiting them in an unpredictable future, what stands out is its radical alienness to everything that would later befall them and plunge them into a profound state of urban commotion. It is as if the sameness of the pose, taken in the same place, with the same type of shot in the same format—the fixity of the identical repeated in all the photos—tacitly exaggerated the subsequent violence of the nonidentical. A contrary direction whose future of contrary movements would patently belie the photographic stature of these poses that in the shot still harbored the belief in the vertical composition and the center, in hierarchies and symmetries. The photographic and urban lines that control these poses would now no longer guarantee the same powers of concentration. Compulsive flows of velocity and spatial displacement daily launch these popular bodies toward a city where life is characterized by the erasure of memories-in-use (previously sedimented in corners and locales). The displacement and erasure are caused by the hysterical multiplication of imported brand names and logos encrusting their metropolitan look on the daily lives of these peripheral bodies who are called on monthly by the seduction of department store credit cards, also reminders of their local debt within the globalization of capital.

What makes these images perturbing has as much to do with the visual anachronism of a temporality consigned to a pose that is impassive to any future as it does with its bygone look of black-and-white photography, almost untranslatable to the language of the international market, overstimulated by so many idioms of advertising. These urban poses, unmistakably local and provincial, have hardened into a greater anachronism by what replaced the photographic gallery, that is, the exhibitionist symbol of the CTC tower, which today from the Plaza Italia dominates the entire city of Santiago, making its lines of perspective converge on an inexorably high point that—technologically and commercially—poses blithely unaware of what goes on beneath: life's incoherencies, panic-induced disorientations, lapses and stutters of identity, existential unravelings, the hollowing out of

history. This new, end-of-century monument to interplanetary satellitiza-
tion, which has revolutionized the scene that was familiar to the women
in Dittborn's photos, virtually underlines how far the out-of-time, out-of-
place look of their poses situates them in a complete state of national
emergency ("the current moment is all that is pending. Today's Chile is the
superimposition of all it has forgotten. The Transition to democracy—the
official name of today's Chile—would become the unmoving oblivion of
transition via satellite, the transnationalization of telecommunications,
amnesias provoked by particles moving at the speed of light."[2]

Social Memories

This series of images collected by E. Dittborn spans, through its diachronic
succession of portraits, ten years of life stories. The artist bought the plates
of these photographic portraits taken between 1970 and 1980 by the photographer Damasio Ulloa, who appears in the last photo (a Polaroid) of
the series: the series is a *mise-en-abîme* of the pasts—subjective and objective—of the Polaroid image, whose development displaced the accordion
camera of D. Ulloa into a prehistory of the portrait, almost entirely gone
from our urban scene. The last Polaroid photo, taken by Dittborn, brings
together the temporal differences that affect what had been photographed
(people, and urban shots) and the photographier (the technical look), all
in the same lapse shared by a premodernity of reproductive media, of visual
grammars and urban figures that recapitulate different types of social
decay in the final synthesis of an image over which is superimposed—in
compressed fashion—multiple events, replacements, and translations of
socially heterogeneous codes. The artist's gesture takes responsibility for
documenting the temporal stratifications of sociohistorical memory visual-
ized through photographic technique, making the preservation of memory
and the enunciation of its disappearance converge synthetically in this last
Polaroid image.

Dittborn's entire work has achieved this minute redemption of precarious and struggle-laden temporalities that are lived in the litigious course
of histories and memories.[3] Without the guarantee of a technical supplement of photographic permanence and duration, these temporalities would
have already fatally succumbed to fleeting transitoriness. But although the
photo grants them the supplement of duration that they need in order not
to vanish in the fleeting moment, these photographic scenes still run the risk
of historical erasure because this small memory is discardable: a memory

Series of photographs collected by Eugene Dittborn (1970–1980).

made of the tiny fragments of a minor historicity only legible from the "clipping" in which Dittborn syntactically isolates them from their totalities in order to investigate—in the details of its details—that which tends to be ignored or repressed in grand social compositions and their visions of the whole. These operations of multitemporal hybridization, in which "signs that belong to different temporal strata and distanced from themselves finally find each other here [in the shot], and when they do find each other they become reciprocally visible,"[4] thereby confirm the strategic role of the photo—a visual marker of appearances and disappearances—battling between past and future as does every moment of the present. Dittborn has systematically managed to join the befores and the afters of each technical sectioning off performed by modernity in order to reconstruct a microscopically convulsed surface of social experiences where the old and the new, the bygone and the actual, the passé and the advanced, the expired and the relevant, are read in a maximum conflagration of its perceptual schemata, visual models, productive forces, and vital energies. Thus the work evokes the multitude of burials and exhumations to which each image is exposed, releasing pasts apparently sealed beneath the crypt of remembrance toward mobile articulations that bring about a retroreading of its inconclusive meanings; these retemporalize the mnemonic trace of the past, so that the actuality of its occurrence and emergence shake up the historicist continuity of tradition with the disruptive intervention of its "Now-time" (Benjamin—"Time filled by the presence of the now").

The technosocial memory of the productive mediations of modernity staged by Dittborn's work narrates a history of substitutions and dismissals whose metropolitan rhythms point to the passing fashions that are quickly dispatched one by another so that the straight line of progress can advance without coming up against forking, divergent, or contrary temporal realms of lagging localities and temporalities. By bringing together the anachronic and synchronic of different and crisscrossed times within the fractured interiority of a single sequence of images, Dittborn confronts the interior realm of the sequence of multiple historical abysses that divide their social chronology, in order to make the actuality of modernity remember the historical obliterations from which it edits the news items of change. But Dittborn's work forces pasts and presents to correct each other from the perspective of the demands and protests that each time period virtually directs at the other, thus making their respective models of technical comprehension and social intelligibility confront one another: "to work simultaneously with various techniques, showing how they are assembled, means

working with different sets of understanding, it means working accompanied by a group of memories. The joining of memories makes each one
think and reflect when faced with another memory, inducing them to
exchange their memories. What they emit jointly is the vision that each
one has gained against the others, and becomes the work that they have
jointly done."[5]

The Polaroid that self-reflexively concludes the series of photographic
portraits by Damasio Ulloa with a new technique that portrays him in the
condition of witness to his own past as photographer makes the "camera
turn back on itself" to stratify the look with the discontinuous subtext of
a local history that superimposes progressions and regressions in a disordered fashion, outside a framework of organic development and temporal
coherence. "If the development of photography depends on a substitution
of the daguerreotype process, a direct positive on metal plates, through the
process of positives and negatives, where one can imprint an unlimited
number of copies (positives) from an original (negative)," and "if the
Polaroid revives the principle of a daguerreotype camera,"[6] the Plaza Italia
series mounted by Dittborn takes the history of photography back to its
origins (from the Polaroid to the box camera that foreshadows it), abbre-
viating the technical development of the rationality of progress, which
should be marked by intermediate stages. And it is the brusqueness of that
leap which communicates the disjointedness of Latin American modernity,
its grafts and transplants of processes bastardly mixed by the transcultural
citation.

The image of urban time evoked in the photos of Damasio Ulloa has
become almost irretrievable. Today the Plaza Italia has suppressed from its
optical center that small factory of portraits through which an entire gallery of urban types paraded as collectible items, different, say, from what
happens with the Plaza de Armas, where still (but only until the new urban
redesign requires a subway station?) you find an accumulation of certain
remains of social cohabitation, although unmoored from their original
contexts and mixed together with no sense of hierarchy and tradition.
Despite the ritual interweaving of their meeting points being interrupted
by the explosive emergence of dialects (tourist, evangelical, commercial,
prostitution, magazines, etc.) whose barbarisms have unsettled the foundational myths of the urban center, the street painters and itinerant mer-
chants, the au pair and the soldier, the retiree and the secretary still "make
a date" with the box camera photographer, who portrays them all in a collage—hybrid and popular—of the transmodern sedimentations that the

Plaza de Armas reflects. None of this occurs in the Plaza Italia, which has erased the historical and social remains of everything that came before its arrogant reign of architectural novelty. The CTC tower, erasing precedents and origins, has disconnected its shining technological and satellite-like image from any archaic remnants of identity that could question the success of the facades of the hyperurbanization of Santiago, with the shameful dyslexia of poverty and backwardness.

Urban Landscapes

Wanting to be photographed has to do with the desire to perpetuate a circumstance in which the person deems the moment worthy of being remembered by means of an image memory that cuts and frames a special occasion, withdrawing it from the regular and ever-changing flow of anonymous lived realities to show off this specialness within a framework of exclusivity. The popular use of photography tells us that it serves "to make the great moments solemn and eternal,"[7] conferring on them the value of an event, a memorable slice of time worth commemorating.

The monuments built in plazas and on avenues evoking the grandiosity of a national past habitually serve as a backdrop so that photographic tourism can give a solemn air to the experience of being-in-the-city. One of the most popular plazas of Santiago as a place to be photographed is the Plaza Italia, "because it has a monument to a national hero," according to the national president of the Chilean Photographers Union.[8]

The leisure time of the Sunday stroll in the photos collected by Dittborn gravitates toward a photographic citation that traverses these feminine bodies with the hard lines of power mapped out to divide the city into hierarchical partitions of places and social standings. The Plaza Italia is a capital cite/site,[9] since photography took the domestic bodies of these women and made them intersect with the severe north-south, east-west axis, which divides not only geographic sectors but also urban roles and public identifications. Segregated by the diagonals of social power, the body occupies the "center" of operations of the plaza as backdrop, symbolically defying—with their "centered" posing—the sum of daily marginalizations to which it is condemned by the discipline of citizenship. The scenic backdrop of the monument to a national hero elevates a foundational symbol to the heights of that photographic "appropriation." If a public statue is made to glorify transcendental figures and episodes of the patriotic narrative, what better example than the illustrious reference of its monument projecting onto the small photographic document the certification of a posteriority that will save the scene from oblivion, making a permanent photographic bond between contingency and eternity?

The capital cite/site of these women with the city is enacted by photographing the event of a battle as worthy of celebration as those that figure in the calendar of national heroes. A matter of celebrating the act of liberty, of "going out into the street." The transgression of borders that divide social organization into private worlds and public places, according to the scripted role of feminine and masculine sexual ideology, gives the phrase "going out into the street" a subtext of risks and adventures contained in the expression "to get lost in the city" (lose oneself), and in the urban traffic controlled by men. For a woman to "lose herself in the city" carries a double meaning, of wandering aimlessly to get involved with the unknown, in unofficial networks of streetwise promiscuity. The way in which these women order their stroll, starting from the monument as an urban guide that serves as photographic referent, lets us guess (from the secret, lateral derivations, hidden out of frame) everything that exceeds the image's format, that is, the dangers and temptations that would upset the order of that constructed pose surrounded by a safe centrality. The wanderings and meanderings through the nooks—cavities, porosities—of the irregular city transgress the convention of the limit between private and public, family and citizen, the domestic and the social, with the ins and outs of curiosity.

The photographic portraits taken at the foot of the monument in Plaza Italia show their subjects supported by a point of urban reference imbued with the maximum of historic symbolism, trying to conjure the anonymity of their life of anybody with the proximity of a glorious legend of an unforgettable destiny. Currently none of the terms articulated by this chain of territorial reference (geography) and national traditions (history) to which the photographed women credulously subscribed remains in vogue. It is no longer possible to geographically control the panorama of the city from an isolated locality that is sufficiently distanced from the chaotic proliferation of multitudes; the exemplary lives of illustrious citizens are not remembered by the landmark of monuments that glorify their historical transcendence but instead are commented in the day-to-day news that builds a legend of ephemeral celebrities that irradiate from the media spectacle. "Chilean leisure time"[10] is consumed no longer by the family cult of the souvenir photograph to be shared with a group but in the impersonal rite of shopping for discardable goods.

Surrounded by the solitude of an empty milieu that should not interfere with the concentration of their absorbed poses in the transcendent
symbol of the Center, the photographic heroines of Plaza Italia show
themselves to be completely alien to the future upheavals of Santiago's
urban modernization. Without a doubt, these strollers of a "sad Sunday
captured on hot photographic plates" would today be distracted from the
social exhaustion by rituals more eccentric than concentric.[11] Whereas in
the recent past "one went to the center from the neighborhoods as a special activity, on a holiday, as a nightly outing, as a shopping expedition,"
because "going out and to the center promised . . . the exploration of an
always different territory,"[12] today it is the peripheral character of the malls
that attracts the Sunday journey with its false streets and avenues that simulate a city within a city, without a sense of direction other than that
graphically marked by ads that orient the intramural transit of strollers
under commercial vigilance.

The desire to resort to a monument situated in the middle of Santiago to
affirm a photographic identity points to a controlled relationship between
urban geometry and its rationalization by means of perspective that still
belongs to the imaginary of the city panorama. The tourist and urban
imaginary of this city panorama inhabited by these photographic clients
of D. Ulloa has disappeared. The labyrinthine expansion of circulation
networks, infused by "velocity regimes" (Virilio) with their flow of bodies,
money, and messages, has erased all reference to a central hierarchy that
orders an overall vision of the city, bringing together all its planes into an
integrated and encompassing whole. The axis of the monument and the
centrality of a plaza that fixes these photographic bodies anchors the urban
representation within a topic that made the lived nexus between locality
and totality legible. This topic has been disarticulated by the hypermobility
of the coordinates of sign transmission that nowadays circulate through
the city's space-time without stopping at any stable point, impeding the
subject from fixing his or her position within the map and from reading
the map from a clearly situated place.

The photographic pose of the women of Plaza Italia represents, perhaps,
the last attempt of identity repetition that obtains its graphic legibility
from an urban perspective traced out before the city exploded into multi-
directional networks of images and signs that are immaterially superimposed and crisscrossed, disintegrating the cohering nucleus of the subject's
corporeal unity and disorienting his or her symbols of a recognizable identity.[13] Today the cognition and recognition of the city collide against the

urban velocity of multispatial and ahistorical transits, which leave behind, in the solitude of oblivion, those bodies that are still subjected to the unity of a central axis of temporal and geographic organization of the gaze.[14]

Photographic Bodies

City, gaze, and photography build their complicities of meaning thanks to the protagonistic role of sight that runs through all modern experience of urban life.[15] Street scenes exacerbate the ocular displacements solicited by the proliferation of visual stimuli—signs, shopwindows, faces, signals, et cetera—that continuously submerge the gaze into multiple and fragmentary planes of optical representation. The visual traffic of bodies that cross each other in the street creates distances and proximities according to the chance rhythm of encounters made possible under the primacy of the gaze, as a network of exteriorities. This optical network proliferates until it traverses all the urban surface, forcing each face to participate in a visual reciprocity of seeing and being seen, which compels the eye to decipher the urban subjectivities according to an erotics of the fleeting and the casual.

The solitary pose of the photographic heroines of Plaza Italia places them at the margin of this ever-changing game of visual interactions, of face-to-face encounters caused by chance pedestrian rhythms. They look fixedly at the mechanical eye that depicts them in that *being seen* of the shot, as if only the immobility of the person and her concentrated effort to reflect an interior and profound psychology of self could act as a refuge against the fragmentary dispersions of the street, whose contact zone of gazes is a mere trafficking in surfaces.

In the rhetoric of photography, the pose—the technical armature of the portrait—is the photogenic mold of an identity whose characteristics should reveal the supposed individuality of a subject brimming with the fantasies of self-expression. We know, however, that individuality is only expressed under the condition of making that untransferable uniqueness of personal traits pass through the collective nature of an identity matrix whose photographic norms are repetition and massification: "the face of man is submitted to a maximum extortion; under the pretext of registering that face in its uniqueness and distinctiveness, the shot, in fact, does exactly the opposite: by applying a one-and-the-same photographic norm, it standardizes the face, cutting it up to order, and massifying it, multiplying the order in the visage so that order can be reproduced unlimitedly and definitively through the face."[16]

The pose molds the human expression according to visual stereotypes of the conventions of photographic portraits, and the photographic portrait serves as a technical metaphor that charges modernity with turning an original into a copy, the unique and singular (the human face) into something multiple and interchangeable (its serial repetition). This is the identity dilemma posed by the women photographed in the Plaza Italia, who are, without knowing it, doing battle with what is individual within the standardized format of the collective, summed up in the generic nature of the portrait. The serialized, professional shot taken by a box camera photographer (a shot identical to itself) has obliged them to renounce any idea of personality, submitting the women to the blackmail of a depersonalizing pose, making interchangeable what none of them would have ever changed for anything: their desire to self-express an image patiently studied and modeled in order to reveal what was different in each one, that is, what was proper to each (and what could not be appropriated) and is now converted into the common denominator of the series.

Frontality and centrality are the photogenic coordinates of a ceremonial identity subjected to a strict protocol of predefined gestures and attitudes, so as not to run the risk of exhibiting the awkwardness of an improvised corporeality (natural) that has not had the time or the ability to harmonize itself visually to purposefully express its traits in the pose. The posteriority of photographic memory will consecrate the idealization of what the "I" (self) has calculatedly prepared and framed as identity: interior truth, human essence, an individual mask, and psychological depth. These fabricated interpretations of the "self" are not only mediated by the stereotypes of the technical language of the pose. These interpretations are also ruled by the norms of dominant socialization daily transmitted by cultural ideologies and their microtechniques of body and identity formation that call on subjects to dress themselves officially according to an inflexible typology of classes, genders, and sexes. Here the fixity of the pose also speaks to us about the rigidity of identity patterns that articulated the regime of Chilean sociability portrayed in those photos, pointing out the structure of domination that was exercised "first, over the Indians, then over the peasant, over women, nature, peons and sharecroppers, the workers, and the truly destitute."[17] This is the vertical weight of authoritarian tradition endured by the bodies of these women who inadvertently re-cite the canonical text of inherited subjugations.

These women photographed by D. Ulloa belong to the Chile of the seventies and were severely governed by laws of identity stratification whose antagonistic segments delimited class roles and positions through exterior languages (conduct, clothes, gestures, etc.) that needed to be mutually incommunicable. Today, such a framework seems to have acquired more plasticity and creative mobility, stimulated by the spectacle of hyperfragmentation and the combination of diverse advertising styles, which appear to dynamically infuse the old signs of social presentation with their new mixed rhythms. The static definition of identities, previously defined by a valorizing-normative authoritarianism of the political code, gravitates nowadays toward the socioeconomic realm, attracted by the seductions of advertising, which promises to multiply horizontally the relations of consumption and participation. Even though the market does not fulfill this promise, since it again segments the signs of identity behind an apparent flexibility of lifestyles, it is true that the network of connections of transnational visual advertising has disorganized the compartmentalization of tastes that traditionally marked fashion's scale of "distinction."

The photos collected by E. Dittborn denote the resigned obedience of its models to a fashion system that in the past distributed identities according to key elements of economic power that drastically separated rich from poor, making them unmistakably identifiable one from the other by the marked differences that should separate their respective dress codes. Nowadays, the imported fashions disseminate and extend their no-longer-select grammar of styles to the underclass that flocks to the great department stores in the working-class sectors of the city. Through credit, poorer consumers deal in the same market offerings as richer consumers, without the item purchased revealing the social rank or privilege of the fashion user who wears them daily. Women from different social backgrounds display similar accoutrements, making each article of clothing blur the social distinctions of the body that wears them, making the recognition of the pecking order more difficult to discern. Both the hybridity of the styles and the proliferating confusion of clothing signs generate ambiguous readings that place women halfway between a uniformity of fashion and the nonuniformity of manners, almost always leaving open spaces, so that certain creative inflections will deviate from the grammar of social backgrounds, as is the case, for example, with the fashion of wearing used clothing.

One of the effects generated by these mixtures and upheavals of style is demonstrated by the current fascination with retro fashion that has made seventies styles popular, a style seen in these women photographed at Plaza Italia. However, despite the affinity of their clothing with the retrospective tastes of today, there is something in these poses that declares

itself untransferable in the play of cites/sites with which we could reactivate their appearance. Maybe it's the lack of syntactical discontinuity in
the overall dress code of the epoch that keeps us from interpreting it as a
postmodernist collage; maybe it is the photographic armature of their
pose in the linear prolongation of a severe urban composition that makes
these poses untranslatable into the airy and eclectic playfulness that rotates
mutating and provisional identities that are now so much in style. With
its engraved disobedience of provincial anachronism, Dittborn's photographic series exhibits a certain recalcitrance of the pose that insistently
belies the visual plasticity of the electronic catalog of globalized identities
and the oblivion-laden fluidities of its market recyclings.

CHAPTER FIVE

Dismantlings of Identity,
Perversions of Codes

The dominant culture's conjunction of codes with subcultures whose access to hegemony is usually blocked by its cultural marginality produces a peripheral person, who is the sum, and not the lack, of all the codes that he or she selects.

Identity, in this universe, is not something essential, homogeneous, or fixed, but instead a transitory and multiple condition that becomes an event in the confluence of ever-changing cultural amalgams.

—CELESTE OLALQUIAGA

Clothes, dress fashion codes, are one of the languages through which cultural identities are expressed in a dialogue of voices (canonical or parodic) with the already-constructed discourse of social classes and sexual representations. Cultural identities become aware of themselves when they select, among different bodily presentations in society, ways of dressing that speak of their roles, genders, and social positions, and display local lifestyles and customs that are now redesigned by multinational images from everywhere.

The mass commercialization of used clothing during the past few years in Chile seems to have multiplied the confusions between what is national and imported, the local and the transnational, to the point of submerging the clothing of the urban poor into a kind of dyslexia of uncoded articles that circulate thanks to the cheapness and casualness of the mixtures: bastard remainders of imported clothing, cheap leftovers of metropolitan serial fashions that are reassembled by popular bodies that stroll in them, forming a visual spectacle of a collage identity without a coherence of style or a unified vocabulary. The noncohesion between the contextual references to which the clothing is so dissimilarly associated has given way to a new cultural multiplicity of hybrid significations that chaotically weave through the popular urban sectors, reorganizing local segmentations and social differentiation according to unexpected arrangements of signs, uses, values, and styles.

The Wearing Out of the New

The interpreters of modernity associate the philosophical and cultural definition of the modern with the absolute predominance of the New, which symbolizes the idea of progress, with its temporal dynamism that moves in accelerated fashion toward the future. The central spirit of modernity lies in a "longing for change," "an enjoyment of mobility," and "a struggle for renovation."[1] Innovation, change, and renovation form a series of replacements and substitutions that posit the New always breaking with an *expired past* tradition. Modernity thus acquires the form of a fashion show, of a succession of changes whose visual rhetoric celebrates the diversity of lifestyles, patterns of taste, and social rules. The fashion industry exhibits that metropolitan example of modern life as a catalog of novelties, all of them discardable, and renewable, according to the laws of the market, which dictate "an obsolescence of style" to consecrate modernity as something that is in fashion and that will go out of fashion: as something to be consumed and spent before its currency becomes the past. The triumph of the sign-fashion mode authorizes this meaning of modernity as a vector of change that revolutionizes the temporal series in order to impose its metropolitan slogan of "keeping up" while, in the periphery, the newness of the center is received as the imported sign of a failed contemporaneousness. This constitutive mark of Latin American backwardness reveals the lag of noncoincidence between sign and experience, the current and the residual, novelty and untimeliness.

With used clothing—which offends the metropolitan slogan of "being modern" as "being up to the latest fashion"—the periphery finally finds itself: it ultimately coincides with its hidden truth by laying bare that in Latin America the simulacrum of the new is always consumed in a deferred manner.[2]

Used clothing is sold as if it were new, but its "as if" registers a worn-out memory that refuses to idealize the "actuality" of the New made absolute by a modernity seen "as the nontemporal value of a sign cut off from all anteriority."[3] Used clothing changes the diachrony of a programmed succession of novelties made to substitute one modernity for the other by the synchronic coexistence of articles that were once in fashion, and that now all together exhibit—without shame and in disorder—their noncurrentness or worn-out styles (postmodernity). The metropolitan fantasy of the "pure actuality" of the "sign-fashion" mode has been rewritten by a kind of Third World allegory of recycling, which opens up its critical interval of cultural simulation and double readings in order to belie, ironically, that the modern tale of the New must always be pure innovation.

Disuniformity, Restratification

In Chile, U.S. secondhand clothing was first a solution to finding cheap clothing that allowed people deprived of economic access to modern shopping centers to dress inexpensively.[4] After jeans, the used clothing brought from the United States became the second-most-important North American export product as a popular article of mass consumption.

The popularity of jeans was first due to their functionality (durability, comfort, etc.) and to their ability to cross sexual, class, age, and racial categories, without encouraging undue attention. Jeans dismantle the connotations of sexual and social belonging by crossing through all identities with their neutral definitions. It is a standardizing and democratizing sign that renounces class distinction. The logic of jeans assumes that men and women, young and old, poor and rich, First and Third Worlds, share the same garment as a symbol of "community integration."[5] Despite the effects of advertising that generates differential subcodes through brand-name competition, jeans tend to deindividualize. On the other hand, used clothing breaks the mass-produced monotony with articles that are mixed together in a maximum of heterogeneity of articles and styles, thereby multiplying the possibilities for each buyer to individualize and make a unique statement of his or her sartorial image. While jeans deactivate what is singular-personal in favor of the multiple-repeated, used clothing activates the imagination around a fantasy of the unrepeatable that is symbolized by the unique article, discontinued, outside the catalog.

But in today's Chile, used clothing represents not only a low-cost alternative worn by low-income majorities. As social prejudices against used clothing begin to give way under the international pressure of the fashion industry and its fantasies of style, recourse to used clothing extends to the upper classes.[6] As they move up to the wealthy neighborhoods, used-clothing stores adopt new codes of visual and social presentation, re-creating a hierarchy of relations between original and copy that have been reshuffled by the anarchy of a dress code that promiscuously mixes in different uses.[7]

The elevation of used clothing to the wealthy areas of the city attempts to reposition the rank of taste against the chaotic. The restratification of fashion bargains yields to a new aesthetic of distinction that converts finding a cut-rate price into a renewed class privilege. High-income groups justify their recourse to secondhand clothing by saying that such clothing allows them to enjoy the mix of the exclusive and the casual stimulated by the whims of fashion, the fantasy of a great find. Thus they rob from the needy the benefits of low prices on remaindered items and of sales, hiding their theft of opportunity behind the hypocritical argument of a selective and exclusive refinement of taste.

The Bazaar's Narrativity

The "fashion system" orders the sartorial language of dress, following a predesigned logic of use and circumstance that governs wardrobe selection.[8] The great stores that commercialize the fashion industry tend to classify dress according to function and distribute them, separately, in areas that pertain to each group: underwear, coats and raincoats, dresses and skirts, blouses, sporting wear, et cetera. Used-clothing stores break with that scheme by having in the same field of vision the anarchic conviviality of a bathrobe and an elegant suit, of beachwear thrown in with an overcoat. The different articles of clothing are brought together in the disorder of heterogeneous accumulation that breaks with the industrial syntagma of dress wear classified by sex and size, place and climate, mode and circumstance.

The chance principle of this irregular sum joins articles designated for activities that are incompatible among themselves according to the official script of life in society, which cuts down and limits roles in strict adjustment to the realistic expectations of each circumstance. The chaotic juxtaposition of unclassified articles in a used-clothing store, its anarchic overturning of the most dissimilar modes of sartorial presentation, uncouple the representational model of the body onstage that the social script canonizes daily. To lose oneself as a customer among that confusion of clothes and the incoherence of its lifestyles breaks with the monotony of the serial dress codes by engaging a fantasy of multiplying images of the person combined according to a whimsical rhythm of improvisations that deprograms the rigid segmentations of daily conduct.

The industrial language of dressing is faithful to this logic of the system that fixes "fashion's textuality" (industrial dress wear, women's magazines, advertising, etc.) while the used clothing sold in more-modest shops— tossed into bins—appears cut off from any signifying matrix, unlinked to the general repertory that classifies the signs traditionally summed up in the fashion show, the shopwindow, and the mannequin. Used clothing all thrown into a bin is an assault on the figurative nature of the shopwindow, erasing the scenic ploys of the showcase window that places the model in passive exhibition(ism), removed from the contingencies of physical manipulation. The mannequin in the shopwindow idealizes the body of fashion as pure *sign*. It visually synthesizes the sartorial discourse of fashion, creating a distance between touching and looking (between matter and concept, substance and ideality). Used clothing tossed into bins beckons the proximity of a primitive tactility and exploration, making the body nar- ratively live the encounter with the disordered multiplicity of temptations that clog the locale according to the overaccumulative model of the bazaar.

Nothing is further removed from this bazaar's narrativity and the pro- miscuity of senses (narratives and sensations) of used-clothing stores than the shopping model fixed by the signal postings of the mall, where the relationship between shopwindow, desire, and brand name is governed by market universality, without the slightest hope that the dissimilarity of an article outside the code could upset the serial programming of advertising taste. The malls, which decontextually reproduce their own systematiza- tion without their architecture ever taking into consideration the physical or local characteristics of their urban surroundings, have artificially erased the social division between the center of the city and its peripheries with a new model of urban extraterritoriality that re-creates a space and time "without qualities."[9] The abstractedness of this model—reaffirmed by the homogeneous order of geometries functional to the exclusive needs of consumption—is the opposite of the sedimentation of experiences whose signifying use values continue to adhere irregularly to a narrativity that, for example, traverses the bazaar of used clothing.

American Residues

In March 1983, the Chilean art group CADA (Art in Action Collective) exhibited an installation in Washington, D.C., called *American Residues*.[10]

The work dealt with the "relationship between U.S. used clothing sent to Chile for resale, and brain surgery on a destitute person," a recording of which was retransmitted on audiotape, which also formed part of the installation.[11]

In the work's dialectic, the used clothing had the value of commercial surplus, since it was leftover merchandise that designated an affluent country, while the brain operation revealed the stigma of a double lack and a shattering (misery and sickness). As part of an international show that took place in the capital of economic exchange (Washington), the work could be read as mocking its market economy: as art that returned to this great center of financial power, the peripheral symbol of a negative resale (that is, not consumed) that denounced, inversely, the arrogance of multinational capitalism that aspires to buy everything. Ailing Chile—the Chile of the dictatorship—donates to the United States its ailment as sole possession: something whose symbolic value exceeds what can be adjusted to the language of the market.

The work thus resignifies the residual in two senses: as a denunciatory tactic, since it accuses the disequilibrium that obliges the Third World to live off the consumerist leftovers of the First World, and as vengeful parody by designing a counteroffensive that feigns participation in the exchange with something leftover but useless to its receiver (a damaged brain).

The crossed itineraries of used clothing—from the United States to Chile and back to the United States—that CADA's work converts into a support for its artistic production also stage the conflict between metropolitan neovanguardist discourse and the resemanticizing strategies of Latin American art. By using the product of market recycling as artistic support, CADA's installation plays with the metropolitan commonplace of déjà vu that habitually disqualifies Latin American art, and infuses its aesthetic mechanism of recycling with critical meaning. The work expressed irony within the rules of international artistic market competition by using secondhand clothing as artistic material and as a perverse symbol of peripheral performativity that mocked the metropolitan demand for the new. By critically reconceptualizing used clothing as a worn-out symbol of a commodity out of fashion, CADA's installation mocked the relationship of hierarchy and subordination between original and copy that the international dogma of faith in the superiority of metropolitan origin(ality) professes, and in the foundational authority of a model to imitate and submissively reproduce.

To Contaminate the Suspicion of the Unknown

It is not surprising that the habit of buying used clothing is principally reserved for developing countries. Having been previously inhabited by another body, clinging to used clothing's fabric is the imaginary web of physical evocation and corporeal associations that always threaten to filter through beyond the industrial guarantee of what is clean and disinfected ("for many, used clothing provokes an unconscious rejection. As if this type of clothing had belonged to someone repulsive, which has led to situations where buyers have submitted the articles to all kinds of washings, with the object of avoiding physical contact with microbes or bacteria").[12]

By having been in close contact with another's skin, by having rubbed against the surface of another body, the fabric of used clothing is a repository of odors and secret stains. Odors are always suspicious because they are emblematic of the most intimate aspects of the natural body and because they refer us to a diffuse animalness that the regulatory body of civilization has not been able to domesticate completely. Odors also carry the stigma of an unknown race: culturally speaking, judgments about race tend to express themselves sensorially around issues of bad odors or strange smells. Aside from smell, used clothing also carries the threat of stains that reveal the skin-induced accidents of a body that might carry skin diseases.

Used clothing introduces doubt, it posits uncertainty, it casts a suspicion that infects the sterilized vision of the world supported by "the increasing medicalization of the hygiene of existence":[13] a vision of advanced societies that seek obsessively to control the danger of trafficking bodies in a time apocalyptically marked by the AIDS plague. The idea that germs and microbes can hide in the secrecy of the fabric and interlinings of local commercial outlets of used clothing contaminates the paranoid ideal of the healthy body that the prosperous center seeks to isolate from any epidermic contact with the epidemic flows of underdevelopment.

Parodies and Recyclings: San Camilo

The reconversion of identity to which secondhand clothing lends itself illustrates one of the dynamics of peripheral consumerism that consists of using transnational commodities according to domestic variants that modify their original logic of precedence. The peripheral consumption of used clothing would be one more example of how the popular subject deals culturally by "constructing his/her own sentence starting from a received vocabulary and syntax,"[14] thus separating the forms from their functions: deforming the antecedents dictated by their original context and generating new, local configurations that transform the imported matrix.

The elements for dressing selected by the consumer of used clothes derive from a heterogeneous source of repertoires—geographic, sociocultural, aesthetic—which are mixed together by chance by selecting and combining realities that, at first glance, seem dissimilar. The stylistic montage of various fragments of dress wear dissociated among themselves make the body of the user into a *body of cites/sites*, traversed by hybrid languages. The used clothes function as a concept-metaphor of a peripheral identity plotted by discontinuous languages, which recombine their signs without the referential guide of an organic totality: they are disseminated remains of languages severed from their circuits of traditional habits and tastes that are reassembled by a postmodernist collage that critiques fixed and homogeneous identities, deeply linked to originating spaces and times.

The poor transvestite of San Camilo Street resorts to used clothing in order to fantasize with borrowed or stolen identities. He mounts her/his simulacrum of glamorous femininity with the cheap ruse of secondhand clothing that allows her/him, by copying gringo dress styles, to accomplish an imitative fantasy of repetitions. The peripheral transvestite finds in the bazaar of U.S. clothing her own code of impropriety and of counterappropriations that degrade the correct rules of dressing well exhibited by bourgeois femininity, with coarse, carnivalesque exaggerations and maskings.

New York transvestites from the movie *Paris Is Burning* (Jenny Livingstone, 1994) show how a marginalized black man dresses like a woman, imitating the stereotype of a top white model who illustrates the conventions of an advertising-style-market femininity. Transvestism is used by drag queens as a camouflage so that the alternative discourse of ethnic, social, and sexual marginality can—almost without detection—infiltrate the codes of dominant culture; they blend in with its official identities so as to be able to saunter more freely by the central byways of the system and secretly infect the boundaries of required models of identification.[15] Fashion and elegance are the *boutiquelike* watchwords of a femininity commercialized by the fashion magazines that marginalized New York transvestites imitate to perfection in their desire to mix both sides of the coin (sexual and social) in order to throw off not only the system of dominant identities but the entire group of stereotypes of marginality fashioned by the market of multiculturalism to commercialize the representations of "difference."

On the other hand, the Chilean transvestite on the street makes fun of the pattern of normative sexual identities at the same time that s/he de-idealizes the femininity of haute couture with the vulgar satire that makes *the copied* violently clash with *the original,* placing in crisis the imitative footnote of doubling that the New York queens revert to with such perfectionism. Leftovers and scraps are part of the Latin American carnival through which the poor Chilean transvestite assaults the cosmetic facade of imported femininity with the grimace of an outré personality who can't be made to fit in. Used clothing gives Chilean transvestites on the street a syntax of discontinuity that exalts their fantasies of noncoincidence of identity, revealing the multiple infidelities of code between sexes, genders, and sexual representations of their peripheral and declassified bodies.

PART THREE

Academic Borders and Hybrid Knowledges

Interdisciplinarity cannot be accomplished by a simple confrontation of knowledges; interdisciplinarity is not something at rest. In effect, it begins when the solidarity of the old disciplines breaks apart, perhaps even violently, to benefit a new object, a new language, neither belonging to the domain of the sciences that they sought to peaceably confront; it is precisely this malaise of classification that allows us to diagnose a definite change.

—ROLAND BARTHES

It's a question of putting into play local, discontinuous, disqualified, and unlegitimated knowledges to counter the unitary theoretical analysis that seeks to filter them, to give them hierarchy and to order them in the name of true understanding.

—MICHEL FOUCAULT

The battle between critical subjectivity and official subjectivity is a battle that brings together various forces inside institutions that are themselves heterogeneous, with certain tendencies that are dogmatic or conservative and others that are not. One must continuously reevaluate the hegemonic powers under construction, and break them apart progressively without deluding ourselves that we are going to get rid of hegemony permanently. Weakening one hegemony can also mean reinstituting another, which is why critical vigilance can never falter.

—JACQUES DERRIDA

CHAPTER SIX

The Academic Citation and Its Others

> I believe that the university consists of a tension between a regular, legitimated knowledge and a plurality of irregular knowledges, defining itself in the capacity it possesses to support reflection over its own foundation, a reflection with a tendency to irreparably disturb the bases of legitimacy over which it rests. It is essential to return eccentricity to the university, to enmesh it with externals and to submit it to a critical process of delegitimization.
>
> —PABLO OYARZÚN

Knowledges, tacitly interlaced with structures of power through ramified intersections of meaning, are regulated by a policy of boundaries that delineate the borders of social recognition and the valorization of knowledge. The university machine is the dividing line between legitimate (authorized) knowledge and illegitimate knowledge. This machine protects the reserved realm of certified knowledge from the dangerous disorder of unregistered language that circulates outside the university enclosure with no guarantee of a known domicile.

During the years of the dictatorship, there was a sharp division—engineered through several mechanisms of territorial segregation—between authorized knowledge and unauthorized knowledge. The rearticulation of the university project in postdictatorial Chile not only raises organizational challenges of institutional politics, for the curricular design of programs of study that should become today more flexible; it also implies removing the marks of exclusion and repression that previously separated radically the "inside" of regular knowledge from the "outside" of irregular knowledge. This inclusion will form a new zone of dialogues and interpellations that rearticulate, in the plural, diverse theoretical-intellectual configurations, a zone that can "put into play . . . *unlegitimated knowledges* . . . to counter the unifying theoretical analysis that seeks to filter them, to give them hierarchy and order them in the name of true understanding."[1]

The new series of the *Anales de la Universidad de Chile* chose to reinaugurate its publication in September 1995 with a special issue dedicated to the university of the Transition, analyzing its role and significance as a producer of knowledge.[2] Various authors were invited to reflect on the changes that affect the traditional definitions of the university "when there is no longer a center for practically anything, when the state has a tendency to vaporize, when information slips away freely through the electronic networks, and when the real and the factual dilutes the social project or plan."[3] The *Anales de la Universidad de Chile* invited us to rethink, in the midst of such changes, "the place that the university occupies in the new settings of the generation and diffusion of knowledge" and "the organization of areas that do not fit into any of the traditional colleges, or the true meaning and function of the humanistic disciplines."[4]

By asking itself about "the organization of areas of study that do not fit into any of the traditional departments," the appeal made by the *Anales de la Universidad de Chile* seemed to be a way of opening up critical reflection on the relationship between the "interior" and "exterior" of disciplinary design; between, on the one hand, the academic control of university knowledge and, on the other, the extraterritoriality of other discursive regimes, capable of disturbing the university's regular format. But it suffices to examine the *form* under which the publication invited "everyone"[5] to reflect on the role and function of knowledge, in order to realize that "the university was making a special plea in light of the exceptional crisis it was undergoing, a crisis that would affect the overall design of the university as a modern state university. [A] crisis that would oblige it to ask itself a series of questions about its historical meaning, necessity and relevance; and also the relevance of its way of conducting itself, the way it had designed its genres and disciplines, its organic culture, and the contemporary codification of its tradition. And yet, despite all this, *it would appear that simultaneously it wanted to neutralize that exceptionality, emphatically inviting us to function under its norms, its normality.*"[6]

In effect, the invitation to write on the subject of the university came with a document entitled "Editorial Standards Guide" that requested that authors restrain themselves to rigid norms of presentation (titles, summaries, notes, bibliographies, etc.) destined to render the texts of the invited authors uniform, under the same written convention. The publication of

the *Anales* invited reflection about the university regarding the crisis of
its traditions, but without abandoning the discursive conventions of the
traditional university model, symbolized, in this case, by the rigor of its
editorial guidelines. In other words, the university showed itself ready to
review critically the "contents" of its model, but not its "form": its pattern of speech and composition of knowledge, the written signifier of
its academic-institutional discourse. However, to debate the enunciative
methods of the mise-en-scène of knowledge (techniques of discourse,
expositional rules, methods of presentation) has vital importance when
one wants to mobilize new theoretical practices capable of shaking up
with their rebellious *écriture* the institutional routine of standardized disciplines. It is thanks to this debate of form and style that we dare to ask
the university to give us "*all the expressions and all the idioms that we need*
in order to think against the realities that do not convince us."[7]

I would like to illustrate here certain conflicts between, on the one hand,
"local knowledge, discontinuous and disqualified, not legitimized," and, on
the other, "the unifying theoretical authority" that hegemonizes the value
of learning set in place by the official discourse of the university, through
a particular reference to certain sublocal forms of making theory that
are untranslatable to the norm-laden idiom of Chilean academia: critical-
reflexive forms that do not demonstrate but instead interrogate, maintaining themselves tense and maladjusted in relation to criteria of the discursive
legality of academic thought.

Inadequacies: The Body, the Photocopy

I particularly recall one of the many events convened in order to make
thinking an act of resistance in the convulsive landscape of the dictatorship:
an event convened by the Arcis Institute (1986), which had the distinction
of being almost the only instance during the long period of dictatorship
in which the subject of exile was debated, although with an almost unsus-
tainable vehemence. I bring up the memory of the event to promote reflection on the relations between university knowledge, on the one hand,
and, on the other, the cultural style of the critical practices that were conceived in total isolation from the academic hierarchy, knowing that in
doing this, I manifest a certain lack of conformity to the editorial tone
solicited in calls for papers like that of the University of Chile. First, when
I say that "I remember" the event of 1986, I introduce a subjective memory that betrays, with its first-person verbalization, the objectivity rule of

academic knowledge, whose pretensions of validity and whose systematic nature rely generally on the nondefinition of the person. This nondefinition of the personal guarantees the abstraction of the philosophical and scientific metadiscourse entrusted with transcending the precarious detail of the enunciative contingency of the subject, silencing the *accident* of its modes, voices, nouns, persons, and genders from its discourse.

Speaking of gender and accidents: the image that I want to bring forth is the memory of the Chilean philosopher Patricio Marchant, who participated in the aforementioned Arcis Institute seminar and dramatized one of his reiterated criticisms of "university discourse" with his emotive trembling, his bodily panic, and the gesturing of failure that generally accompanied his public lectures. Criticisms involuntarily marked by all that the mastery of philosophical knowledge denies: the body itself and its vicissitudes, its bonds, which mock the higher illusion of the transcendent "I" of philosophy with the shameful symptoms of physical materialism of a revealing and betraying flesh. P. Marchant was displaying a supplementary body that contaminated the philosophical reading, inopportunely calling attention to the foregrounding of the enunciative "I" that the magisterial text strives to keep under wraps. As he was reading, P. Marchant surrounded his text with trembling signals that were, in their trembling, obscene, because they were feminine, since all the ritual of academic authority demands that its subjects maintain a solid and sure (virile) discourse concerning the unique and final truth of meaning. What was "unpresentable" in the presentation of P. Marchant was what he himself called *the body*; in other words, that which the academic model of philosophical knowledge conceals, considers indecent, suppresses, views as scandalous ("Body is there where a terrible, imperious, unbearable need imposes itself, presents itself, herself. Body is necessity: not all body is necessary, but all that is necessary is body. Where there is desire, there is body: hiding itself so as not to be discovered, it trembles in its desire to avoid, trembles in being discovered, or not discovered. The body is necessary thinking. To discover how it is constructed, what forces are in play, is the inexorable necessity. Compared to the bodily imperative, formal logic and necessity seem a mere curiosity").[8]

It was the formality of this logical necessity for an *adequate* knowledge (functional to the truth of knowledge) that censored the writing from the body of P. Marchant in the name of an academic morality, and that marginalized his book *Sobre árboles y madres* (On Trees and Mothers) from the Chilean university discussions of literature and philosophy.[9] The somatic characterization of lack in the living body of P. Marchant dramatizes the gesture, theorized in his book, of converting the *lapsus* and the errata into rhetorical artifices of a discourse that aspires to be hesitant, tottering: "an antiuniversity discourse," ready to be judged as a *slip of the tongue*,[10] in the precariousness and frailty contained in the double meaning of the verb "to err" (commit errors, wander without a known path). Marchant's text contains poetical errancy and deviations that deform the straight and correct ideal of the demonstration-of-knowledge, philosophically supported by a "logic of the erection, of the position and the truth,"[11] that shows itself incapable of valuing the creative risk of the uncertain, the tentative, the inexact: the sinuous plurality of "metaphor-concepts" that prefer to renounce the all-too-clear uniqueness of the finite truths of "thought-theorem" (Deleuze). "University discourse" judged *Sobre árboles y madres* as if it were a "degenerate" book:[12] an unclassifiable book that mocks the borders of academically recognizable genres; a book of perversions that breaks exhibitionistically from the academic protocol of the much-belittled body while multiplying, in its pages, the marks of the unconscious (the manic rhythm of an obsessive biography that extracts from writing its desiring impulse) in order to contradict the philosophical dominion of a knowledge that is in complete mastery of its abstract reason.

In another talk from the Arcis Institute seminar of 1986, the poet Gonzalo Muñoz read a text, a theoretical-poetical manifesto distributed in photocopies that sketched out the conditions of an emerging critical scene in the artistic and literary milieu of Chile in the 1980s.[13] A scene of writing—perhaps the most daring artistic expression of all—that surged forth from a devastating "crisis of speech" when, given "the interruption, the rupture of all narratable history," the poetic narratives turned back onto themselves, contorting themselves in order to "postulate the utopian supplement of the word" and to overturn, with their figurative excess, the national condemnation of the misery of meaning.[14] In that document, G. Muñoz highlights the aesthetic criticism of art and literature of the eighties dedicated to the explosive search for a rebellious speech, when "solitude and deterioration were the wounds of access to one's own language."[15]

This critical aesthetic of the eighties considered its theoretical material and its cultural operations from the viewpoint of the maximum upheaval of meaning provoked by the innumerable breaches of the social representation machine. While other social and cultural practices sought to patch these fissures with the compensatory discursiveness of a metasignified and its representational ideologies, the theoretical-critical scene of the eighties dedicated itself to restylizing the residue in order to speak of the ruin of meaning with pained metaphors, sympathetic to the catastrophe of naming. G. Muñoz spoke brilliantly about this, theorizing a Chilean writing scene (situated outside the university) very conscious of the corruption of the official lexicons, while the literary criticism of the academy continued to rely on doubtful formal technicalities and methodological purisms to protect its specialized knowledge from the antagonisms of the outside world.

If we want to be careful about "the nondetachment of knowledge from the *vital* and *experimental* contexts" that determine it in a material sense,[16] we need to remember, as we imagine new dynamics of reflexive thought in the postdictatorship university, the conditions of critical emergence of that Chilean scene of theoretical-cultural thought referred to by P. Marchant and G. Muñoz. An out-of-boundary scene, whose wounds came from names and concepts that traveled through high-risk zones, in the dangerous company of artworks, all of them extreme in their gesture of reimagining themselves politically after the failure of the ideological totalities that in the past guided the macrorepresentation of the social.

But how can we remember the antecedents of these texts (necessary for a reflection about academic knowledge, the university discourse, and its others), and the "new Chilean scene" of the eighties that situated us in the period in which academic discourse and antiacademic discourse dramatized more strongly their theoretical conflicts, when everything in them rejects the editorial formality of an appeal like that of the *Anales de la Universidad de Chile*? These conflicts range from the typographical erosion of many of its writings that still maintain themselves in the clandestinity of the photocopy, to the blurred memory of defiant practices whose insertion as material for study in the disciplinary programs of today's Chilean academy remains completely residual.

Plurality of Knowledges and Theoretical Mixtures

I mention a theoretical-cultural past to which we cannot refer without mentioning how its texts were written in clear antagonism to the valued authority of Chilean university discourse. And I speak about the aforementioned texts in order to reflect on the *untranslatability* of their writing to the university requirements of editorial norms, of the unpresentability and unrepresentability of their forms and contents.

One of the recommendations published in the "editorial norms" guide that accompanied the call to contribute our texts to the journal of the

University of Chile was the following: "the title should contain the maximum number of words that define the content of the article. If a fantasy
title is desired, it is necessary to include a second subordinate title, that is
explicative of the content."[17] This recommendation was made so that the
definition and the *explanation* of the content of the argument, in the sub-
title charged with clarifying the goal of the text, would correct the vagary
(the vagrant meaning) of a "fantasy title" with the criteria of rational representation of an objective knowledge that must comply with the norms
of consumption of university disciplines. For the academic model of disciplines rationalized by the logic of the demonstration-of-knowledge,
the "content" is the substantial nucleus of the truth of knowledge, while
the "form" is the decorated, insubstantial element that "loses itself" in the
digression of artifice and metaphors. The law of gravity (seriousness) of
the content that provides knowledge with its rational equilibrium scorns
the tangle of metaphors, the signifying obliqueness of the "as if" (Derrida), and punishes the inconsistency of style, further demanding that the
decorative surface of the form return to reason (referential clarity and exact-
ness) in the name of an economy of profundity of content. An economy
that believes in the logical demonstration of a thesis whose arguments
must be summed up in the synthesis of the title, censoring the self-reflexive
deviating turn of the writing in the name of a linear transmission of didactic knowledge.[18]

Not surprisingly, the publication of the University of Chile attempted
to regulate the format of the encounters between the official knowledge of
the academy and the other nonstandard knowledges that might respond
to the call for papers, equally forcing on all of them the same university
publishing norms and normality. "With said guidelines, the university appeared to guard itself from 'exterior' styles, academically unacceptable, still
unpresentable in the ivory tower"[19] owing to their lack of compliance with
the protocols of academic transmission, which mandates a single voice of
knowing legitimated by official knowledge.[20]

While attempting to regulate the disposition of meaning through a polic-
ing of form that subjected the essays to editorial guidelines, the invitation
of the university weighed down its repressive hypothesis over those forms
of theoretical thought that had defended their polemical difference against
the traditional university knowledge by posing "questions of style";[21] that
is to say, defending the use of allegory and metaphors as intensive figures
of its aesthetic-cultural symbolization.[22]

The memory of the theoretical scene of the eighties that invokes the names of authors like P. Marchant and G. Muñoz is not only useful to me here to defend the critical force of texts that knew how to break the closure of the disciplinary specializations with intractable (uncontractable) games of writerly passions. The mention of their practices has relevance as well as a local unorthodox antecedent to the reshaping of borders of knowledge to which cultural criticism now tends.

In effect, the Chilean theoretical scene of the eighties presents the characteristic trait of having woven its knowledges into the in-between of the organized disciplines, mixing references thus omitted or censored by traditional academic discourse (Benjamin, psychoanalysis, art, Foucault, deconstruction, feminism, etc.) with the heterogeneous network of a social exteriority penetrated by political confrontations and antagonisms. By detaching the citations of university philosophy from their traditional bibliographical underpinnings to connect their disassembled formulations with rough and conflicted experiences and localities, the scene of the eighties used knowledge to "make cuts" in the surface of understandings (Foucault), and not to rationalize processes of knowing with the sure techniques and methodologies of a disciplinary truth.

The theoretical antidisciplinarianism of this Chilean scene, its way of placing itself on the edge of academic disciplines and conventional genres in order to fire away wild metaphors that gave legibility to the hidden-repressed elements of the social landscape and its destructive violence, made it attempt transversal gestures, unforeseen positionings, and emerging surfaces that did not fit on the map of institutional culture. And it was these antinormative breaks, operated through *conjunctural* forms of making theory, that provocatively managed to unleash the conflicts of idiom between formal knowledge and informal knowledge, between systematic learning and extrasystematic conceptualizations, between endowed repertoires and interstitial readings, that articulated a certain debate about different critical positions on intellectual work in Chile under a waning dictatorship.

The "new scene" searched for fragmentary knowledge that slipped over the surface of the institutional mechanisms in order to experience, at its edges, a freedom of movement that is generally censored by the cartography of sedentary idioms, set by the specialization of disciplines and by means of pedagogical rules that only pay attention to the social utility of knowledge.[23] In disordering the map of the functional knowledges and their objective truths with the force of critical interrogation in order to work with inconclusive (suspended) meanings, the Chilean critical "new scene" was able to encompass materials that lacked a finished formalization and to explore *the folds of sensibility* of a cultural narrative made up not only of constituted discourses but also of floating discourses, of diffuse practical ideologies, of sketchily outlined body languages, of incomplete symbolizations. The deprogrammed texts of the "new scene" came very close to what Raymond Williams called a "structure of feeling" (an unstable mixture of categories and experiences still not crystallized into sure conceptual definitions), while weaving their critical knowledge into the breaches and fissures of disciplinary learning. And it was this mobility of theoretical idioms that worked over the ravages of category-based knowledge with fortuitous pieces of hybrid vocabulary that marked the otherness of the critical scene of the eighties, in relation both to university philosophy and to academic literary criticism, as well as to research in the social sciences.

The differences between controlled knowledge and the uncontrolled thinking (between the mechanisms of sure understanding and the experiments with knowledges located in the most disobedient of the disciplinary bodies) that caused such vibrant conflicts of discourse between the academy, the centers of alternative studies, and the micro-critical-intellectual scene of the eighties should be worthy of study by the new university discourse, at least the discourse that is convinced that the university "consists in the tension between a legitimized, regular knowledge, and a plurality of dispersed knowledges" that are outside the bounds of the controlled perimeters of validity upheld by magisterial reason.[24] To analyze the dispersed knowledges—their theoretical codes, their writing machines—it is worthwhile to reflect on the "crisis of the university" not only referentially as a "subject" but also by deconstructing the hierarchy of power-knowledge that separates the discussion "about" the crisis from the discussion "from within" the crisis to ensure a radical critical suspicion that would affect the shape of its academic discourse and infect, as well, its system of nominations and denominations.

CHAPTER SEVEN

Antidiscipline, Transdiscipline, and the Redisciplining of Knowledge

I return to the debate between intellectual work and academic work: they
coincide partly . . . but they are not the same. I return to the difficulty of
instituting a real practice of cultural criticism that should not attempt to
reinscribe itself in the metanarrative of knowledge accomplished inside
institutions. I return to theory and politics, to the politics of theory. Not
theory as a desire for truth, but instead theory as an assemblage of embattled
learnings, localized and of the moment.

—STUART HALL

Although still scanty and often precarious in their achievements, certain
attempts to modify the rules that configure traditional knowledge are shaping themselves in the context of a contemporary reflection that critiques
the academic model in postdictatorial Chilean universities.[1] These experiments that aim to decentralize the mechanisms of hierarchy and control
of official understanding—pluralizing the forms and the styles of creating
theory—speak of "oblique perspectives on inter- and multidisciplinary
intersections, which serve as bridges between the academic and the sociocultural polyphony; of knowledges that are neither authorized nor con-
solidated, but instead open to the critical-creative errancy of the unstable
and fluid fin de siècle imaginaries."[2]

Plurality, mobility, and flexibility of understanding are some of the traits
that these recently designed practices of knowledge oppose to the rigidity
of the traditional academic format, appealing to *transdisciplinarity* as an experimental and creative vector for the reconfiguration of new theoretical
instruments for the critical analysis of culture.

95

Cultural studies and cultural criticism would represent two new practices that participate in the same search for transversality as much in the redesigning of the borders of academic knowledge (cultural studies) as in the critical rearticulation of theoretical discourse (cultural criticism). Both practices—and the relations of dialogue, resistance, and questioning that connect them—invite a currently needed reflection that overruns the format of university knowledge and academic discourse to interrogate the critical borders of intellectual work.

Intermediate Texts, Border Knowledges

Why call it "cultural criticism," and how can we avoid the fact that by repeating the name, we make it sound like something restricted, like a program, as if it were intended as a model to apply to, and purportedly be endowed with, a homogeneity of form and content?

We can leave the definition of what *is* cultural criticism in abeyance (first, because the term designates a varying ensemble of practices and writings that do not answer to a uniform design, and second because keeping open this mobility of differentiated positions that open up contrasts between heterogeneous discourses helps to break up the homogeneity of the academic will that continually seeks to order typologies and nomenclatures). Still, it would be worthwhile to specify some of the traits that these texts share, in spite of the heterogeneity of forms and dissimilarity of content, as texts of "cultural criticism."[3] They are texts situated midroute between essay, deconstructive analysis, and theoretical criticism, which blend these different registers to examine the crossroads between social discursiveness, cultural symbolizations, power formations, and constructions of subjectivity.

First, let's say that it's a question of "texts that overflow—above all in their moment of production and circulation—an easy inscription into the meshwork of knowledge and thereby vindicate their marginality. These are marginal to constituted disciplinary fields—sociology, psychoanalysis, semiology, anthropology, literary theory, etc.—even though they are dependent on the concepts generated in these fields. In a premeditated verbal register that distances itself from the institutionalized doctrine, these texts are animated by a conceptual vision of significant moments that either: (1) are not yet analyzed; (2) up to now have been considered according to discursive frameworks whose ideological assumptions have not been subjected to criticism; or (3) are excluded from all analysis by the boundaries passively reproduced in the formation of disciplines. [They are] texts that unfold at the margin of institutional backing, that is, discourses where—either through their framework, format, syntax, or grammar—the institution as subject is not expressed, but instead these academic texts define themselves in critical tension with the university."[4]

The texts of cultural criticism would thus be *intermediate* texts that don't want to let themselves be situated in the institutional parameters that define orthodox learning; texts that claim the right to their impropriety in relation to the traditional disciplines and the traditional notion of "discipline" conceived as a body of learning whose rules of specialization set and control the relation (disciplinary, technical, and professional) between objects, knowledge, and methods.[5] Far from being a discipline, cultural criticism would be a *practice*, that is, a way of doing, a way of acting, a strategy of theoretical-discursive intervention that chooses its own critical instruments as a function of the conjuncture of signs that present themselves as material for analysis and disassembly. "There is a politics of intellectual weaponry in cultural criticism, a politics of resourcefulness in laying hands on poststructuralism, semiology, psychoanalysis, gender discourse, etc.," according to the specific nature of the materials dealt with and the meanings that come forth from these localized contexts.[6]

Bound to this *conjunctural* dimension, we should also emphasize the character of *intervention* that animates the project of cultural criticism. It would not be enough for the project to analyze the texts of culture in their intradiscursive dimension, but instead it should always attempt to engage its reader in a critical task of disassembly and rearticulation of meaning in order to examine the local and specific connections that link the signs to their political-institutional networks. This intervention would be a matter of being suspicious of the discursive mechanisms of the constructions of power that plan the different chains of social production and reception of the messages in circulation; of involving the reader in a shared task of critical vigilance that teaches him or her to uncover the artifices of dominant representation and to produce, at the same time, counterreadings susceptible to refuting its system of values and canonical hierarchies.

In a line of thought derived from poststructuralism, cultural criticism would work to *politicize* the question of discourse, causing it to be viewed as a correlation of violence, control, and struggle that surrounds the symbolic authority of the power of the word and the control of representation. But cultural criticism would not only be satisfied with deconstructing the discursive figures that impose meaning in which social ideologies base their normalizing power. Its critique would also claim critically to discover and activate that which resists them: the discordant potentiality of the most rebellious between-the-lines reading of the cultural texts that enter into conflict with the legitimating accounts.[7]

Cultural criticism would be interested in taking a position in favor of the antihegemonic—noncentral—meanings that emerge from writings and readings in conflict with the official tradition, the dominant canon, the institutional norm, and that appeal to a politics and aesthetics of the edges, margins, and borders. (This explains the alliances that usually form—in a disorganized manner—between cultural criticism, deconstruction and feminist theory: because of their shared intention to disorganize the binary machines that move around the "function-central" of the hegemonic representation in order to rescue the plural and the disseminated that reside, as minority positions, in the fringes of exclusion and subalternity in relation to the geography of official knowledge.)

Cultural studies—as it has been defined[8]—also tends to be cross-disciplinary as a model of academic reorganization of knowledge that incorporates knowledges that until now have been marginalized by the canon of the traditional disciplines. Cultural criticism and cultural studies would share the same interest in certain theoretical combinations that both use to analyze (and defend) social representations and identity formations that are habitually segregated by the hierarchies of official culture. Both practices would be interested in provoking an "insurrection of the subordinated knowledges" (Foucault) destined to empower the decentralization of the margins and the peripheries that border institutionalized culture. But whereas cultural studies perhaps defends the practical objective of academically revising programs to institutionally transmit new fields of knowledge, cultural criticism might enjoy a greater freedom of movement to enter and exit the academic map—to travel along its borders—placing a special accent on the critical transversality of its *textual practice*.

On the one hand, cultural studies and cultural criticism might come up with a common response if we confronted them with the question of which practices are capable of opening new contexts of discovery that modify the lines of inclusion-exclusion of dominant knowledge, since both lean toward subjects and objects discriminated against by the abusive predominance of centrality (the metropolitan, the Occidental, the masculine, etc.). But cultural criticism might also be interested, above all in asking itself more specifically *how* one should tackle these new objects (through certain new registers of knowledge and writing) in order that the relation between theory and novation be questioned—that is, not only conceptually but also rhetorically—regarding the forms of speech that overdetermine the fields of knowledge inherited from the disciplines, since faced with the codifying language of the academic program, these are the forms that place them in "degrees of exclusion and inclusion, of complicity and resistance, of domination and letting-be, of abstraction and situatedness, of violence and tolerance, of monologue and polylogue, of quietism and activism, of sameness and otherness, of oppression and emancipation, of centralization and decentralization."[9]

Faced with a cultural studies basically preoccupied with amplifying and diversifying the university's scheme of knowledge, cultural criticism should accentuate the need to reflect not only on the social formulation of the new objects being theorized (democracy, feminism, globalization, citizenship, postcolonialism, etc.) but also on its own devices of theorization: on that which the use of theory mobilizes and transforms *in* and *from* the networks of disciplinary knowledge; on the respective positions of academic-institutional authority that obey or disobey the texts according to where the critical knowledge situates its voice. These voice positionalities and speech registers define and articulate the politics of writing of the critical text.

Theory as Writing

The relation between academic knowledge and the nonacademicization of knowledge also surfaces in the issue of critical writing, and the politics of the written text. However, this theme is generally disregarded by cultural studies, whose academic standard tends to produce a uniform sum of investigative materials—governed by the technocultural action of the datum—that encounters its dispassionate symbol in the academic paper. The functional reduction of the Text to a *paper* has broken the emblem of a dense tradition of essay writing with the new predominance of sociological inquiry that sacrifices the rhetorical and figurative density of language in the (strong) sense of what Barthes called "theory as writing."[10] Such theory reflects on its enunciative forms in order to deinstrumentalize the simple "refer to" of practical knowledge with words that retain, in their reflexive composition, the memory of the making and unmaking of meaning. Contrary to the paper that predominates in the departments of cultural studies where one pursues the mere calculability of meaning, the simple manipulation of cultural information for its economic conversion into a descriptive knowledge, the "theory as writing," dreams of opening lines of flight where critical subjectivity could divert the straight line of useful knowledge to explore certain meanderings of language that overload the borders of speech with opaque intensity.

Literary studies, we know, saw themselves brusquely shaken up by the decentralization of the modern ideology of literature that founded, in Latin America, the critical conscience of the continental and the national, exactly as it appears symbolized, for example, in *La ciudad letrada* by Ángel Rama. This ideological-literary conscience of Latin American modernism (its images of the function of intellectual activity and of critical thought) sees itself threatened today by the dispersive effect of the global networks whose mass-media images daily fragment the outlines of integration between nation and citizenship, increasingly diffuse and unstable.[11] Literature and literary studies have had to get used to this displacement of their leading role, now superseded by the visual and the technologies of image making. This exchange of verbal thickness for visual flatness marked the unthinking triumph of superficialities without symbolic fissures or tears, created solely to consecrate "the disillusion of metaphor,"[12] by eliminating all the marks of profundity (the enigma of the fold, the creases of multiple voices) that associated the literary with subtle protocols of aesthetic deciphering.

But literary studies have felt the effects of another confusion. They have been affected by the attempt of cultural studies to enlarge and extend the notion of "text" to any social practice—or articulate network of messages —without really specifying the distinction between "narration" (volume) and "information" (surface) that formerly separated the direct from the indirect, the literal from the metaphoric, the simple decoding stages of communication from the complex interpretative games of aesthetic symbolization.

The "linguistic turn" that caused the notion of the text to overflow the exclusive boundaries of what was consecrated as literary in order to encompass any discursive practice has given us a theoretical vision of the social sphere, more attentive to the details of how signs, codes and representations gradually construct their symbolic, discursive, and institutional connections. On the other hand, this unlimited opening of the Text (in the Barthesian sense of the word) to the "textuality" of any signifying practice has eliminated the need to discriminate between "text" and "discourse" and has also dissolved the specificity of the aesthetic-literary around which literary studies revolve. The semioticization of the everyday world that invites us to decipher the rhetorical artifices of fashion and clothing or a television program with the same techniques with which, in the past, we analyzed a poem or a novel has subordinated the value of the artistic and

the literary "to the relativistic point of view of cultural sociology";[13] a point
of view that admits commentary on the institutional effects of production-
circulation-reception of the works but does not allow us surprise with a
will to form and style that defines an ideological-critical stance that each
work chooses to oppose itself to others, and postulates certain values of
signification. The sociology of culture—whose criteria amply predomi-
nate in various regions of the academic map of cultural studies—fails to
take into consideration the disputed forces of the ideological, the critical,
and the aesthetic, when it is precisely this state of tension that art dramatizes in staking its values in opposition to "aesthetic relativism, laden with
indifference" fostered by the mass-produced pluralism of the culture market and industry.[14] The sociology of culture and cultural studies trivialized
the reflection about texts and their aesthetics by neglecting the value of the
difference between "text" and "discourse." They refused to specify why certain indirect modes of speech (full of ambiguity and multiplicity of voices)
say what they say, with the formal and semantic intensity of a "more" that
is totally unredeemable to the demands of the communicative practicality
of the sign that only carries the value-information of knowledge.

The crisis of the literary paradigm, exacerbated by the media flows
of audiovisual culture, has motivated the questioning—formulated by
J. Beverly—of "what will happen when literature is simply one discourse
among many others,"[15] that is to say, when the borders completely dissolve between the ordinary speech of the instrumental message and the
poetics of writing that carries the sign of autoreflexivity and ambiguity. In
other words, when all that is spoken and written ends up conforming to
the same banal register of a deadly flattening of meaning; a register in which
the word will have stopped being theater or event in order to become a
mere currency of practical exchange, lacking all brilliance, fire, or drama.
This questioning about the destiny of the aesthetic-literary realm as a figurative dimension of an explosive sign (diffracted and plural), capable of
criticizing the homogeneity of the communicative market, also affects the
fate of critical writing now threatened by the instrumental domination of
a practical knowledge that censors the depths of the autoreflexive folds in
the relationship between subject and language.[16]

The Politics of the Critical Act

The leitmotif of "trans" ("beyond," "from the other side," "through," etc.)
today runs through multiple layers of academic culture, speaking to us of

border crossings, of identity migrations, and of hybrid knowledges that are displacing and reformulating geographic positions, social classes, gender definitions, and theoretical knowledge. And cultural studies takes up, as conceived initially, the critical impulse of this diagonal severance traced out on the map of the traditional disciplines.[17] But the rapid academicization of the "trans" already tells us that the nonsettled space exalted by the first critical desire for nomadism and errancy indicated by the prefix "trans" (as being opposed to the sedentary formations of institutional knowledge) is not as inconvenient as it sounds. The coming from another place and the critical otherness of the knowledges that were born fighting against academic centralization today find themselves being reintegrated into (at least in the international academic circuit) a discursive standard that administers "the institutional political effects of the inscription of the intellectual work in the interior of the academy" by means of the professionalizing language of the university critic.[18]

Cross-disciplinarity is one of the theoretical rules that today stimulate the systems of knowledge in their desire to extend and diversify the scope of objects for study, all in order to enhance their inclusiveness in an increasingly mobile and complex reality. But the greater plurality of objects for study that cultural studies seeks to conquer does not always imply a reflection about how to pluralize the modes of discursive configuration of knowledge so that the writing of the heretically new does not remain captive to the old molds of expression. It seems as if the free-trade zone between the disciplines proclaimed by the interdisciplinary method has simply resigned itself to composing an order for a peaceful summation of complementary knowledges destined to integrate a new, more inclusive and functional totality of learning that finally leaves untouched the contours of each inherited intellectual discipline. However, Roland Barthes already warned us that interdisciplinarity "cannot be achieved by the simple confrontation of specialized knowledges; the interdisciplinary is not a comfortable affair: it begins effectively . . . when the solidarity of the old disciplines breaks down—perhaps even violently—to the advantage of a new object, a new language."[19]

The academic formalization of cross-disciplinary study implemented by a good share of cultural studies has ended up erasing from its processes of reorganization that which Barthes called "the malaise of classification,"[20] in other words, the critical experience of a disorder that one must keep in mind in order to ward off the risk of new predetermined knowledge paradigms reinstalling themselves. More so when the renovation of objects of study ends up answering to the technical imperative to produce only a new ordering knowledge (a knowledge that reclassifies), without allowing the language responsible for transmitting this knowledge to be questioned by the estranging force of the declassified, of the unclassifiable, which positions itself in the unraveling and raveling movements of critical writing.

Cultural studies was born with the idea of mixing, collaboratively, pluridisciplinary approaches (plural combinations of flexible knowledges) and transculturalism (opening of the borders of knowledge to problematic concerns heretofore marginalized from the monocultural paradigm of dominant Western reason). It thus responds to the new slippage of categories between the dominant and the subordinate, the masculine and the feminine, the learned and the popular, the central and the peripheral, the global and the local, that traverse current geopolitical territorialities, symbolizations of identity, sexual representations, and social classifications. Cultural studies reformulates in this way a new democratizing project of academic transformation that permits the reading of the subalternity (exclusions, discriminations, censorship, peripheralizations) at the crossroads of "an ample range of academic disciplines and social positions."[21] That is to say that cultural studies—in the version most strongly motivated by what J. Beverly calls a "political vocation"[22]—claims at least two things: (1) to disassemble the hierarchical structure of knowledge and modify the borders between the disciplines in order to produce a more plural and flexible knowledge, or, in other words, a mixed knowledge that allows more adequate comprehension of the new—hybrid—realities of a social landscape in extensive mutation of categories and identities; and (2) not only to study but also to intervene in this landscape, making the field's engagement with the social movements and the cultural practices of counterhegemonic subjects (postcolonialism, feminism, multiculturalism, etc.) explicit, something that runs counter to the desire for autonomy in traditional disciplines. This political vocation of cultural studies led it to construct a type of "organic knowledge" (Stuart Hall) destined to strengthen the demand for citizenship of the minority group, and also to rearticulate politically the cultural significations rasied by their new conditions of social emergence in the terrain of the academy.

The idea of a knowledge that uses interdisciplinarity to combine different models of analysis of the new problematics of gender, multicultural, and postcolonial issues, et cetera, is a constructive and organizing knowledge, a knowledge that strives to perfect the utility of certain instruments

of theoretical and social reflection in order to make a certain dynamics of
academic and extra-academic change "functional."[23] In its zeal to "criticize
the disciplines, to democratize structures, to modify requirements, to dismantle the canon, to create new spaces in order to work freely,"[24] cultural
studies fights for the practical effectiveness of changes that would modify
the most conservative rules of traditional university teaching that continues to govern departments and programs. "To democratize knowledge"
(Beverly) means, then, to favor the plural incorporation of knowledges until
now devalued by the hierarchies of learning of canonical culture: knowledges
whose emancipatory potential is capable of overflowing the academic text
with new energies of social transformation that connect theoretical-political
streams of thought with a living reality outside the university. And there
is no doubt that the democratizing movement of cultural studies that reor-
ganizes learning in complicity with identities that until now were underrepresented by the canon of the metropolitan university has altered the
system of authority of the university institution with its reevaluation of
the noncentral and of the counterhegemonic. But it is also true that the
practical nature of knowledge of cultural studies generally tends to annul
the tension between subject, theory, and writing that ought to bring about
a vibrant reflection about the critical text today repressed by the dominant
sociological paradigm of the new academic research.

F. Galende debates this point,[25] affirming that cultural studies would
do nothing other than "put into circulation the other . . . into the market
of the known"; "remove the heterogeneity of the other, its unheard episode, all that which this other is, when it extends beyond its useful life" in
order to finally "beckon it to appear in the form of a category"[26] and thus
to domesticate its rebellious surge within a functional reordering of the
discursive bureaucracies of criticism that cause knowledge of the new to
advance exclusively toward calculable and manageable meanings, avoiding exposure to the risk of the untimely. According to F. Galende, the
academic criticism institutionalized by cultural studies would only permit the illustration of "the official metaphor of an inert epochal realism"[27]
that seeks to adjust its knowledge to changes, instead of empowering the
change as a force of maladjustment that should shake up the normalized
language of knowledge and its corresponding academic discipline.[28] It
is true that many exponents of cultural studies believe they contribute
something to knowledge by simply describing the changes of the present,
without ever asking themselves about what radically disturbs the satisfied
adaptation between reason, method, and objectivity, about what shakes

up the dominant vocabularies of the academy and its indices of legibility. Perhaps a possible difference between cultural studies and cultural criticism—if we understand the latter as a "critique of criticism"—is related to this tension between the explanatory knowledge that formulates and expounds the reasons why our present is as it is, and the questioning knowledge that does not content itself with these demonstrations but instead seeks to perforate the order of its proofs and certitudes with the speculative incision of doubt, of conjecture, or indeed of utopia, making, in each case, writerly protests against the didactic claims of knowledge content to apply only educational techniques.

Just as insufficient, however, is the deconstructionist fashion of a knowledge that contorts itself into arabesques of doubt and of eternal self-questioning, without risking an affirmation or a negation that, provisional as it might be, dares a decision: to exercise the practical responsibility of *an act of meaning.* To lose oneself in an infinite slippage of meanings frustrating all possible encounter of the signifier with the signified obviously conspires against the possibility that knowledge can have a transformative action on the material structures of the institution.[29] Such an action requires that the doubt leave behind its introverted reserve and pronounce itself in favor of (or against) certain decisions, interrupting the suspension of its unlimited chain of nondefinitions, and thereby stop in some determined location from which it might draw out lines of demarcation, mark out positions, signal and communicate changes. The organizing moment of any academic-institutional struggle depends on the capacity that knowledge possesses to work with concrete connections of meaning and references, in order to intervene in the support structures of the institution in their concrete materiality;[30] the "desire called cultural studies" (Jameson) could never be expressed without passing through these practical maneuvers. Imagine something both dual and combined: a gesture that, on the one hand, would dare to materialize change, necessarily passing through the application of localized operations in an institutional setting, and, on the other, is vigilantly conscious of the danger that unnoticed conformities of style might end up with the language and knowledge of the "new" to simply illustrate the academic realism of the official politics of change. This double gesture is what Derrida reflects on when he evokes the tension between philosophy and institution, when he affirms that "the extra-institutional realm should have its own institutions without belonging to them," and when he asks himself: "How can we reconcile the respect of the institutional limits with their transgression? How can we reconcile the localizable identity with the overflowing ubiquity,"[31] both dimensions equally necessary to construct a politics of the critical act?

The relationships between the academic institution and its borders, between the centralization of knowledge and the forces of dispersion, between the ritualization of the "university discourse" and its precarious and hybrid "others," are not fixed relationships but are instead mobile and changing, made up of lines and segments that are variable as much in their consistency of principles as in the equilibrium of their locations. To revise this alignment of forces in order to calculate the mode in which the changes carried out in the interior of the academy (be they gender studies or cultural studies) are capable of affecting—and to what extent—its machine of knowledge, to examine the conflicts and the antagonisms of knowledge that emerge from the fissures of authority of the centered discourse, are part of what that same cultural criticism proposes as deconstructive work, that is to say, as a work that cannot be summed up with a simple method of analysis of texts but that instead searches to intervene in shaping the forms and the underpinnings of relationships (practical and institutional) of the discourses. For this reason, it is only a situated critical practice of theory that can decide the value of the enunciative disorder that its discourse wishes to enact within the institutional format of academic knowledge.[32]

PART FOUR

Polemics and Transvestisms

Neoliberalism becomes internally self-contradictory, and this contradiction is increasingly easy to see. On the one hand, it constitutes one of the principal forces that eliminates tradition on all sides, as a consequence of driving market forces and of an aggressive individualism. On the other hand, its legitimacy and its links with conservatism base themselves in the persistence of tradition in the areas of the nation, religion, the sexes, and the family. . . . It is no surprise that the doctrines of the new right mix the liberal freedoms and authoritarianism—even fundamentalism—in an unstable and uncomfortable way.

—ANTHONY GIDDENS

Free market would not imply here "free interpretation." The goal is to have multiple meanings drown in orthodoxy.

—KEMY OYARZÚN

While defrauding the expectations and subverting the model of the predictable, fragments of discourse demand to be heard in a different way, anticipating that which in a society remains obscure as they illuminate with another kind of light a past that appeared definitely organized. A political gaze could also work with what appears to be unmotivated, to the extent to which the unmotivated does not respond to the interrogations that are considered legitimate.

The political gaze pays attention to the alternative and sketches paths between the diverse and sometimes almost inaudible forms of the new. It discovers and relates things. A political gaze would also discover disputed virtual spaces of the new. And from there . . . the scattered voices of the alternative and dissidence.

—BEATRIZ SARLO

CHAPTER EIGHT

❧

The Graphic Model of an
Advertising Identity

The iceberg was the sculpture of our metamorphosis. The iceberg represented
the debut in society of the New Chile—cleaned, sanitized, purified by the
long passage through the sea. It was as if Chile had just been born. The
iceberg was a successful sign, architect of transparency and of cleanliness,
where the damaged had transfigured itself.

—TOMÁS MOULIAN

Chile's presentation at the Expo Sevilla '92 indicated the nation's first
opportunity to shine internationally, an opportunity for the government
of redemocratization to represent itself through a performance of identity
that had the peculiarity of condensing—graphically—several of the official
meanings connoted by Transition policies. In retrospect, Chile-Expo Sevilla
'92 is much more than a celebratory exhibition: it is the first practice of
identity that the redemocratized Chile makes into a spectacle in order to
give form and style to its "discourse of change."

There were many meanings that opened debate on themes of modernization in the Chilean Sevilla exhibition.[1] But perhaps the most significant
was the formal and rhetorical supremacy of languages used to give style
to the first great cosmetic refashioning of the Transition with commercial
graphics and advertising technologies. The superficial effects of these flat
languages illustrate the work of denarration of memory to which the political consensus and market forces were jointly dedicated, orchestrated through
the emptying of historical context.

The Exhibitionism of the Pose

The prologue of the corporate book *El pabellón de Chile: Huracanes y maravillas en una exposición universal* (The Chile Pavilion: Hurricanes and Wonders in a Universal Exhibition)[2] sketches an introductory framework of the Chilean presentation in Sevilla that tells the history of past world's fairs—London, Paris, New York, et cetera—as a history of audacious dealings with the future whose success is based on the necessary conditions of "megalomania, superproduction, exhibitionist display of resources in a blatant zeal" to "encompass everything" and to "put everything in view,"[3] thus saturating the display areas with exacerbated references to the complicit role of the gaze.

The introduction to Chile-Expo Sevilla '92 retraces the cosmopolitan desire for a universal modernity that impels countries to exhibit their advances and progress in the "showcase of the world," inasmuch as they share the vitality and optimism of a metropolitan ideal of expansive industrial and technological growth, a desire that is satisfied with the excitement of the New as product for exhibition and commodity for consumption. The story of Chile-Expo Sevilla '92 put the Chilean adventure in serial correlation—historical and international—with the grandiose displays that illuminated their evidence of progress to the world and filled their showcases with novelties. This story took as a model the proven dimension of spectacle that guided the competition in the world's fairs in order to thus justify the fantasy sustained by the Chilean Transition of *showing* and *showing itself*: in publicizing its image through a presentation filled to the brim with multiple effects of visual seduction and attraction.

What was new for exhibition in the showcases of international modernity was not any achievement in particular but rather the image of Chile itself as a superachiever that acknowledged its executive passage to democracy. For Chile, only two years after its recently premiered democratic Transition, the Fair of Seville was the opportunity to demonstrate that it was a "new country": to make the rest of the world see the apparent transformation of a country confident in the supposed equivalence between the signs *to be* and *to appear* with which, in its vanity, the representation of all advertising plays.

The promotional story of Chile in Seville throws into relief this discourse of ostentation: a discourse that recurs to appearance and the cult of appearance as dimensions of recognition, of an identity projected as a brand name, that is, as a signal of particularity and difference that singularly identifies its bearer. The discourse of change of the Chilean Transition flaunted the New through this specular speech of the spectacular, where the gaze of the other is called on to ratify the brilliance of self-representation. It was a question of "showing the best face," "projecting an image," "seducing the other," "calling attention," "creating a mirror," "provoking a type of reflection"[4] in which the country could recognize itself and be recognized as *image* through the smooth and brilliant superficiality of the visual planes in which the valorizing definition of the brand name–country reverberated semiotically.

Multiple references to the visual grammar of advertising design settled the issue of identity as *expression* and not as *signification* (as perceptual schema and not as trajectory of experience), through a culture of the look that consists of "being an image, possessing the value of exchange, being esteemed in the visual market" (Baudrillard), in other words, calling the other's attention to the artifices that construct a posed superficiality made to be consumed as an icon in the parade of representations.

Because in fairs "that which is traded are images," whose competition is principally through exhibition,[5] in order to conceptualize its project, Chile conferred a leading role on experts in brand names and logos. The tone of the advertisement was relied on to correct old prejudices (of content) about the Chile of underdevelopment and dictatorship, replacing it with the new visual stereotype of the language of international graphics; a language whose flat colors rejected the adherences of textures that had been too roughened by memory and history and needed to be smoothed over photographically for the tourist-commercial pose of modernizing development, its success-oriented technologies leaving out of the picture the elements that could not be synchronized.

To Label, to Classify: The Standardization of Meaning

The novelty of the *stand* that Chile wanted to expose at the Discovery Fair was the new content of the Transition: "Chile Now" (T. Moulian). But the novelty of present-day Chile kept in reserve as key to its success the subtext of continuity through a figure who secretly linked the past and the present: the former economic minister of the Pinochet government, Fernando Léniz, was designated commissioner general of Chile-Expo Sevilla '92 by the president of the consensus government, Patricio Aylwin. The new content of the Chilean Transition in Seville blended the triumphal appearances of a discourse of change, synthesized by the public relations renovation of the "Chile" image, with the modernizing past of the dictatorship, whose technical and economic successes indulged in self-congratulation in the secret between-the-lines image of the democratic metamorphosis.[6] Such a metamorphosis had already been announced by Joaquín Brunner, whose cultural sociological texts explain that the more gradual rather than brusque character of the Chilean Transition was due to "the 'moderate' disposition widespread in civil society created through discipline, the integration into the expectations of consumption, and the desire to find a continuity for the basic economic adjustments inherited from the authoritarian period."[7] This training of the collective subjectivities to be a part—be it obligated, convinced, or seduced—of an economic competition that resocialized them through the politics of consumption and the mass media best explains the *reasoned* substitution of the dictatorial model consisting of "market, repression, and television" (Brunner) (with its effects of triple social deactivation) by means of the new model of market, consensus, and television with which the political Transition realized its economic path of adaptation-integration to the modernizing pact of neoliberalism.

The election of F. Léniz as commissioner sanctioned the successful continuity of the politics of economic macrorealizations whose shining achievements could now be internationally applauded, without their being clouded over by the questioning of the dictatorship on matters of human rights that the lights of Seville left behind in the dark past. This choice also highlighted the economy's new technocratic leadership role as dominant language, and the entrepreneur's role as metaactor of a reconstructed Chile.[8]

In Seville, the "imagined community" (B. Anderson) under the "Chile" brand name was the result of a showy combination of businessmen and advertising executives who coincided in projecting the image of a country that was both efficient (in performance) and attractive (in visual seduction, scenic display, play of representations), whose full-color screen set the tone for the new times, without the bothersome background of an experiential depth wounded by memories in black and white.

Although the dictatorial past bound the economic narrative scheme of market policies that defined the facade of Chile in Seville, it was important that the ties with such a problematic past should go unnoticed. For this reason, it was necessary to disencumber the image of "Chile Now" of all mnemonic residue and to simulate the rebirth of a transfiguration: one represented by the iceberg that, "cleansed, sanitized, purified by its long trip through the sea," caused one to believe that "it was as if Chile had just been born."[9] The "discourse of change" should fulfill the inaugurating role of a *discourse of foundation*, charged with reopening a new historical temporality that would place the future in a hitherto-unheard-of—virgin—pact of recently discovered meanings (it would be necessary to "clear the mind and to start to look with the eyes of a child" and "simply . . . give things a name").[10]

The semantic break with the world of the dictatorial past (the world of the pre-Transition) was achieved by rebaptizing things and legalizing their names in order to normalize their definitions, by captioning again and again the photographs in the display cases that reproduced different visions of Chile with didactic headings charged with transmitting stock meanings: "Country Life," "Bran Bread," "Pedro de Valdivia," "Astral Road," "Southern or Spanish Hake," et cetera.[11] After the historical trauma of the dictatorship that generated a loss of speech ("a lack of common words to name the experienced"),[12] it was necessary to "reconsensualize" the communicative order with references free of all vagueness and imprecision so that the danger of ambiguity and discursive conflict would not slip through the semantic fissures. The didactic captions of Chile in Seville symbolized the necessity of *generating consensus about names* so that the social exchange could move about within the preguaranteed limits of a reconciliatory discursiveness.

It was necessary as well to erase the "bad image" that the stereotype of Latin America projected over Chile as a country like others filled with "chaos and disorder," and to avoid at all cost the promiscuous register of confusion that only knows how to mix and lump everything together. In this manner the Chilean designers justified their obsession with multiplying the mechanisms for ordering names, labeling, and classifying.[13]

With the certainty that "the unequivocal signal of modernity" is the "decision to avoid confusions" and that "the connected meanings or associations are made today on the basis of knowing what each one is and how one looks,"[14] the representatives of Chile in Seville brought extreme discipline to the display with methodical principles of visual and conceptual order. Subjects and sections imposed limits on the uncontrolled multiplicity of the collections; labels affixed the name of what the exhibits assembled under a generic description that delimited the collection while the boxes separated the contents of each from the field of signifying dissemination surrounding it. Such insistence on standard procedures, on laws of numeration and enumeration, acknowledged the need for the reborn Chile of the Transition to rely on everything being definitively consigned to its place;

each identity differentiated and recognizable, each definition closed by a stable repertoire of unique meanings that would permit the regulations of the consensus to operate over a world that was happily free of ideological disarray and insurrectionary voices.

Bright Light, without Shadow

The idea of modernity that Chile took to Seville derives from a central model of technical rationality, ordered by processes and identities along the straight line of development. This simplified model of "rationalization, commercialization, contractualization, and technification" (Brunner) restates the economistic version of modernization understood as a simple performative law of technico-operational efficiency that can only "make a clean slate of cultural history and *ethos*."[15] By cultural *ethos*, we imply all that Chile in Seville left outside its visual and conceptual framework: the peripheral fragmentation of contexts where "modernization has not operated in general through substitutions, but instead through attachment, rupture, partial superimpositions" that articulate the heterogeneous multi-temporality of "snippets, truncated developments, grafts, new buds."[16]

In the catalog published for the trade fair, the designers of the Chile pavilion talked about the blend of "the empanada and the cheeseburger" or "Coca-Cola and boiled wheat with sun-dried peaches" as a supposed heterogeneity of dissimilar planes that juxtaposed themselves irregularly with our daily social life, and whose dissimilarity should express "the Chileanness" in a disordered superimposition of crossed referents.[17] However, the presentation of Chile in Seville was far from resembling this Latin American collage of a residual and peripheral modernity that blends discontinuous processes of social advancement with the precariousness of zones foreign or refractory to the metropolitan paradigm. The fragments of memories, traditions, and experiences of a Chile truly made up of contradictory space-times were all leveled by the recycling graphics of advertising that canceled out the "cultural depth" (Subercaseaux) of these ruptures of sense that mix folklore and market, oral tradition and telecommunications, premodernity and postmodernity. The standardizing language of advertising that smoothes surfaces and flattens contents continually erased the hybrid and discordant identities in conflict that referred to the maladjustments and the asynchronies of startled temporalities.

The stylistic form that the representatives of the Chile pavilion in Seville gave to their messages deployed all the resources of the graphic arts in advertising and industrial design in order to create smooth images, with-out pores or textures, whose orderly glow—that of a brightly lit reality (without shadows)—should not be seen as overshadowed by confusions or a jumbling of layers. The images of Chile's modernizing development in Seville (rapid and airy images based on a pure circulation value) needed to omit the jumps and discontinuities that interrupt every historical sequence; to erase the remains of times past and suppress the dark spaces of the preterite and of what is passé that obstruct the visual flow of simultaneity that capitalist globalization celebrates.

Scene and Monument

The two motivating ideas of the Chile pavilion in Seville were the super-market (as scene) and the iceberg (as monument). Guillermo Tejeda, one of the principal representatives of the trade fair, defined the "contempo-rary supermarket" as "a very attractive place of modernity where . . . there are no discriminatory relationships. Things are in abundance. At arm's and eye's reach."[18] The idea of the great market representing Chile as an "installation chock-full of products" synthesized the horizon of consump-tion in which the neoliberal politicians lost their vision, blinded by the vocabulary of advertising brand names that exhibit themselves all day long everywhere as values falsely shared by a social pseudoidentification.[19] The omnipresent and repetitive syntax of consumption saturated with brand names finally convinced the designers of the pavilion that in general the market is—by extension—universalizing; that is to say, the market equally brings together all the differences into a shared totality of consumption that extends itself by a simple, contiguous mass-produced series. As if the simple visual contact with a diversity of products—based on the advertis-ing illusion of the "the equality of all spectators faced with the image"[20]—were sufficient to guarantee the equitable and participatory inclusion of the consumer in the decision-making world of citizens.

The supermarket was intended to create the illusion of an interactive cir-cuit whose metaphor of game and adventure would prepare the spectator for a labyrinth of products "at arm's reach": the exaltation of the tactile and the sensorial ("we have made a great effort so that people can touch, get close, return again")[21] should have compensated for the abstraction of the computer-computational code of the design, simulating a physical contact with the material dimension of a certain value of experience even though such a value could only be realized on the banality of "buy and take away."

All Chile, its national history, its cultural traditions, its geography, its art and its politics ("don Francisco, the kites, José Donoso, Claudio Arrau, Rugendas, the empanadas, the Magellan Strait, the Virgin of San Cristóbal, the architecture of Chiloé, the tamales, etc."),[22] became, in Seville, the graphically and commercially rendered material of a photographic promotion that cut all the country into postcards, posters, and boxes for sale on the shelves of the supermarket. The "Merit Market" mounted the graphic simulacrum of a Chile fragmented into icons of consumption as souvenirs, to commemorate a successfully commercial Transition. The only "souvenir" that was not collectible by the tourist market was, of course, the pained memory of the dictatorship, whose pathos is out of tune with the lite dialects of the new entertainment culture of the democratic market.[23]

The second motivating idea of the Chile Pavilion in Seville grounded itself in the desire to create an impact with a surprising, extraordinary idea that would—in its originality—powerfully call attention to Chile's "difference," not so much in relation to Europe but in relation to the rest of the Latin America countries.[24] For this reason, a hundred-ton iceberg captured in the Chilean Antarctic was transported to Seville, after a voyage across the sea of almost thirty days. The iceberg idea attempted to highlight the creative audacity of the Chile-Expo Seville project with something unheard of. But the iceberg was also tied to the hype(r)contemporary nature of publicity's discovery of the most legendary dreams and fantasies of the Latin American continent, woven together—in filigree—by an oblique mention of the supernatural magic of the literature of the boom. Exhibiting the iceberg in Seville was like repeating the same gesture, although inverted in its geography, described in *One Hundred Years of Solitude* when José Arcadio Buendía pays to touch what he believes to be "the biggest diamond in the world."[25] In full hyperreality, the iceberg of Chile must have offered premodern memories of the moment in which "the heart swells with fear and joy on contact with the mysterious."[26] And it must also have surprised the international public with its postmodern blend of mythic residues and high technology, of magic realism and hyperconceptualism, of virgin nature and special effects.

The polemic unleashed in the national press over the iceberg was concerned above all with discussing whether it was pertinent to represent Chile as a cold country, with this image of coldness that conjures up associations with the calculation and efficiency of technologically driven rationality. The image of cold sought to contradict as neatly as possible the old stereotypes of disorder that the European gaze was apt to project on Latin

America: the cold opposed to the hot, the rational to the irrational, and the civilized to the barbaric. But perhaps the most decisive factor of the symbolism of the iceberg was its condition as "virgin object, white, natural, without precedents," exactly as it was defined by one of its creators involved in the project.[27] The "without precedents" left no doubt about the double historical break with the past that the Chile of the Transition in Seville claimed to trace: with the utopian-revolutionary past of 1960s Latin Americanism, and with the traumatic past of the military dictatorship.

In the first case, the ahistorical surface of a *natural* monument (the iceberg) situated outside social time and space enacted the cancellation of all reference to the historical Chile of the socialist revolution and the suppression of the Third World memory of conflicts of meaning that were contrasted under the contestatory ideology of underdevelopment, the periphery to the metropolis, the traditional to the modern, the popular to the lettered, the native to the foreign, the subordinated to the dominant. It was a question of "distancing cultural images tied to the decade of the sixties, images like folklore, testimony, 'Macondism' or denunciation, images whose capacity to evoke outrage and commitment had gone out of date and that would be dysfunctional in and for the world of business."[28] It was a time to say good-bye at all costs to the image of underdevelopment: the "southern scum, painful, remote, dusty, infectious, revolutionary, counter-revolutionary and confused," that denotes "periphery" in the version of unhappiness and demands for justice, of disorder and insurrection.[29] The mission of the natural and unpolluted whiteness of the millennial ice of the Antarctic was to *decontaminate* the image of Chile of any Third World ideological reminiscence and to cancel at the same time the rebellious attitude of the "peripheral defiance" that radicalizes this remoteness as inequality of power. It was necessary to redraw a fluid map of multilateral movements whose continuous line would not be interrupted by the obstacle of old antagonisms of positions and identities, in order to benefit freely from the growing multiplication of circulatory flows of messages and capital in the world economy in which the Chile of the Transition so festively entered as a participant.

The second historical break was a notorious attempt to remove any reference to a "pained and conflictive Chile" that had encouraged a compassionate gaze on its "many deaths and many poor," which during the dictatorship were the bearers of "bad news and dirty images."[30] It was a question of urgently replacing these bad and dirty (negative) images with other positively good and clean images, made for the occasion thanks to a mixture of computer design, graphic visualization, and industrial design meant to erase the recalcitrant opacity of a reflexive memory susceptible to clouding and disrupting the political-commercial optimism of the Transition with the malaise of its historical breakdowns.

The exposition of Chile in Seville was not only a "proposition that had the character of an advertising campaign."[31] It marked the triumph of a language (that of advertising with its marketplace of styles) that was characterized by its sacrifice of any depth or substance, in favor of the superficiality of the ungrounded images (without background) whose power of appearance speaks to the eye, to the exteriority of the gaze. This language was entrusted with translating excessively all the images of Transition Chile into the culture of *look* and *performance;* a culture that celebrates the nihilistic victory of the apparent by means of the superlative recourse to a mis-en-scène of the discourse of forms and their artifices.

If we remember that the hegemonic discourses of transitions are usually discourses "of halfhearted measures, not having brought about a true historic rupture, [that] find themselves constantly inflating the accomplishments in progress and their recent acquisitions,"[32] it is easy to understand how ambiguities accrue to the word "change" in the context of the post-dictatorship and democratic Transition. The tension between "real change" (transformations that should be perceived daily as such by the social body) and "formal change" (change announced by the official politics without experiential correspondence to the daily universe of practice) generates multiple zones of disassociation and contradiction between reality and discourse, between the daily and the political, between experience and representation.[33] To counteract the social perception that real changes are too slow or insubstantial, political officialdom produces a discursive over-representation of the word "change" that emblematizes its reference. Chile-Expo Sevilla '92 emphasized this value-sign with the aesthetic-advertising surplus value of a visual coup that would allow the performativity of the image to bring about the "new" of the Transition, through a politics of change that was simply a renovation of style.

CHAPTER NINE

Turbulence, Anachronism,
and Degenerations

Each society delineates various systems of more or less normative values with
which to judge itself. Once one has stated how the manner in which taste and
corresponding values are interrelated and compete in society, the problem of
judgment remains open.

The three barely pronounced emblem-words are intellectual risk, conflict
of acceptability, work on the aesthetic material.

—OMAR CALABRESE

A conflict from the art world seized popular attention both in the press
and on television during more than two weeks in August 1994; the pretext
was the aesthetic transgression of a work that satirized for the first time
the patriarchal ideologemes of Latin Americanist discourse in Chile. This
debate—even if for mistaken reasons—took the arts out of the secondary
role they ordinarily play in our cultural debate. It all started with an
extravagant anecdote: the Venezuelan embassy complained to the Chilean
Ministry of Foreign Relations about the mailing of reproductions of an
image of Simón Bolívar portrayed as a transvestite (signed by the artist
Juan Dávila), part of a project of the Santiago School that was financed by
the Ministry of Education through Fondart.[1] Rationales and arguments
about various aspects of the controversy were (un)leashed: freedom of creation or artistic censorship, state financing of art, discrimination against
homosexuals or respect of differences, ideological pluralism and cultural
modernity.[2]

The party alignments of the Chilean Transition, compromised around the too-visible and predictable contents of the national agenda, broke ranks and got lost in the deviation of aesthetic metaphor, bringing to light what the regulating core of the political debate generally kept out of sight due to fear or expediency. Beyond the provincial anachronism of the news story sensationalized by the press, beyond its awkward caricatures, the *Simón Bolívar* case and its allegory of transvestism as cultural and sexual parody caused the overflow of compressed hidden margins of meaning that provoked the sudden explosion of myths related to nationalist histories and hysterics, ideologies of (good) artistic taste, sexual repressions, Latin American mythologies, political officialdom, and cultural bureaucracies at the ministerial level.

Crevices, Subversive Infiltrations

Although the question of artistic procedures (of the productive materiality of the postcard as editorial support for the work of Dávila that sparked the controversy) was completely ignored by the commentaries on the *Simón Bolívar* case, the conditions of printing, reproduction, and circulation of the mailing of the Santiago School foregrounded a first way of nonaccommodation with the conventional schemes of a traditional artistic system.

The four artists brought together in the postal mailing of the Santiago School (Dávila, Díaz, Dittborn, Duclos) come from Avanzada scene, whose critical, leading role in the 1980's shook up the nonofficial borders of the artistic-cultural realm devised under the dictatorship. The first mailing of the Santiago School, entitled "The Decade of the Eighties,"[3] published the still-dispersed memory of conceptual fractures that gave all the analytical rigor and expressive brilliance to the Avanzada scene's ruptures of language; it was a scene traversed by the question of how to repoliticize art, after having taken on the formal convulsions of linearities of sense formerly programmed by the discourse of ideological representation, in order to reveal, alternatively, the constellations of signs of what had been broken, fragmented, and wounded.[4]

The first mailing of the Santiago School registered the effective force of an artistic memory that re-creates itself by editorializing its fragments, reinscribing in this way variations of meaning around the past of the works thanks to new intervals of deferred gazes that reactivate what had been sedimented with their *desire for the present*. In addition, this first mailing made a visibly staged paradox that its authors were "the four Chilean artists least esteemed by the media, and, on the other hand, those who have the most consistently successful artistic careers abroad."[5] This paradox was activated by transforming the mailing of the work into a small appeal for attention; into something that finely parodied the news of an event from the self-promoted event of its own news, seeing as how the Santiago School was inaugurated as an artistic group by the performativity of the name that created it.

But the project of the Santiago School informed us principally of its desire to create a form of exhibition and reception for works that would

Simón Bolívar the Liberator, by Juan Dávila. Detail of the installation *Utopia* (Hayward Gallery, London, 1994), reproduced on a postcard by the Santiago School.

not necessarily involve their display in an art gallery. In this way they secured an exit from the predesigned circuit of artistic consumption. The mailing of four cards of printed works mapped out a *mobile* gesture that overflowed the regular format of the museum or the gallery, causing the movement of its difference, its critical alternative, through a multidimensional space-time of social receptions. It was also a gesture that exercised independence and freedom of movement, as it circulated images according to networks of destinations whose places and positions did not coincide with the official directions of the artistic map of museums and galleries. By choosing who would be the addressees of the work by means of a list that selectively configured them as an audience, implicitly embedding in its model a receptive subject constituted according to a certain hypothesis of an addressee, this postal "framework" created a horizon of receptivity open to new encounters. The postal aspect of the work was able to convert its itinerant project into the critical operator of this desire for new configurations of readers and readings that would mark its nonconformity with the passive and resigned setting of the art gallery. Perhaps the disorder of these crevices opened up by the unpredictable circulation of postcards throughout the length and breadth of the cultural field emphasized the character of infiltration that Davila's subversive image took as it crossed irregular channels in order to make itself actively desiring and summoning, imploring in its search for an addressee outside the official realm. The circulation of the *Simón Bolívar* image, multiplied by the postal distribution that carried the surprise of the work beyond the circuit regularly authorized by artistic convention, brought about a proliferation of the transgressive virtualness of the image by disseminating its readings outside of institutional control.

Mixed with the moral sanctions with which they castigated the "sexual deviation" of the image, the public interventions around the *Simón Bolívar* case caused the embarrassing emergence of an artistic ideology wrapped up in mediocre layers of anachronism. Broad sectors of the public rejected the work for the way it violated the supposedly inviolate limits of "good taste and of good manners."[6] The opinions disseminated in the press entered into the reactionary defense of a model of the so-called fine arts, largely discredited by the vanguard and the neovanguard movements of this century, a model that postulates artistic taste and value as *natural* (not ideological) categories, thus erasing the preconstructed web of social rules and conventions that institutionally determine and regulate the dominant significance of art.

We know that the artistic institution and the legitimizing mechanism of art history are the means used to formulate the system of categories and judgments that grant social value and worth to certain conceptions of art while discrediting others. They regulate the battle between signs, values, and powers by means of an "ideology in images" that fixes the manner in which the classes and social groups recognize themselves in symbols and representations. This ideology in images possesses, among other responsibilities, that of forming *taste* and at the same time hiding the manner in which ideology informs taste by means of a whole influential system of cultural norms that mark individual sensibility (the biographical specialty) with the social markings of multiple learnings, impositions, and prejudices.[7]

When the president of the Chilean Senate insists that works of art should respect the limit of "good taste and good manners," he is only revealing a class ideology that confirms the aristocratic privilege of the fine arts, a perspective that contemplates the artistic as a sublime and transcendent expression of the idealization of Beauty: art as pure expression, noble and disinterested, that detaches the works from the historicity of its condition of social inscription and circulation.

The "distinguished" taste as it pertains to art is the sign of distinction that reconfirms in elitist fashion the class superiority entrusted with imposing its hierarchy of vision and division between the cultured and the popular, the refined and the clumsy, the educated and the vulgar, and so on; a sign that passes itself off as the spontaneous manifestation of a sensitive individuality and thus erases the manner in which the normative schema of the habitus (Bourdieu) restructures the individual sensibility through its social ideologies of artistic perception and consumption. The ideology of (good) taste transmitted by the artistic judgment of the president of the Senate in the name of an elevated conception of art did nothing but empower "the public extension of the private desires for an aristocratic representation of culture and of the role of the artist in society,"[8] to which all the cultural establishment adheres and whose institutions hold regular photo-op meetings recorded in the social pages of the daily *El Mercurio*: Municipal Theatre, Friends of Art, Cultural Institutions, et cetera. An invitation to celebrate the myths of talent that ritualize the belief in the "quality" of the work as value in itself (transcendent, universal, ahistorical), as well as to celebrate the images of art that adorn the social with its bonus of imagination and sensitivity without ever managing to attain the power of a critical leadership role in the scene of democratic culture.

These consensually bourgeois visions of art defended by the political sectors that pronounced on the work of Dávila, these visions foreign to the dislocations of the iconographic repertoire of the dominant history of art and defenders of a canonical order of official reading, castigated the manner in which the work opened up the images to a disturbance of codes that brought on a crisis—conceptually and figuratively—of high art's montage of discourse, authority and, representation.[9]

Carnival of Identities

Which interpretations legitimated by the artistic tradition were violated by Dávila's *Simón Bolívar*, and why did it cause such a commotion in the predominant system of cultural legibility and appreciation?

The "indecorous and criminal attacks on the immortal genius of the American independence" supposedly expressed by the work can be attributed to the act of painting the Liberator "as if he were a deviant" (with the body of a woman) and making a streetwise gesture, popular and obscene, with a direct sexual connotation (i.e., giving the finger).[10] But there was also the racial mixing of his facial traits (*mestizaje*) that indicates the indigenous nature of the person. The indigenous, the feminine, and the popular exhibited the traits of subidentity so long censored by the academicism of universal art history in complicity with the interests of a whitewashing ideology of official Latin Americanism: traits of impurity that contaminated the official image of the hero, of the independence legend of Latin America, integrating "the subordination (the Indian, the woman) to the criollo centrality (oligarchy, masculine) of the national project."[11]

The *mestizaje* of the facial traits of Dávila's *Simón Bolívar* transgressed the sublimated model of Latin America, creating a tension by invoking indigenousness and colonization within the same scene of identity (the mestizo face), where blackness struggles against the cosmetics of whitening that was responsible for the official simulacrum; it cracked the mask to exhibit the other it covered and hid.[12] But the juxtaposition of styles practiced by Dávila in the interior of the image also overturned a certain Latin Americanist discourse of the "autochthonous." In dividing Bolívar's horse between realism and abstraction, in mixing the modernity of the vanguard movements—and their cosmopolitan engagement—with popular and folkloric realism, Dávila rejected the vernacular demand for the "Latin American identity" based on a Manichaean polarization between the indigenous and the foreign, founded as the originating nucleus of an ontological purity of being. Ironically, Dávila shows us that "patriotism is

also a commercial construct, based on the wholesale packagings and a trafficking of poses, gestures, styles and clothes"; his artistic bazaar pokes fun
at "the state's commerce in nostalgia and invented tradition."[13]

Dávila's Simón Bolívar in drag posed Latin America as a mestizo construction not only in terms of ethnic mixings but also in the hybridizations
of codes that join—and collide—modernity and traditions, vanguards and
folklore, metropolitan aesthetics and popular cultures ("Dávila's postcard
is not, then, the representation of Bolívar, but an attempt at creating an
identity. Stirred up and excluded bric-a-brac meet there, pieces of rubbish
that adorn the bazaar of Latin American identity. Mixed up, patched, stuck
together").[14]

In addition, the patch of identity is mixed in with the feminine ("How
is it possible that Bolívar is also a woman? And that the founder of so
many Fatherlands should have suddenly lost the martial composure, the
military virility, and acquired women's breasts, earrings, panty hose and
women's rouge?").[15] The feminine retouching that degenerated Bolívar's
image points to the following hidden truth: "the discourse of history is
gendered: no one doubts, from the first school texts, that history is written in the masculine."[16] We know that the sociomasculine hierarchy that
affirms itself in the inequality of values attached to sexual identifications
reserves for masculinity the privilege of occupying the rational and productive side of culture and society, while the feminine side continues to be
confined to the reverse: to the irrational and merely reproductive side
(body and nature), which does not partake of the universal transcendence
of the Logos or in its grandiose achievements. On the side of the foundational heroic metanarratives, there is the patriarchal cult of the virile masculinity of the conquistador and the legislator: these are the rites and
emblems that recount the history of the great events whose public slogan
(nationalism, Americanism, etc.) is written in monumental letters. Giving
Simón Bolívar a woman's body was a betrayal of the story written in capital letters of the heroic deeds and battles of the Founding Fathers, making
it fall into the decorative superfluousness of a nontranscendent body.

The "indecorous" and the "criminal" dimensions of Dávila's work derived, as far as official Latin Americanism was concerned, from how the
inversion of gender made vulnerable the virile protocol of a history that
reproduces the masculine ideologemes charged with safeguarding the civ-
ilizing pose. The distortion of signs that committed the barbarism of which
the work was accused boiled down to the figure of transvestism;[17] a figure
that blends paradoxically the masculine and the feminine in a zone of

sexual ambiguity that carries the mark—always disturbing—of indefinition, of tumult and uncertainty suggested by a "perhaps." Transvestism breaks the binary of sexual opposition while superposing and undermining the representations of gender and produces disequilibrium between the terms in the dual system of fixed categorizations of gender by official culture and its masculine-feminine dichotomy. Moreover, transvestism disarticulates sexual identity from the realism of the original body in order to rearticulate the marks of the masculine and the feminine through a rhetoric of artifice, masks, and simulation. The image of a transvestite Simón Bolívar and the transvestism of its author ("the way he too signed with a woman's name implies that he is a person with problems")[18] produced, in the registers of propriety and identity of the official culture, a semantic disorder that blurred the border between the One and the Other—as homogeneous substances and absolute opposites—a border whose sure demarcation seeks to safeguard conservative morality.[19] There is "something precise and taboo that formally questions, frustrates, confounds, infuriates, and disorders in Dávila's postcard. Something that shook up high officials of the Chilean government and of the countries liberated by Bolívar":[20] this taboo is concerned with the ritual of the separation between the pure and the impure that hegemonic culture uses to ward off the menace of the plural heterogeneity of the Other.

The transvestism of Simón Bolívar disturbed the definitions of gender with its cosmetics of retouching (of parody and simulation) that desubstantializes sexual identity; at the same time, the cross-breeding and bastardization of traits of the hero painted by Dávila in a body "half white, half black; half woman, half man; half dressed, half naked in the poverty of Latin America; also part wise guy torn by the economic power of other centers" also frustrated the glorious allegories of nation and identity upheld by official Latin Americanism.[21] In addition, the hybridization of codes between the cosmopolitan modernity and the popular folklore that fragmented the work disordered the classifications of styles of European art history with its jumble of lexicons. Faced with gestures so disrespectful of the orthodoxies of language and the representation of national, cultural, and sexual identities, the conservative forces of Chilean culture called for the preservation of certain "indestructible values" around which conventional families (among them, the "Chilean family") should renew their ties of obedience. Whereas Dávila's work used the metaphor and the double entendre to criticize the dogmatism of the official truths, the democratic press used the work of Dávila to revise subject limits that censorship can impose on the liberty of meanings ("Should a government use or not use state money to support a work that could be offensive, or cataloged as immoral?").[22] The public flap caused by Dávila's work cataloged as "offensive" and "immoral" only showed how desperate the moral traditionalism of Catholic discourse is today in Chile; it is desperate to reinsert its sacred values into the demystified landscape of economic liberalization where the market's power of abstraction has already dissolved all consubstantial links between sign and value. It was again necessary to demonize the danger of the lack of sexual definition as something "immoral" in order to realign loyalties around the equivalence—conventionally regulated—between the natural, the human, the normal, and the moral ("because being a woman . . . is normal and being a homosexual is not").[23] The exemplification of "natural" behavior as the foundation of human normality, defended by Christian morality and its rigid paradigm of the disciplining of the self, censored the problematization of identity-propriety unleashed by the metaphor of transvestism. The normativity of sexuality and the moralization of art combined their categorical imperatives to dogmatically fix the principle of a univocality of meaning, castigating critical paradoxes, ambivalences, and disseminations: all that is likely to disobey the monolithic reason of moral and social ideologies with their carnival-like play of parodic forms and styles.

There are various meanings—lesser and greater—that a cultural analysis of the discourses of the Transition could retrieve from the controversy generated by the *Simón Bolívar* case in order to comment on the anachronisms and the trivialities that fill up the Chilean cultural milieu and conspire against the possibility of a real critical debate about the power of art. There are also various hypotheses and suspicions that could be assembled to explain all the exaggerated publicity around the *Simón Bolívar* case; enough ammunition to accuse this overactive media of having dangerously relegated central subjects and matters to new margins of silence and concealment.[24] But beyond the raw evidence, the sharp suspicions or the quiet machinations, the controversy over Dávila's *Simón Bolívar* opened up a cultural fissure that allowed an oblique approach to meanings deliberately obscured by the media glitz of the national news. Once more, it allowed us to measure the incompetent criteria of the critical languages of art and culture that the political class profess when they have to think outside the box of approved subjects of parliamentary debate.

Postscript: Margins and Institutions

After the 1994 *Simón Bolívar* scandal, whose controversy involved the Ministry of Education as the entity that financed the postcard project signed by the Santiago School, the Gabriela Mistral Gallery—a space dependent on the same ministry[25]—officially invited the artist Juan Dávila to put on a show. The exhibition entitled *Rota* (Broken), in November 1996, included a reproduction of *Simón Bolívar* and again brought together various critical motifs that had been used—and censored—in it as artifices of parodic construction: the mixture of high culture and the popular that confronts the figurative canon of cultural authority with the turbulent images of social exclusion and discrimination; the dislocations of the iconographic repertoire of art history and the fragmentation of styles recombined according to a jumble of bastardized proceedings; the contamination of the symbols of the dominant culture by the decentralization and peripheralization by languages that criticize the dichotomization of meaning between model and reproduction, original and copy; the metaphor of transvestism that conveys retouchings, simulations, and masks as fictional strategies of a changing and reversible identity, without fixed harmonious characteristics between body, identification, and belonging; and so on. In the case of the *Rota* (literally, "broken"; Chilean slang for poor [wo]man) exhibition, it was the poor Chilean (wo)man (*el roto, la rota*) that served as a deconstructive paradigm in order to undermine the legitimacy of the official system of representations of "national identity" and to sarcastically set at odds everything canonized by their hierarchies that ordered the being and purity of the nation.

On the other hand, despite the fact that the exhibition in the Gabriela Mistral Gallery reproduced the same type of operations that had earlier been judged unbearably provocative by the official cultural milieu, and despite the fact that said operations were directed against the moral and national foundations of the "Chilean" paradigm, the work was not only tolerated by the artistic institutions but also given a prize by the Art Critics Circle that "considered Juan Dávila, and his transgressive stance, the most notable Chilean artist of the year," according to the official communiqué that justified the awarding of the prize.

What happened between the sanctions against *Simón Bolívar* (1994) in the name of "good taste and correction" and the prize given to the work *Rota* (1996) that ended up being applauded by artistic officialdom, despite the fact that it recurred to the same parodies that had scandalized in 1994?

What explains the institutional about-face that transformed Dávila into an official invitee of the art gallery of the Ministry of Education when the same artist had earlier been qualified as a "degenerate" by cultural official-dom? The answers to these questions could only be tentative, resorting to extremely varied logics, all confusingly intertwined. A preliminary hypothesis (limited to politically relevant data about the bureaucratic evolution of the conflicts between the sectors of Christian Democracy and of the Socialists that faced off during the earlier debate on the role of Fondart and how to manage cultural institutions)[26] would perhaps explain the change in institutional policy and refer to a dynamics of applied pressure, opportunistically taking advantage of the Dávila affair to settle partisan scores. This hypothesis only sadly confirms the already known: the political-administrative functionalization of culture called on to serve interests independently of the specificity of their discursive operations; the subordination of the cultural-symbolic realm to external demands in relation to politics, which denies art a leading role in critical confrontations and interpellations in the social arena. It is also possible to imagine that the success of the work was simply the product of a misunderstanding, occasioned by the blindness of official readings (the art critic of the daily newspaper *El Mercurio* and the Circle of Art Critics) faced with the most subversive dualities of the work that questioned, without their knowledge, their hierarchies and classifications of taste, value, representation, and power. Or perhaps, on the contrary, the dialectic between norm and infraction ends up always reinstating the rebellious position and its iconoclastic gesture into the museum catalog of permissible deviations, due to the almost infallible capacity that artistic institutions possess for neutralizing critical provocation. Underlining other suspicions about margin-institution relations, one could suggest that in Dávila's case, the governing apparatus's persuasiveness in establishing well-defined limits were directed to "make excesses into borders. They acted like a membrane to filter and translate external elements, adjusting them to the coherence of the system."[27]

One can't ignore the fact that something within the work itself could have eased its assimilation into the categories of official readings; something perhaps related to the iconography of the popular *roto* from the magazine *Topaze*, which classified its cartoon character with an overly familiar Chilean identity of picturesqueness, in which this representation of the popular functions graphically only as a "symbol of the domesticated exterior."[28] In contrast to what occurred in the *Simón Bolívar* case, whose denigration of identity became scabrous when it attacked the solemnity of the official portrait and violated the superior ideology of purity with the obscenity of signs violently proscribed by the canonical representation of the model (signs that unleash—in the portrait itself—a conflict of forces between the idealized and the demystifying), it would appear that only the pop recuperation of "the malicious, obscene, drunken, idle, menial, servile" traits of the popular cartoon character Verdejo the *roto* could motivate the politically deactivated laughter of the large audience that came to the Gabriela Mistral Gallery.[29] This image of the Chilean *roto* (paternalistically recuperated by the overly festive reading of the relations between humor, people, and nation that prevailed in the general commentaries) permitted, in fact, the criticism of the daily *El Mercurio* to rejoice in the changes to "this new, less aggressive and tragic tone" that would finally make it possible for "the debate over Dávila's painting that for years centered on his political, historical and social merits, and was considered by many offensive to certain moral and national values, to situate itself once again around the true value of his work."[30]

Most likely, none of these explanations is enough in itself, and logic and circumstance have become so entangled with the rationality of the system, with the contingency of the details and the accidents that always make it less uniform. In any case, the paradoxes of the *Rota* exhibition of the artist Juan Dávila may serve (1) to demonstrate that the institutional logic is not as complete or as unified as it appears, and that each one of its chains of practical relations presents irregularities and noncoordinated elements of meaning that make its bases of action much more heterogeneous and discontinuous than they appear at first glance, with breeches through which these irregularities virtually turn around its hegemonic pacts; and (2) to refine the vision of how the "margins" and "institutions" should permanently renegotiate their positions according to the modifications in the power relations between totality and fissure, between center and border, between demarcations and rupture, between regulation of authority and significant disseminations.

CHAPTER TEN

❦

Gender, Values, and Difference(s)

> In the discussion of the SERNAM document, one of the women senators declared the term *gender* ambiguous. The senator is not mistaken, except perhaps in her belief that there exist other less ambiguous terms. The "ambiguity" does not imply imprecision; it is a consequence of the struggles for interpretative power that leave their traces in the play of signifiers.
>
> —JEAN FRANCO

In August 1995, the word "gender" polemically interrupted the national public debate centered on the Chilean Senate's response to the official policies that the National Woman's Service (SERNAM) would bring to the Fourth Beijing Conference. During that same month, the Department of Philosophy and Humanities of the University of Chile inaugurated its postgraduate degree in gender studies,[1] amid a tense discussion about academic politics, the state apparatus, privatization, and the autonomy of knowledge. This discussion occurred in the context of a neoliberal democracy that today subjects the university project to a menacing process of segmentation, technification, and commercialization of knowledge, without consideration of the critical-reflective (nonutilitarian) dimension of thinking. The local conjunction of both situations (the public debate about official Chilean participation in Beijing, the academic inauguration of the Gender and Culture Program at the university) gave the concepts of family, gender, feminism, woman, and difference controversial accentuations, both ideological and social. These words, in turn, were pulled apart by the conflicting forces of moral traditionalism, market diversity, and critical pluralism.

The Rearticulation of the Mother-Family Syntagma

In the military regime's past, the signs "woman" and "family" were the object of a double and contradictory treatment. The dictatorship sought to bring cohesion to the ideological nucleus of the family with the doctrinaire identification of woman with the fatherland as the national symbol that guaranteed and upheld continuity of order, while the dictatorship broke up the physical and corporal contours of the family by submitting persons and relatives to the violence of its homicidal repression. On the one hand, an emblematics of the mother as natural guardian of the sacred values of the nation was officially elevated as the patriotic representation of life, while on the other hand, the political war against the enemies of national security used the figure of death to submerge the mothers of the detained-disappeared in the clandestinity of mourning. Maternity thus lent its sign so that the mother-fatherland relation could enact an extreme polarity of opposing values that led women either, in support of the dictatorship, to translate the "maternal instinct" for the conservation of life to a conservative search for official security or, on the other side of totalitarian/authoritarian power, to fracture the patriarchal mold with their civic disrespect.

Working with the remains of this fractured link of nation-woman-order-dislocation, the government of the democratic transition needed to hyperbolize the discourse of family to forge new links of community stability that would be responsible for *naturalizing* the reencounter of the country with itself. The base of the family unit, in the postdictatorship, was intended to "unite, to reunite the social bond" with the help of "the rites, symbols, and associations representative of union and integration."[2] The ideologeme of the family would thus repair the political and ethical damage of death committed in the military regime's past against the material and affective integrity of the person and at the same time ward off the moral damage committed, in the present, by economic neoliberalism, whose globalizing rhythms dissolve community values that moral traditionalism tries to symbolically safeguard in the family institution.

Street rebellions were organized during the years of the military regime, whose official policies glorified woman—mother and wife—in her role as defender of the regimented fatherland. Other women (family members of the detainees-disappeared) decontextualized the traditional motherhood-home nexus and resignified politically the symbolism of the mother in the public space of the street, traditionally reserved for men. The women "effected their maternal politics" by "flight" that "usurped the space of the citizen and formally questioned the political order steeped in death, questioned it, precisely for transgressing the order that life legitimated and that was represented by the *mater*."[3]

Accompanying these women's social movements associated with human rights issues in socialist circles in Chile, a feminist line of thought that emerged from the nonofficial academic centers imbued the problematics of gender with a primary force of political questioning.[4] The feminism of the antidictatorship not only sought to mobilize women to activate the social struggle against the system of sexual discrimination of the patriarchal ideology. It also engaged the "woman" category in order to design new axes of critical reconceptualization of political thought and action that took into consideration the whole cultural network of subjugations that overflowed the merely economistic code of social class exploitation to which leftist orthodoxy remained attached, with its traditional monopolistic reference to the power of the state. And it was the decisive slogan that "the personal is political" that pointed out the invisible chains of repression that run through the daily details of personal life and the subjective theorized by feminism.[5]

The feminism of the eighties had taken pains to redesign the political according to axes transversal to the linear features of institutional politics. The politics of alliance and negotiation of the democratic recomposition of the nineties broke away from the disaffiliating mark of this political and critical transversality in order to recycle the demands of feminism in a new language agreed on by institutional agreement and party arrangements. The women who during the dictatorship had impugned the traditional political model later during the Transition reclaimed identity and legitimization inside the same system of categories, expressing a desire for recognition by and in the order whose rationality they had previously questioned. They sought political legitimization in the bureaucratic-institutional circuits of the government of redemocratization.[6]

The creation in 1990 of the National Women's Service (SERNAM) sanctifies this politics of institutional administration on the subject of women, leading the Transition government to delegate to SERNAM the task of designing, coordinating, and evaluating public policy about the family. But the rationale of SERNAM's creation not only has to do with this political-institutional recomposition of a discourse about women that renounced, by and large, the agitational and contestatory dynamic of feminism in order to limit itself to a new pragmatism of instrumental agreements and alliances.

The SERNAM that administers the "woman" sign in a landscape traumatically divided between the past (the disintegration of bodies and families) and the present (the necessity of reintegration of social and sexual roles to paradigms of stabilization in the social order) bases its legitimacy on the complicity of points of view that brought together the official politics of the Reconciliation, hegemonized by the Christian Democrats, with the defense that the Chilean church makes of the family as a symbol of reunification and consolidation of a new sexual morality.[7]

Unorthodox Words

Supported by the symbolic and ethical prestige engendered by its actions in defense of human rights during the dictatorship, the Chilean church recovers, during the Transition, a power of discourse whose hegemonic voice allows it to pass judgment on and sanction the conduct of the social body, taking as a reference point the teachings of the Vatican on evangelical matters of morality.[8] The church launched a "great moral campaign to illuminate consciences and to sanitize morals," an effort "that is an integral part of the New Evangelization of the country, to which the pope urgently appeals to us," recalls the archbishop of Santiago, Monsignor Oviedo, in his Pastoral Letter.[9] The Christian dogma of the church rearticulates the whole symbolic-cultural plan of Chile in the Transition, converting the religious theme of *values* into the crux of an intense political normativity that censors sexualities, bodies, and identities: a politics subscribed to by politically conservative sectors—and not only by them— that defend this leading role of the Catholic Church in the definition and regulation of a sexual morality capable of protecting "the dignity of women and men"; a morality whose fundamentalism attempts to counter the rising risk (promoted by the same market that these sectors defend when it concerns the economy) of a progressive liberalization of customs, social permissiveness, and degradation of values.

Although the official policies of SERNAM to be presented at the Fourth Woman's Conference in Beijing were very moderate, the majority of the Senate signed a rejection that criticized those policies for not being sufficiently categorical in their defense of the family as an institution and as the "basic cell of society," founded "in the monogamous and stable union of a man and a woman in matrimony."[10] An ample political block closed ranks around a definition of family that recognizes it only as a group inseparably formed by the mother-father-child triad, whose links—stably classified—should not suffer alteration in form or content, since, in the words of one representative of the political Right, "the family is what is destined to endure, and does not change";[11] a moral family, legally consti-tuted, that ought to bring together (in an essentialist sense) the natural-biological destiny of every body with the transcendent ideal of universal values. This was the framework for the ideological-sexual conceptualization of the masculine and feminine identities within which the word "gender"— mobilized by the discussion over the policies of SERNAM—controver-sially intervened with its unfamiliar inflections. Inflections whose lack of familiarity first caused suspicions about their origin (international femi-nism), causing ample political majorities to mistrust this exogenous cultural model that, according to these majorities, did nothing but confirm "the penetration into the social framework of lifestyles that clash with our cul-ture and all that which has been considered positively traditional."[12]

As we know, the concept of "gender" was theorized by feminism to open an analytical breach between the *sexual body* (natural substratum, biological determination) and the *marks of representation* of masculinity and femininity traced by social codes and their cultural norms; a breach that feminist criticism uses to intervene in the discourse about the body and to politicize the signs of sexual definition. Gender as sexual represen-tation and self-representation brings into view the "varied social technolo-gies and institutionalized discourses" whose semiotic scheme models the significations of the "masculine" and the "feminine," which are then acted on by bodies and subjectivites in relation to dominant codes of symbolic power.[13] Highlighting sexual gender as *representation* (in other words, as effect of discourse and a mediation of codes) has brought to feminism a double benefit: (1) it allowed a de-essentialization of sexual identities, that is, it broke with the determinism of an identity preconstituted by some invariable signification of the masculine and the feminine that causes a linear correspondence of sexual origin, body, substance, and value; and (2) it has been critically helpful in denouncing the work of concealment that cultural ideologies enact when they disguise as *natural* the *conventional* manners in which hegemonic masculinity fixes its interpretations and val-uations of the sexual, as if these were not what they are: interpretations and valuations that are historically constructed and therefore can be decon-structed and opened to rearticulation.

If we take into consideration the critical potential of the concept of "gender" that dismantles the sexual naturalism of original masculinity and femininity, we should not be surprised that "gender" turns out to be so profoundly irritating to those who claim that "what is essential for women is being a mother,"[14] or even that a woman ought to fulfill "her feminine essence that is naturally directed toward motherhood."[15] Gender analysis highlights the marks of construction and interpretation of sexual value that is regulated by fixed codes of social and historical signification. A gendered perspective disorganizes the conventionality of the maternal applied to a universal-transcendent feminine essence and also introduces the dangers of change in a world of continuities and traditions up until now based on the certainty that "natural moral values should be absolute and permanent."[16]

The defense of the moral values and contents of traditional sexuality that "gender" introduced into Chilean public debate thanks to the Beijing Conference was based on the semantics of the *proper* and of the *natural* (of the "familiar") that were supposed to fix a standard of meaning and conduct through known and recognizable words, and without strange (foreign) connotations or ambiguities of meaning that contaminate the systems of homogeneous categories tenaciously upheld by the nationalistic purism of tradition.[17]

For conservatives, the debate about Beijing demonstrated that both the conceptual legitimacy of the words and the morality of their use values have to do with the capacity to guarantee a permanent and definitive meaning: an invariable meaning. The Chilean Senate reproached those who use the word "gender" for its link to "equivocal terminologies and ambiguous positions" that allude to sexes and identities "of diffuse or uncertain limits,"[18] treating it as a "contraband" (clandestine) word trafficking in multiple and forbidden meanings along the ideological borders of the dominant code of identity. The word "gender" was basically condemned for its lack of orthodoxy in matter of definition, whether lexical or sexual; for opening too many margins of imprecision that threaten to deregulate the center of authority of a single (predetermined) truth. The ideological discomfort created by the semantic rupture that the word "gender" introduced in the realm of sexual designations, the vagrancy of the word that wandered outside the definitions regulated by cultural authority, led ministers and delegates to demand of the Dictionary of the Royal Academy of the Spanish Language (the supreme authority of canonical meanings)[19] and of the Senate (official guardian of political legality) that they perform in tandem the firm task of putting a stop to this subversive-errant-proliferation of *vague* and *strange* meanings, and bring them back into the "authorized and legitimate territory of the voice of the *Father*, a place capable of containing the paradoxes and heterodoxies of marginal voices."[20]

Transvestisms of Difference

While on a national scale the church and the Senate condemned the conceptual legitimacy of the word "gender," the university's Gender and Culture Program was inaugurated to fight for university legitimization of the knowledges born of feminism; knowledges until now precarious, fragmented, and discontinuous, whose regrouping as a corpus of teaching should have granted a basis of academic certification to their still-precarious body of historical knowledges.

The formation of the Gender and Culture Program (GCP) aimed to bring into the postdictatorship academy knowledges and experiences that had been generated unofficially outside the walls of the university during the military period and to ensure that these feminist materials finally gained scientific autonomy and institutional validity. These knowledges and experiences were linked to the citizenship struggles of the women's organizations and with the investigative work of nongovernmental organizations. The challenge was double: on the one hand, gender studies needed to bring about the convergence of marginal forces and practices formerly separated from all academic legitimacy in the academy, and thereby obtain a deserved recognition; but on the other hand, they needed to be careful that the machine of university reterritorialization did not end up erasing the political tension of their minority and militant formation of knowledges indelibly linked to the desire for social transformation.[21] With the inauguration of the Gender and Culture Program, the knowledges of Chilean feminism entered from outside the walls into the enclosure of the academy in order to benefit from its mechanisms of institutionalization of knowledge, but they did so surrounded by multiple contradictions. In effect, these knowledges—those of gender, those of feminism—sought to achieve their theoretical and conceptual autonomy as academic materials not only while the church and Senate were censoring, on the national scene, all reflections that did not canonically conform to the official terminology of their rehearsed truths, but also in an atmosphere in which the new regime of neoliberal privatization in Chile was effecting "the transition of the modern state university to a poststate neocommercial university." This implied the liquidation of "all the modern university values and hierarchies starting with the 'autonomy'" of knowledge.[22] In other words, at a time when the modernized university of the Chilean Transition complied with the privatizing forces of liberalism and made the decision to translate the value "education" into the economic, it exchanged the reflexive value

of critical thought for a technical market of radically uncommitted professions. All the more reason to redouble suspicions regarding certain
circumstances that now appear to favor the formation of gender studies
programs in different parts of Chile: if the postdictatorship university,
propelled by a commercializing logic, appears so easily to tolerate the
inclusion of knowledges formerly discriminated against as marginal (feminism and the problematics of gender), perhaps it is because the "novelty"
of "different" knowledges contributes to filling a menu of options for
learning that are needed for the university market to be increasingly flexible and diversified. Although late in the game, the system of novelties that
regulates the oversupply of different offerings invites the options of women
and gender to be part of the "liberalness of the supermarket" that today
governs the university of the Chilean Transition.[23]

   Margin, difference, and otherness are categories that the Gender and
Culture Program assumes—in the name of feminist criticism—in order for
them to be included in the horizon of the democratic debate of the Transition, but without ceasing to be alerted to certain dangers: (1) of moral
conservatism that, faced with the detranscendentalization of the signs operated by the dissolving forces of the market, resumes the debate over "values" only in order to defend the fundamentalism of tradition; (2) of the
pluralism of the market that neutralizes the values of difference to undif-
ferentiate them under the serial abstraction of its product form; and (3) of
the academic recodification of university knowledge that institutionalizes
"the other," adapting it to the mold of an already-classified difference.
Margin, difference, and alterity should thus have been capable of imagin-
ing small tactical movements, escapes and ruptures of meaning that would
have known how to thwart this triple mechanism of appropriation and
domestication of otherness.

   At a time when the voice of the *Pater* defended in the Senate resolved to
prohibit "equivocal definitions in matters of such ethical transcendence,"[24]
the inaugural session of the Gender and Culture Program in the University
of Chile marked, first, its dissidences with the national slogan of having to
agree on the unanimity of meaning. Jean Franco, the professor invited to
give the inaugural lecture, read her address in the Ignacio Domeiko salon
in the main building at the University of Chile: a room on whose walls
hang the effigies of the historic university presidents, whose stern gaze
symbolically re-created the same patriarchal control over bodies and knowledges exercised outside the university by the Senate of the Republic. J.
Franco started her address by projecting a slide (the reproduction of a work,

The Two Fridas, by the Mares of the Apocalypse),[25] and this gesture condensed in itself various transgressions of gender(s) and genres. First, the
projection of the slide shattered the magisterial format of a university
lecture with a marginal visual nature that committed an outrage against
academic solemnity. The projection of the work of the Mares of the Apocalypse collective also subjected the patriarchal authority of the knowledge
of science and philosophy—represented by the image of the university presidents—to the spectacle of a homosexual turn created by performance art.
The feminizing obliqueness of the transvestism was destined to upset the
control of the truth-of-knowledge, with its cosmetic confusion and intrigues

The Two Fridas, photo-performance by Las Yeguas del Apocalipsts (1992).

of simulation. Moreover, the work dislocates the market of representations of identity with its transvestite parody that carnivalized not so much the feminine as the feminist iconization of Frida Kahlo that, after having been emblematized as a flag of feminine struggle and resistance, ended up being commercialized through the "Frida" fashion.[26]

The text read by J. Franco reminded us how the projection of the same Mares of the Apocalypse postcards in an earlier international conference had caused problems among some of the women attending, who posited that "introducing transvestism into a discussion of gender was not appropriate, because . . . gender is only about women."[27] It is true that transvestism radically subverts the conceptualizations of sex and gender also defended by a certain kind of feminism, which even if it distinguishes between the body as biological reality and gender as symbolic marking, continues to linearly imply a continuity of experience and conscience between sex and gender, woman and feminism, without ruptures of representations or discontinuities of signs. Transvestism mocks in a spectacular fashion all the claimed unity of meaning of the "woman" category, with its antinaturalistic rupture of the distortion of the sign that overacts the identification of feminine gender in order to emphasize the rhetorical norm of sexual conventions. With the photograph of the work of the Mares of the Apocalypse, J. Franco's inauguration of the Gender and Culture Program acknowledged the truth—parodically—of the conservative fear that the word "gender" was deceitful and concealed a series of "trick(s), masking(s), costume(s), ideological and sexual transvestisms," to perversely entertain that it was scheming with identities that were more fake (constructed) than real (natural).[28] The photograph of the Mares of the Apocalypse shamelessly exhibited the sexual trap in order to excite the critical imagination around the secrets of the folds and doublings of unregulated masculinity and femininity. The carnival-like recourse of transvestism that ventures in the transgendered "between" of the formulations of sexual identity and propriety subtly ridiculed the monological rigidities of discourse around the masculine and the feminine, in whose name the church and the Senate in Chile censored feminist theory and the word "gender," having found both of them guilty of giving rise to uncertain definitions and ambiguous categories. While deploying an infinity of polysemies and multiplicities of voices in the breaches of the portrait of Frida, the image of transvestism not only criticized the essentialism of *one* sexual identity (defended on the national scene by moral traditionalism) but also the academic recodification of *one* gender difference, as institutionalized by university feminism.

Politically, gender studies contribute to the widening of the university borders under the pressure of new problematics of identity that question the hierarchies and censoring tactics of traditional knowledge. And this critical contribution to the dehierarchization of knowledge speaks clearly to the need to fight for the entry of gender studies into traditional university frameworks. But at the same time, certain tendencies of gender studies, too attached to the politics of "identity representation," have simplified the question of identity and representation, reducing it to the monotone formulation of a predetermined condition (to be a woman, to be a feminist) that has to express itself in obligatorily functional terms, that pursues legitimacy and power within an institutional struggle. When gender studies speak only the normative language of classified marginalization (to be a woman, to be a feminist), they tend to steer conscientiousness to an obligatory "we," and to repress the free and changing play of the selves about to be invented in the plural interior of each subject. By listening only to the univocal language of the linear correspondences between "to be" and "to speak as," they end up forcing the discourse to follow a pedagogical slogan of identity that represses the zigzags of fantasy and its errant meanings.[29]

If identity and difference are categories in process, that form and rearticulate themselves in mobile and provisional crossroads, opened by each subject between the given and the created, and if neither identity nor difference is a fixed repertoire of natural attributes but instead an interpretative game that draws on multiple dramatizations and theatricalizations of the self, no "politics of representation" ought therefore to close the breaches of indefinition that the categories happily maintain in suspense. The appeal of a certain feminist sociology that the subject "woman" sum up and coincide with its representation of gender blocks lines of flight and rupture that the symbolic representation of cultural poetics is capable of unleashing in unorthodox fashion.[30] To let the relation between politics, identity, and representation open itself to experimentation in form and style, to mutations of speech and searches for expressiveness, liberates within each subject's unity an internal deferment that maintains in an incomplete state both the "self" of women and the disciplinary knowledges that speak about women. The incompleteness, the nontotalization, the noncoincidences between the "self" and its roles or classifications are what constitute a scene of multiple entrances and exits where the difference "woman" and the difference "gender" can enjoy the paradoxes and ambivalences that impede the closure of overly finite categories of identity and representation. And these are the creative paradoxes and ambivalences that resonated in launching the reproduction of the work by the Mares of the Apocalypse against the monological discourse of sexual value (call it "identity" or call it "difference") that renders absolute the fixed discourse of representation, crafted from a normative moral tradition (the Senate) or indeed from the normalizing constraints of the academization of gender (the university).

The deconstructive metaphor of transvestism was what contributed—with its disruption of gender—to deprogramming both the natural identities of metaphysical essentialism and the representation of "woman" as difference, which is overly schematized by rights-driven and institutional feminism. The critical gesture of exhibiting the image of a transvestite *performance* in the inaugural lecture of the Gender Studies Program, whose title contained the word publicly censored by the Senate and the church, used transvestism as an antiofficial metaphor: a metaphor that displayed, with its asymmetric game of sexual sides and flip sides, the multiple voices of meaning that are so feared by these discourses that seek only to capture and lock down identity (or difference) in a representation without fissures. The playful transvestite spectacle went on performing—as counterscene—its difference of the difference of the difference: a difference that, hypothetically, traverses the margins of critical otherness to disseminate them even while the censorship of difference, the knowledge of difference, and the market of difference attempt to control their transgendered position. The critical metaphor of transvestism opened its lines of flight in the middle of blocks of predetermined signification so that what is undetermined (the variable or the fluctuating, the oscillating) in matters of sexual identity, gender, and representation might critically reactivate the elusive and fugitive potential of difference.

PART FIVE

Points of Flight and Lines of Escape

A mode of production is not a "total system" in an intimidating sense; lodged
in its breast are various counterforces and new tendencies, forces that are
"residual" as well as "incipient," that seek to dominate or control. If these
heterogeneous forces were not endowed with a proper efficacy, the hegemonic
project would be unnecessary. In this way the model presupposes the
differences, distinguishing itself clearly from another trait that complicates the
model, e.g., that capitalism also produces the differences or the differentiation
as function of its own internal logic.

—FREDRIC JAMESON

The great ruptures, the great oppositions, are always negotiable; but the small
fissure, the imperceptible ruptures that come from the south, these are not.
We say "south" without giving it a lot of importance. Everything has its south,
and it doesn't really matter where it is situated, that is, everything has its line
of fall or flight. Nations, classes, sexes also have their south.

—GILLES DELEUZE

Art bestows a function of meaning and otherness to a subset of the perceived
world. In sum, we need to rarify an enunciation that has too much of a
tendency to become shipwrecked in an identifying seriality that infantilizes or
paralyzes it. The work of art is an endeavor of decentering, of rupture of
meaning, of baroque proliferation or of extreme impoverishment that drags
the subject toward a re-creation or a reinvention of the self. The event of the
encounter can irreversibly mark the course of an existence and generate fields
of possibility far from the equilibriums of daily life.

—FÉLIX GUATTARI

CHAPTER ELEVEN

ॐ

Take the Sky by Assault: Political Transgression and Flight of Metaphors

The exemplary action opens a breach not because of its own efficacy, but instead because it displaces a law all the more powerful in its unexpectedness; it discovers that which remained latent and makes it unbeatable. It is decisive, contagious, and dangerous because it touches this obscure zone that all systems postulate and that it would not know how to justify. A symbolic action does not change anything; it creates possibilities relative to then admitted and not elucidated impossibilities. It manifests a disarticulation between the said and the unsaid. It exits the structures, but in order to indicate what is missing, namely the adhesion and the participation of the subjugated.

—MICHEL DE CERTEAU

The most insidious effect of the officialization of consensus effected by the discourse of the Transition could be the flexible revision of articulation and thought through common technologies of regularization and standardization of the social. This ordering of speech and thought controls both the tone of the voices, their registers and inflections, as well as the force of expressivity of inhibited subjects in their small or large desires for otherness. It was a discourse born under the festive slogan of diversity and plurality (the "rainbow" of the NO voters, who voted to end the Pinochet dictatorship in 1989) that later occupied itself with quickly reintegrating the diverse and the plural into the homogenizing serialization of consensus and market, which promoted the commonplace of formula-prototypes that would standardize tastes and opinions, judgments and postures, bodies and aesthetics, according to a passive agreement between model and series brought together by acritical consumption, faithful repetition, the submissive copy, the mechanical reproduction of the identical.

The sensation of a monotonous lack of distinction and contrast in the ensemble of social idioms, political slogans, communicative exchanges, vital modulations, and subjective expressions derives from a "consensus achieved forcibly by formalized politics [that] creates a plane resistant to any excitement or enthusiasm" while installing the predictable, the foreseeable, as a unique horizon in the fulfillment of meaning.[1] There are various reasons that coincide in the leveling formation of this plane, beginning with the ideological loss of all that, in the past, sounded like promise or utopia and is now replaced by mechanisms, procedures, and results that speak the resigned language of calculation in order to better serve the new equation of democratic realism that understands only professional contracts and statistical tables: "corresponding to a time that no longer finds itself divided by a promise [of change] should be a public space free of divisions. *Center* is its name; this does not designate a party among others, but instead the generic name of a new configuration of political space, a free unfolding of consensual power that corresponds to the free apolitical development of production and circulation."[2] The "center" is no longer the center, nor an intermediate point that might control the threatening disequilibriums of extreme positions, but instead is a diffuse, vast, and equilibrated territory where what rules, almost without obstacles, is the *average*: that which adjusts itself—in form and proportion—to the rule of not disrupting the social ranks, of not departing from the script, of not losing the composure of democratic order that is now reduced to an airy syntax of contractual arrangements stripped of all shadow of malaise or indignation.

The center, the "center function" and its dominant representations (common sense, practical reason, the laws of the market: the force of the facts), produces the rotation of the images of political, social, and economic stability around this unifying paradigm that shows us that maturity is common sense, common sense is moderation, and moderation means being resigned to the consensus and the market, both of which project a continuous present of readjustments that are infinitely diverse and equal among themselves: "the plurimorphic spectacle of multiplying varieties produces boredom with the fixed rotation to which all events are subordinated, as in a kaleidoscope. The variety of events in the Transition, although very diverse among themselves, did not make a difference, since the Transition remains identical within its multiplicity. Modernity was history's entertainment, the expectation and the enthusiasm for everything that was not assimilable to its revolution. The Transition is a definitive boredom expressed in an unlimited verisimilitude."[3]

Without precise edges, without a clear beginning or ending to mark the calendar, this sequence appears to us as indefinite in time. Since there is no visible ordering of ruptures or emergences of meaning to dramatize the breaks, the Transition extends its time frames thanks to an intermediate regime of signs already free of all historical urgency, of all vigor and passion. To break this conformity of the same, of the always similar, implies the formulation of something sufficiently unexpected that the daily rationality of the system finds itself taken by surprise, disoriented in its plans and calculations: something unexpected, whose earthshaking tremors are capable of producing leaps of the imagination that disorganize the tedious programming of reality that would appear to have definitively erased from its operational surface the expectation of any surprise or transformation, anything that ruins the balance sheets of moderation and resignation.

An Action Film Rescue

Between Christmas and New Year's of 1996—in other words, at a time when the political agenda becomes relaxed and is in a festive parenthesis—a news item rocked the political system: the escape of four inmates of the Manuel Rodríguez Patriotic Front (MRPF) who fled by helicopter from the Santiago Maximum Security Prison. I want to put aside the politico-conjunctural meaning of the flight as well as the moral and ideological judgments about the phenomenon of terrorism, in order to explore instead the symbolism of the event that the news story placed center stage, and its fictional capacity to liberate romantic fantasies of rebellion that stood out, in high contrast, against the programmatic design of the consensus in order to contradict its objective linearity.

According to the MRPF, which narrated in ample detail the episode of the flight in a special edition of its magazine *El Rodriguista*, the objective of the operation was two-pronged: on the one hand, "'Flight of Justice' was the operational expression of a political and ethical decision of the MRPF to liberate its imprisoned brothers," and on the other hand, it "formed part of the historic rescue of Rodriguism that guided the organization on new paths that corresponded to changes in the world."[4] Double rescue, then, of the prisoners and also of the history of a party in the present-day context of the Chilean redemocratization—a party reorganization riven by multiple debates and internal questionings about the validity and efficacy of the strategies of armed combat (employed during the antidictatorial struggle in order to accompany "operations of self-defense, settlement of accounts with traitors, armed propaganda, minor sabotage, and assaults on banks, financial institutions, and various businesses in order to partly finance the activities of the party")[5].

The "historical rescue" operation signaled by the MRPF spoke the double language of the past and the future: it wanted to remain faithful to a militant past whose heroic value should, according to its protagonists, be recognized (continuity) and at the same time sought to reorient the party line—"to revitalize and refresh its structure and ideals"—starting from new impulses and renewed forms of action (reactualization).[6] In the story of its protagonists, the account of the flight offered the mythological value of rupture and foundational act while demarcating a separation of time that redefines, in an inaugural sense, the nexus between past and future. The delimiting emphasis of the new that leads *change* and *origin* to quote each other in the threshold of an "other" temporality projected a mythic aura of a foundational story onto this episode of flight, a story that was told with all the narrative suspense and lyrical fancy that would merit its own "space odyssey."

But "Flight of Justice" not only exalted the sense of its protagonists. Independent of all sympathy for the positions of the MRPF, and taking into consideration the majority political opinion that broadly rejected extremist deviations by the Chilean Transition, the escape aroused "numerous manifestations of affection, best wishes, and celebration."[7] At the same time, it was a metaphor for the flights of fancy of a social body that experienced the episode of the escape principally as an *adventure*, in other words, as a story that mixed risk with fantasy in an exceptional setting that renders it worthy of being *told*. The narrativity of this story (its form) prevailed amply over the contents of the tale, causing the media spectacle to monopolize the imagination of public opinion and to deflect reflection on terrorism by the citizenry. Only the official political sectors took seriously the discussion of the antisubversive struggle and the proper control that had to be exercised by state policy, the intelligence services, the national security organisms, the plainclothes and uniformed police, et cetera, in order to vanquish the danger contained in "all these forces that operate in the shadowy recesses of a democracy."[8]

Since the beginnings of the Transition, *darkness* and *transparency* were the symmetrically opposed terms that mobilized the subtext of the official discourse to signify a polarity of values (order/disorder, rationality/chaos, integration/disintegration, etc.) underlying the recuperation of democratic order. Transparency was the leitmotif of a national call for clear mechanisms and procedures, for sharp borders and sure demarcations between the regular and the irregular, the organized and the disorganized, the cohesive and the dispersed, whereas darkness was charged with the negative connotations that associate the nontransparent with the danger and menace of confusion and upheaval, of anarchy and chaos in the social order. The democratic system could only condemn terrorism as a "dark force," in other words, as a force susceptible to transmitting the subversiveness of chaos within the interior of a social rationality that must constantly produce the required equilibrium for consensus. Its enforced construction of normality and order should also become permanently desirable, using for this purpose new polarities and dichotomies that remind one at every moment of the social precariousness and the political fragility of this order that the system must overprotect. Since the turn to democracy supposedly ended a logic of confrontation that articulated the dictatorship-antidictatorship tension as the binary axis in structuring the symbolic and political world, redemocratization again needed to project a symbolic enemy to underline the constructions of its order against a new background of antagonisms that would justify its efforts in the continuous operations to create social normalization.[9] Terrorism became the enemy symbol that represented the threat of destabilization to the normality of the social contract through the chaotic and subterranean production of disorders, anomalies, and transgression, as opposed to the positive law of full self-reconciliation that sustained the consensus. It was a symbol that, read more critically, also reminds us that under the "uninterrupted production of positivity" responsible for affirming "the transparency of the consensus" lies "an inverse energy that works everywhere to create disorder."[10]

Spectacle was the way of producing this "disorder of things" in the case of the news item of the flight. The recurrent term most used by commentaries in the Chilean press about the flight of the inmates was that of the "spectacularity" that unites the two dimensions that terrorist discourse habitually gives to the production of the event: that of the *act* itself and its condition as *news item*. As we know, terrorism manifests itself socially in the media, creating an interdependency of signs between violence and spectacularity that calls attention to its outside-the-system position in a manner that erupts in the showiest way possible into the networks of informational transmission of current events.[11] At issue is how the newsworthy repercussion of violence helps to dramatize the gesture of provocation with which the extremists challenge the system, bursting the norms of daily life with the excess that consumes itself in the disproportion of the act ("violence, thus, justifies itself in its spectacularity, independently of its effects").[12]

In the case of the flight of the front members, their much-commented "spectacularity" referred as much to the "cinematographic" realization of the operation as to the display of imagination and to the artifices of the mise-en-scène of this event, which, when reported as news, left the social and political community dumbfounded, demonstrating to them that reality is stronger than fiction.[13] The public opinion contemplated this "escape of the century" as if it were at a spectacular blockbuster, applauding as much the technical perfectionism of the details as the creative flights of a story full of suspense and capable of exciting the imagination around the dangers and uncertainties of a narrative of the incredible that upsets the routine of the overly well-known.

Mocking Official Realism

The sophistication of the plan and the rigorous professionalism of its execution—and above all the precision of the means employed to mock the system—caused an impact and used the system's same elements and methods while inverting their logic and functionality, thereby pushing the official project to the limits of contradiction. These elements reversed, so that the deconstructive side of their parodic action revealed the arbitrariness of the conventions that daily fabricate the social pacts of control and authority.

If the techniques of vigilance destined to control the placements and displacements of bodies are what generally characterize the disciplinary machine, thanks to an analytics of space and its "diagram of power that acts by means of general visibility,"[14] then the first thing the extremist plan copied was the supervising dominion of the gaze from the prison system by making "architectural models of the Maximum Security Prison built to scale, which helped the members of the unit to familiarize themselves with the aerial view of the prison and to discuss the best flight and rescue plans, the range of fire of every marksman and the targets to be neutralized."[15] If the helicopter was the instrument that the Chilean army used to distract and confuse the attention of the public during the transfer of General Contreras before his incarceration,[16] this also came to be the (aerial) medium that the front members used to throw into the lap of the national intelligence system its same trick coin of confusion. If the Maximum Security Prison constructed during the government of Patricio Aylwin represented the most advanced of prison institutions ("the prison believed to be the most secure in all of Latin America"), the flight of the terrorists adopted this same language of modernity ("before it was tunnels, now it's escape in helicopters")[17] in order to harmonize ironically with the discourse of the modernizing transformations flaunted by the Chilean Transition, and to compete on the same footing in the use of high-tech gadgetry, as if they shared the same belief in progress through technical success.[18] The undermining effect of mocking the system spectacularized by the flight of the extremists had to do with this reversal of signs as a critical operation that overturns the triumphant rationality of order and ridicules its fantasy of absolute domination through an insidious production of counterstatements that interstitially deconstruct the dominant grammar. The antiofficial criticism of the front members used the parodic accentuation of gestures that decontextualized certain traits of the dominant discourse in order to reemploy them in circumstances that made them serve ends contrary to their original purposes, thus distorting the template of the known; this delegitimized its repressive programming by means of the irony of surprising countersignifications.

The artificiality of the consensus, the simulation of a base of accords that leaves out from its parameters everything removed from the language of administrative politics, was suddenly clear to people whose laughter overturned the gravity of official discourse that strained to convince public opinion of how serious the escape was.[19] The people's laughter deofficialized the logical scheme responsible for constructing the image of the Transition's political maturity, ridiculing the seriousness of the foundations and arguments on which the political system's credibility rests.[20]

The published commentaries about the news item underlined the exemplariness of the action and its symbolic nature as traits that gave an imaginary projection to the story of the event, amplifying its meaning with utopian resonances that transcended the particularity of the concrete deed. Both traits helped to remove the episode of escape from the *operative* code of the action itself and its practical results, in order to transfer it to the *figurative* code of the symbolic representation. The "exemplary" character of an action comes, we know, from the way that the action is capable of creating a model, a sufficiently general and collective reference that contains a lesson useful for everyone. In the discourse of the front members, the exemplariness of the action had to do with demonstrating to the Chilean people that "one can overcome the impossible" when there exists "a desire for change, a decision to struggle and faith in victory."[21] The exemplary value of the escape was situated in how *the story* of what happened could extend the force of its signs beyond the explicit nature of the action itself, thereby creating associative networks of complicit meanings that slipped past the first message to transmit the news that it was possible to beat the system's rationality by drawing on an "excess of the imagination."[22]

According to the MRPF members, it was a question not only of liberating their comrades but also of demonstrating that "the ingenuity, audacity, valor and will dedicated to achieving the impossible toppled in a second the pride and despotism of that symbolic monstrosity of modernity, which until then went under the name of the Maximum Security Prison."[23] On the one hand, to attack the *emblem* of the prison (its representativity as symbol of the capitalist modernization of neoliberal Chile)[24] and, on the other, to produce fissures in the verisimilitude of the officially instituted names—these actions are two "symbolic" gestures that manifest something "that *signifies* more than what it does":[25] something that overflows the practical content of the realized action, in order to fill the borders of the message with suggestions and evocations and lead its symbolicity to discharge the expressive potential of a supplement of indirect connotations. The expressive potential contained in the gesture of wishing "to achieve the impossible" took over the metaphor of the sky in order to make the figure of freedom "fly." "To take the sky by assault" was the poetic motif of an operation whose immaterial support (the infinity of a space—the sky—without limits or limitations) created the possibility of evading the real, of breaking the bonds and subjections of practical life, of abolishing "the tyranny of continuity" imposed by the force of facts. The episode of the flight sought to activate a proud refutation of the paralyzing slogan of the death of utopias, making the dream of the impossible into reality, and for this they chose the sky as an amplified metaphoric horizon that was interspersed with the doubly emancipatory dimension of the *flight on high* and the *flight of the imagination*.

But the flight not only opened the doors to freedom for the front prisoners. It demonstrated as well how the omnipotence of the system could be converted into impotence, thanks to a sudden about-face in the power relations executed by the force of a utopian machine. Those who commented on the spectacularity of the news item agreed in stressing that the libertarian upshot of the flight consisted, above all, in having broken "the sensation that this system is impregnable and that we are all, in one form or another, its prisoners."[26] What most stood out in the news of the escape was how it demonstrated the vulnerability of the system with an action first of all unforeseeable in the system's logical foresight, and then unbeatable in its precise calculations. The escape also showed the community how "ingenuity, audacity, valor and firm will" could render the discourse of power vulnerable, shattering its methods and sabotaging the rhetoric of security that secures the normality of the system with tyrannical chains of protection. The event of the flight made the following obvious: the subversiveness of a "symbolic location" that "changes nothing" but "creates *possibilities* with respect to *impossibilities* that had until then been admitted but not clarified,"[27] opening breaches in a horizon of meanings that appeared hermetically sealed, until a mix of cunning and courage, but above all of conviction, managed to demonstrate that the *force of desire* can win a battle of the imagination against the all too reasonable, of the hopeful against the resigned, of the unsubmissive against conformity. And it was this rebellious coefficient of desire that the flight vibrantly transmitted to the social body as part of a dream that was sketched against the background of the Transition, in luminous contrast to the boredom of everyday living "in a society without heroes or heroism," where "mediocrity is the moral standard that imposes accommodation and artificial consensus."[28]

What the flight did—under the leadership of those who define themselves literarily as "fragments of a strange race, destined to escape from everywhere, addicted to perpetual nonconformity"[29]—was to trace, with its multiple irradiations and transfigurations of sense, a poetics of the event that would metamorphose the regimented syntax of social life; that would open escape paths between the zones of censure and inhibition to deterritorialize everyday life toward unsuspected borders of upheaval and contradiction.

The Art of Flight

This "poetics" of the event was restaged in two subsequent opportunities by the discourse of the Manuel Rodríguez Patriotic Front, which concerned itself with deciding the "form" to be taken by the news item for its reappearance, in order to mark a difference (in *style*) from the habitual ways of "presenting things" employed in traditional politics.[30]

The first of these two dramatizations occurred when, three months after the flight, the first public—and verifiable—pieces of information about the fate of the fugitives appeared: photographs and letters, passed out by spokesmen of the front during a press conference. Whereas the documentary value of the photographic evidence (its certification of reality) lent itself to meticulous examination by intelligence officers, who hoped to extract informative leads that might confirm the whereabouts of the fugitives, the letters played the role of frustrating all expectations of obtaining clarifications through concrete sources of information. The press and the intelligence services instead remained perplexed, disoriented, faced with the enigma of not knowing if these letters contained "poetic reflections, words thrown to the wind, or coded messages."[31] The literary meanderings of the letters provoked great consternation in the representatives of the law, leading them to commit an extravagance. Since the police could not take the referential content of the letters seriously, they asked three Chilean writers to pass judgment in the press on the letters' poetic value. From the standpoint of the literary institution and its conventions of style, the writers consulted by the newspaper sanctioned the excess of wordiness that converted the letters into a "literary product highly overwrought . . . with rhetorical display, excess of imagery, symbolism."[32] Not only were the letters "literary," but there was also formal searching for lyric pretension (with kitsch) that bordered on a hypergrandiloquent baroqueness that further exaggerated its infractions of common sense and practical messages, mocking the official quest for a uniquely factual "truth."

It was once again the literary institution—this time, the Society of Chilean Writers (SECH)—that served as recipient of the second news event that marked the reappearance of the escape as a political event. Now that the fugitives had remained at large a whole year following the aerial rescue, the political milieu and intelligence services feared a new escape and redoubled their vigilance around the Maximum Security Prison. The fugitives chose to celebrate the anniversary of the rescue with another unforeseeable and disorienting gesture: the presentation of a book by the mother of the author who narrated the story of the flight (*The Great Rescue,* written in hiding by one of the fugitives, Ricardo Palma Salamanca) that took place in the institutional headquarters of Chilean literature. The SECH, as the institution responsible for certifying the literary professionalism of national authors, was parodically reconfirming the *novel* state of the event (its novelistic character), but it ended up blurring the already-confusing limits between utopian fiction and the romantic imaginary with a book that is in itself ambiguous; a book that is "chronicle, diary, epistolary narrative, soliloquy," whose ambiguity opposed the additional obstacle of its undefinable genre to the official will to nail down a single and definitive historical truth.[33]

Both the first letters sent to the newspapers as well as those interspersed in *The Great Rescue* play with the sublimated figure of the mother as recipient of filial love. The first letters published in the press placed the authorial voices in an unexpected feminine register (lyricism and tenderness) that contrasted with the revolutionary emblem of the Manuel Rodríguez Patriotic Front, whose iconographic reference served as the background of struggle in the press's depiction of the fugitives. Photos and letters passed between the double game of the masculine-political (the party dogmatism) and the feminine-subjective (the sentimental arabesque); they executed a surprising slippage of codes marked by this leap from the masculine to the feminine that went from military offensiveness to literary inoffensiveness, from extremist violence to the feminization of voice in the epistolary register of a letter signed by a son who lays down his arms before ritualized motherhood ("love to you, Mother, and thanks for the gift of life")[34] and fills its nostalgic verbosity with romantic encrustations. Both the letters and the book gave the mother figure the adorned place of a symbolic womb (matrix) that displays, in literary fashion, love as a "flight of metaphors."[35]

The feminization of voice that connoted the double reapparition of the fugitive protagonists (a voice sentimentalized by the cult of maternity) also occurred in the elaborate use of ornamental language, full of fringes and convolutions. The inflexibility of militant speech and the ideological toughness that characterize the front's voice in its political declarations and communiqués were exchanged for a language full of folds, sinuousities, and undulations that rendered meaning elusive and its message "uncapturable." A rhetorical trick displaced the secret of the "confessional" for the "confusional" (N. Perlongher) in order to frustrate the curiosity of the police, who were bent on discovering the "useful information" that the practical communicative function of ordinary enunciation must transmit in linear fashion. To render this denotative-referential function of the objective message useless was one of the sophisticated tactics that the front used to throw common sense off the scent with the same skill with which it had conceived its rescue and flight plans. The poetic surcharge of the fugitive letters left the intelligence services with the disappointment of a *nonmessage* when faced with the affected and superfluous speech that had strategically renounced the direct and translatable, the codifiable, the easily graspable by the interpretative machinery of the linguistic code. In preferring the ambiguous to the definite, the indefinite to the definitive, the fugitives put into motion a new flight, this time of meaning; while advocating the signifying mobility and ubiquity of the word, they rendered the operation of confining the truth difficult with a new ironic way of mocking the normative system of ordering facts and words that sought to confine them behind the bars of reason.

The artificiality of meaning, the baroque style of a writing full of superfluous touches and flourishes whose twists and turns snatch the text away from the prison of denotative realism, and the dramatization of the form and its signifying cosmetics, are signs of figurative obliqueness that speak to us of the allusive and elusive vocation of the metaphor that desubstantiates the truth with its "art of flight." And the poetic metaphor was precisely the medium through which, by signifying proliferation and dissemination, the verbal expression of the fugitives could escape from the denotative-referential prison of the univocal message, throwing off track the search for linearity of meaning and objectivity of information by which the intelligence services pattern news of the antisubversive war machine. After the flight, the poetic metaphor was the second fugitive recourse that permitted the subjects excluded from social legality to mock its repressive codifications through the baroque stylization of an elusive "I" and an anarchic verbalization that was also recalcitrant to the subjections and controls of meaning making.

By breaking away from the tough wording of the political communiqué, the letters and the book (its allegories) exposed the partisan orthodoxy to expressive breakdowns that also questioned the paradigm of militant identity that discursively sustains it. The narrating subject of *The Great Rescue* prefers the figurative derivations of symbol and of metaphor to the representational hegemony of metasignification, the oscillations of a voice that declares itself "indefinite" to the declamatory rigidity of authoritarian speech, the ambiguities of a fluid subjectivity to the "self" indoctrinated by the certainties of revolutionary ideology. The novel of the flight led the centralization of the truth (of meaning, of representation) that is situated in the pure, hard nucleus of political ideology to dissolve itself in an imprecise constellation of identity effects full of mobility, asymmetries, and noncoincidence ("making me that which I am not, believing I am another, playing at poetic intuitions, doubting myself").[36] The "slow undulation" of imprisonment and poetry caused the biographical and writerly subject of the story to risk going beyond the strictness of the tone of "engagement"—bound to the unitary voice of the militant's slogan—in order to become "more in tune with the multisignification of life."[37] And it is this speech, full of the double meanings of literary metaphor, that opens the one-dimensional hero of political militancy to these fluctuations of identity, breaking the disciplinary mold of a subject obliged to coincide with himself, without gaps or hesitations of self, without vacillations or incompleteness. In addition, "the sociology of marginal poverties"[38] that habitually focuses on issues of delinquency was mocked by the digressive exuberance of the metaphors and a poeticization of phrasing that created obstacles in advancing the story toward an objective understanding either of the acts related in the book or of the personality of its author ("there is no other thread in this book that helps to straighten things out in order to be able to know, above and beyond the official explanations, what a Rodríguez Front militant is sociologically: A terrorist? A delinquent? A subversive? etc.").[39] The poetic digression evaded the clumsy typologies of the sociology of identity and frustrated the curiosity of those who pursue sure identifications by impeding "the processing of the enigma of intimacy of a subject living on the edges of humanity."[40] The literary digression did not allow the law to verify more about the suspicious individuality of those who situate themselves on the borders of the social contract, in those zones of danger where the tension of forces is most exacerbated between subject (subjectivity) and subjection (the tying down of identity to the grid of normative identification).

As simulated representation, the trope of metaphor works first as substitution of certain displacement mechanisms of meaning, then toward forms derived from analogy and translation. It is the displacements and substitutions of metaphor that permit the triumph of the figurative over the literal. Thanks to this "symbolic" triumph, the metaphor and the metaphorizations evoke a transgression of the social system that modifies the imaginary relation maintained by subjects according to the topology of order set by those in power, and without needing a radical modification of the facts of reality that condition the limits of the possible.[41] And it is this symbolic nature of the escape that was displayed by the story of the Manuel Rodríguez Patriotic Front when they condensed the diffuse and latent meanings of an imaginary of the flight that only awaited a motive (in other words, the insinuation of a figure of escape capable of generating multiple transfigurations of sense) to express, allegorically, their sensation of imprisonment, of narrowness and flatness of horizons in the interior of a reality condemned to the death of the imagination by the antiutopian closure of the consensus that only responds to a reproduction of administered, bureaucratized reality of the Transition. Beyond all discursive thinking about the political contents of the event, the *images* of flight and rescue brought forth fantasies of evasion repressed daily by the impression of closure that manufactures the self-referentiality of the system, and took

advantage of the disruptive leap with which the unexpected, the exceptional, and the risky rend the background continuity of consensus. In exemplary fashion, the Chilean history of "the escape of the century" moved
to center stage the double artifice that traversed the metaphoric transgression of the political system with the literary use of the metaphor as verbal
transgression: on the one hand mocking democratic officialdom, the parodic rupture and dismantling of the discourse of authority, the critical
fissure of the consensus, and on the other, poetry as the denaturalization
of objective meaning, the feminization of speech, the baroque creation of
a network of subjectivity alternative to the interpellation of the discourse
of power. A double political-aesthetic transgression takes advantage of the
ambiguity of literature to subvert the orthodoxies of political codification
of a revolutionary message.[42] It also opens flight paths in the symbolic-
cultural horizon of the Transition thanks to a narrative that, by inverting
the traditional hierarchy of political meaning that normally hegemonizes
the signifier of revolutionary poetry, shows how the Chilean prisoners were
able to fabricate artifices as recherché as those used by "the poet [who]
constructs . . . his metaphors," so that flight, metaphor, poetry, and utopia
might mix their rebellious imaginaries with and against the common sense
of democratic realism in the same literary fantasy of the great escape.

CHAPTER TWELVE

ↂ

For Love of Art: Critical Ruptures and Flights of Fancy

As if the gesture that approximates the word to the body of the madman could somehow guarantee the ethical incarnation of a politics that, even though it is thought from both art and extreme experimentation, a gesture that does not sidestep the problematics of its responsibility, of its insertion in the circuit of the social interpellations.

—JULIO RAMOS

The Chilean postdictatorship orders its landscape without tensions by resorting to pragmatic coordinations of discourses that, while exalting the agreement between politics and the economy, functionalize the social and weaken, with their antinarrative of what is only reasonable and utilitarian, the strong sense—yearning and accusing—of the historical. Languages are standardized by the communicative pattern of technical-instrumental vocabularies and subjectivities normalized by the consensus's operative mechanism, which disciplines the heterogeneous to make it fit passively into the mold of social integration. This homogenization has the de-emphasized traits that mark a postdictatorial landscape with neither accentuations of terms nor variations of intensity, a landscape without marked contrasts between moderation and excess, between disaster and luminescence.

It becomes difficult to imagine that something could interrupt such a leveled-out landscape in order to vehemently and passionately disturb, with ardor and furor, these redundantly programmed forces, geared so that everything stays in equilibrium, without scandalous extremes that force one to live out the critical tensions of the limit. A disruptive "something" might emerge from the "struggles of desire"[1] that pass through the social body when groups and subjects let their imagination wander beyond what is realistically delimited by political reason and decide to move beyond limits to desire the impossible: nor to resign themselves to the fact that images of change need to adjust to the possible, in other words, to the small-minded, previously delineated horizon of what is realizable and verifiable. It could also emerge from art; launched by an aesthetic gesture where forms and meanings manage to disturb expressive registers with conceptual transfigurations to work on the unspoken (the repressed-censored) of the social contract. This disturbance questions the borders of maximum turbulence of symbolic representation, indicating the relative signifying weight of the struggle that sense and the intelligible always wage around figurations of the real.

It is true that the commercialization of cultural goods and their networks of trivial satisfactions would appear to conspire against this subversive power of art. However, certain aesthetic practices know how to generate fissures through which to escape from market specifications,[2] and they betray their clumsy sociology of mass society and its rules of statistical consumption by means of a disobedient poetics that produce innumerable and incalculable affects and effects.

I would like to linger on one of these fissures: the one traced by the book *El infarto del alma* (Heart Attack of the Soul) by D. Eltit and P. Errázuriz,[3] which brings the passivity of dominant cultural reception into conflict with zones of infraction of the gaze, subjective disorders, and gender rebellions, coded in a stubborn *desire to love* ("love" in the double Spanish meaning of "loving someone" and "wanting something"). The desire to love that permeates this book on the edge of art and literature with its anti-neoliberal poetics of waste, excess, and incertitude is counterposed to the linguistic markets that seek only quantifiable meanings.[4]

The critical gesture of associating words and images with subjectivities that are in danger, menaced and divergent, is enacted from the oblique, furtive gaze of the estranged face of a woman who looks beyond the book cover that introduces the text and its images—as a minority force—into the networks of the Chilean Transition's editorial market. A vague, meandering look that leaves the cover and overflows its confining limits. This gaze of a subjectivity in flight toward unknown or unlocalizable territorialities makes its statement in tacit concordance with the strangeness of a book that is also on the border, without a fixed address, without clear definition or a reserved localization: an "unusual book that, for its size and

above all for the commotion (and emotion) that it generates when reading it, proves to be difficult to handle and almost impossible to place in
the preestablished places and classifying shelves of our university libraries."[5]
This academic unclassifiableness is the first fugitive sign that *El infarto del
alma* exhibits as resistance both to the compartmentalizations of identity
and to the segmentations of uses and values with which the institutional
culture and the market want to detain the critical moment of aesthetic
production, confining it to the sedentary (reified) format of a product-
work. The unclassifiableness of the book refers the reader to in-between
codes that convert the uncomfortable sense of place into a dissident stance,
in order to be in solidarity with the erratic nature of the gazes gathered
deep within and with the subterfuge of something very *personal* (love) with
which the asylum inmates mock the punishment of depersonalization that
the social institution inflicts on them.

From the example of these trapped souls that deploy the artifice of the
caress to evade confinement in the psychiatric bulwark, *El infarto del alma*
shows us that there is no subject definitively held captive in the prisons of
order; there is no subject that completely renounces taking small or large
trips to the wellsprings of the self, where the self's imaginary journeys
serve to overrun the guidelines of a standardizing identity and to disorganize its roles.[6] Not all the escape routes in the fixture of unidimensional
subjectivity need to speak the same grandiosely transgressive language.
There are also unorthodox ways of acting that plot their anonymous
disagreement with the serializing paradigm of dominant identity, plotting
intimate and infinitesimal rebellions in the microinsurrectional scene of a
person's life story.

Symptoms and Arabesques

El infarto del alma interlaces a photographic series of couples of chroni-
cally ill psychiatric patients confined at the center in Putaendo,[7] along with
texts, literary hybrids that attempt diverse textual approaches to the hiero-
glyphs of mad pairs of lovers, of mad people in love: lovers who do not know
whether the madness of loving each other in spite of everything will make
their being locked up easier or perhaps more furious. The pages of the book
construct two contradictory effects: the first consists of the extreme visual
rigor of the black-and-white photographs, which synthesize the drama of the
couple in such sharply drawn poses that the smallest physical twitch acquires savage proportions. The second effect is due to the literary refinement

of voice that endows the madness and the love with the equivalent (in words) of something so unreasonable, so out of all proportion, of that which is contrived by these out-of-control minds with which the text shares the desire to be free from being condemned to dispossession.

Culture has woven many private and public pacts between photography and madness. There are internal pacts between sensation and impression (the hallucinatory relation between present-past and past-present that divides the temporality of the photographic trace and rends the temporality of the pose). There are external pacts between demonstration and knowledge (the photographic archives of medical knowledge, with their historic cases of hysterics destined for scientific-professional examination), or indeed between illustration and cataloging (the thematic symbol of madness converted into a human stereotype of social marginality, overly rhetoricized by the photodocument).

The relationship that P. Errázuriz's photographs sustain with madness continues to show the same constructive rigor of a *measured* distance between the camera and the objects photographed that defines all her work: it is neither compassionate nor indifferent, neither too close (in other words, ingenuously attached to the photographic-existential realism of testimony without the mediation of a linguistic calculus that regulates the impact of the confession) nor too distant (coldly separated from the most intimate of these powerless subjectivities who seek refuge in a nearness of feeling). The circumspect look of the photographer, this look carefully opposed to any sensationalist excess, has been constructed by an authorial will whose conceptual rigor disappoints the cheap expectations of an audience attracted by the clichés of the tragic expressionism of madness. And the first thing that this book does is distance itself from the most conventional expressiveness of madness and instead involve us in a refined, double-sided emotional enigma; the enigma of this loving each other *in spite of everything* that adorns the brutal convulsions of the symptom with the delicate arabesques of loving tenderness.

The photographic series of the mentally ill in Putaendo registers the same calculated distance and the same tact with which its author has always portrayed her underworlds of selective affinities (circus artists, transvestites, boxers, the elderly, women, and vagrants) in order to show their differences with deference. Once again, P. Errázuriz knows how to render the eye of the camera almost invisible, an eye that is going to invest these socially discredited subjects with photographic value in order to finally award them a *scene* that compensates, with its surcharge of luminosity, for the lack of these gloomy bodies of "Chileans, forgotten by the hand of God, handed over to the rigid charity of the state,"[8] which "when all is said and done conserve a little piece of human identity" and, in spite of everything, stubbornly devote the rest of their existence and this tenacious little piece of self to the romantic cult of the couple.[9]

When the time comes for the equilibrium of the pose, the central and the frontal are the photographic axes to which these mentally ill persons subject themselves. And the duplication of these frames (doors, windows) that suggest the geometry of the photographic shot within many of the photos is there in order to reframe these borderline apparitions, to draw a frame around them that valorizes and highlights their precariousness with a peripheral aesthetic that renders tribute to the social subjects and the human particles whose remains normally constitute the elements most disparaged by the hierarchies of official reason.[10] The series of images published in *El infarto del alma* perform a recentering of the precarious that moves its marginal corporalities toward the center of the prestigious frame of the photograph, thereby correcting the asymmetries and inequalities that normally victimize these inhabitants of third and fourth worlds now favored by the penetrating and incisive gaze of art.

If (almost) everything in the Chile of neoliberalism arranges its visibility thanks to the cosmetic overexposure of riches and vanities, of privilege, abuse, and distinction, then how can we not avoid seeing the denunciatory refutation of the social lie of democratic renaissance that only values the commercialization of the image, in these bodies deprived of all worldly inscription and protocol, bodies that dwell on the radical fringes of exclusion and reclusion?

These subjects of dispossession and alienation, already without control over their appearances because of the chaotic nature of the physical signals that testify to corporalities in profound mental and expressive disorder— these bodies selected by P. Errázuriz are the bodies excluded from the symbolic repertoire of the promotional values upheld by advertising-laden modernity (force, vigor, energy, health, beauty, youth, etc.) and sanctified by the dominant sexual mores. P. Errázuriz's camera makes up for the effects of social disdain that these bodies without expressive self-control already suffer with the meticulous precision of a visual tension that reinserts them in a selective framework of photographic appreciation. She treats these wretched bodies with the same professionalism (precision of angles, quality of light, rigor of composition) that is used in an advertising photo shoot with the most graceful models. She gives back to these "others" of

Photographs by Paz Errázuriz, from *El infarto del alma* (1994).

power and of carnal seduction the benefits of an egalitarian look that, thanks to the technical impartiality of an exact treatment, puts them virtually at the level of the most privileged exponents of conventional beauty. The photographic tribute of the pose repairs the social injustice documented in the book by using the capacity to irradiate light that a camera possesses in order to show us how, thanks to photography, these mad people madly in love broke free from their condemnation to darkness of sense in order to become gloriously photogenic.

But the relationship between madness and photography contained in these photos also raises acute questions. What is brought to these photographed subjects (and what does it matter to them) by the mechanical certification of a documented existence (the photo as proof of reality) if they diffusely inhabit a world where the real and the imaginary have become equivalent and where one doesn't need the objective certification of provable reality that photography provides? If the pose is the mold that invites us to resemble the image that we make ideally of ourselves, then what is the use of this mold (to be copied) in the case of a "self" that has become simple turbulence and disorder of identity? How can we imagine a photographic album that orders these lives devoid of the connection of a before and an after, without the biographical chain of interlacing relationships? Where is the narrative continuity between the act of "forming a couple" in the moment of the photographic shot and the consignment of the memory of "having been photographed as sweethearts," if these couples don't have families to gather around the ritualistic and collectible support of the album?

Circulating *El infarto del alma* in the cultural markets and fairs of the Chilean Transition means to introduce into its circuits of relaxation and entertainment the critical austerity and sternness of a visual idiom that uses the metaphor in the negative of the photo/album/family relationship to destruct(ure) the illusion of a social group brought together through the solidarity of its members, and to reveal "the zone of defenselessness and piety of bodies, whose exposure to a standard gaze is anything if not violating."[11] The book compels, then, a question: if there still remains a cracked and interstitial space for these destitute bodies, if what reigns as the dominant visual paradigm is an arrogantly standard gaze that leaves out of shot and frame the underrepresented and the unrepresentable, how to retain that which threatens to disfigure the face of self-complacency displayed by a society lit by the radiance of advertising? This book, circulating through the networks of impiety and disaffection of neoliberal Chile, transmits emotion and commotion contained in "the social gesture of selecting and grouping a quantity of images that is confronted by this flip side of the album, on this dark flank of memory constructed by Paz Errázuriz. It is not family memory found here, but instead the memory of social cancellations."[12]

The couples photographed in the book are linked by the sign of a double loss of control that affects the order of reason (psychic disturbance) and the order of feelings (amorous exaltation). P. Errázuriz inserts this loss of control in the parenthesis of the pose. She calls on her subjects to pose. A repose required by the task of holding oneself immobile in the pose to fit into the photographic mold of the typical portrait is a respite patiently set up by the camera in the midst of the crazy agitation that shakes the very fiber of the convulsed souls torn away from their medication. The pose is an applied exercise thanks to which the nervous rictus forgets the involuntary past of muscular contraction in order to entertain by the aesthetic modeling of a seduction: the pleasure of seduction that mocks the condemnation to captivity. It is as if the opportunity to pose in front of the camera gave back to these bodies and minds at the edge of disintegration the reintegrating force of corporal synthesis. It is as if the photographic armor of the pose that helps them overcome the hesitant and startled language of the tic might bring together the most divergent signals in the generic portrait, in order temporarily to slow the savage violence of what remains disconnected. In every photograph, the pose is the scene of a struggle waged between the different parts of the face respectively wrapped in the paradox of the intermittent tic, while the tic reveals the conflict between *subjectivization* and *identification,* where there is an opposition between "a facial trait that attempts to escape from the sovereign organization of the face, and the very face that closes itself once again over this trait, recuperates it, blocks its line of flight, reimposes its organization."[13]

Organization and flight. While analyzing the visual syntax composed by the photos of P. Errázuriz, we realize that the underlying conflict between norm and infraction (in other words, between the anarchic overflow of a subjectivity rebelling against the normal and the codifying matrix of a socially normed identity) is generally insinuated by the tension between, on the one hand, the reiterated verticals and horizontals that compose the demanding visual order of the photo and, on the other hand, the decomposition of that order indicated by the small lapse of a winding gaze that escapes from rigorous symmetries. The many lines of perspective within the photos are not there in vain. Their mission is to hypereducate the eye so that it knows how to measure the way order is formulated through this strict linearity of straight lines that disciplines the look. But they also teach our look to detect the virulent contrast of the minuscule circumstance where the norm of disciplinary integration breaks down. The straight lines designate the convention of the limit at the same time as they highlight the semi-imperceptible way in which that convention can be minutely fractured by those limit cases that exceed the social rationalization of the normal thanks to a secret poetics of disorder.

The insane minds that dwell in *El infarto del alma* found in love a bifurcated correspondence to their lack of logic. The heart, a labyrinth of irrationalities, conjoins love and madness on the shores of nonsense so that both can discover a common language that does not stifle reason's "other" but instead exalts it with their respective incongruities. The first-person voices that run through D. Eltit's writing in *El infarto del alma* insert descriptions, narrations, letters, diaries, testimony, and so forth, multiplying styles, mixing genres and rhetorics, to dilute the borders of a writing self that wanders from repertoire to repertoire, from language to language.[14] These voices create a vague symmetry with the blurry-edged identities of the characters of the book, creating similarities between, on the one hand, the fragmentation of a unitary consciousness and personhood that erases the contours of the subject in the vertigo of madness and, on the other hand, an eccentricity of literary metaphorizations that dissolve the conceptual nucleus of discursive thought with their stylistic ornamentations.

In this book, the disfigurations of identity suffered by the wandering I of the marginalized and the literary transfigurations of speech that have also strayed from literature are derived from a poetics of a nonclassified genre; they require clues of solidarity that can interlace this double and disturbed condition. One of the clues that the writer chooses to share with the insane is the maddening reference to the mother: imaginary womb of the body-sanctuary, archaic source of primary satisfaction, continent of a fusion that threatens to erase the limits that separate the one from the other. "The hunger" is the scenario of the maternal abyss of a bottomless orality that, from chapter to chapter, scans the litany of "lack" that runs through *El infarto del alma* ("the hunger hangs from the tip of my tongue. More than one hundred days, twenty-four nights and the hunger grows and writhes and groans like a furious woman").[15] Lack—literally speaking—designates hunger, which in turn designates the mouth: a zone of passage that joins the organic matter-nourishment (maternal orality) with the semiotic matter-word (literary verbalness). The mouth as zone of passage symbolizes the place where, on the one hand, the name and literature emerge from that amorous duel with the mother's body that must necessarily end in a severing of ties and separation so that language can exist and where, on the other hand, the impulsive pleasure of writing needs to reencounter the intensity of feelings close to the first experiences of the body. The state of madness that is evoked by the chapter entitled "The Other, My Other" has to do with the mother and the unresolved wound of separation and of differentiation; with the failure of the paternal metaphor and its mediating authority responsible for establishing an order of speech to the somatic disorder of the body-to-body contact with the mother. By verbalizing—by making literary—the theme of the mother as cause of conflict between subjectivity and language,[16] D. Eltit separates herself from the body of madness so that her text can freely approach the mental hospital and share with its patients the hallucinatory vertigo of verbal delirium. The aim would be to "deposit an *other and identical* word for the strangest and most uncompromising lovers of the earth,"[17] and *El infarto del alma* responds to this search for a complicity between affect and effect, between affections and affectations; a complicity that is sensitive to, and at the same time hyperconstructed by, a verbal rhetoric that is so strange and deviating in relation to the practical standard of ordinary verbalization that it is analogous to the mind of those who invoke and justify this extravagance of the writing from the dark side, in disorder, removed from the rationality socially instituted by the knowledges, methods, powers, and technologies of science.

D. Eltit's writing of difference seeks to highlight human and social otherness and begins by constructing a primary difference of speech from the direct referentiality of testimony that should have accompanied this visual code according to the conventions of reading that normally govern the relations between text and photographs (the method of complementing the illustration, of subordination to its referential content). The writing of the letters inserted in the book increases the difference from a testimonial register, with a proliferation of literary artifices (poses and masks) that dramatize the signifier and denaturalize the utilitarian sense of the denotative message with multiple folds and drapes, with the distortions of style that are similar to the deviations from the normal of the rambling subjects of the mental hospital.[18] The symbolic-literary perversion with which the writing of D. Eltit disfigures the referentiality of testimony as a genre based on the documentary convention of the objective, and the exacerbated subjectivity of voice that implicates the author in the most personal and unique of the existential margins lived by each confined inhabitant, indicate the infractions of testimonial truth that *El infarto del alma* effects with its border movements that depart from genre classifications. Its effects— aesthetic, political, and critical—are correlated with fugitive identities devoid of law or fixed domicile.

While P. Errázuriz uses the physical mold of the pose as a technical mechanism to intervene between madness and its doubles, D. Eltit searches in the polished detail of style, of literary stylistics, for a constructive mediation that will *transfigure* her aesthetic approach to madness. The medieval love poetry that inspires the writing of the letters gathered in *El infarto del alma* is one of the styles of literary vestment that clothes the sentences in a speech etched by tradition: a speech ritualized by centuries of literary craftsmanship, in other words, by the cosmetic trade of adorning each word with the splendor of codes elaborated by a love for fineness of detail that spreads its luxury over the human misery of the destitute. Words drawn from the courtly love lyric and mystic poetry, which parade through the medieval symbols of the wounded heart (the bleeding heart) and the burning heart (the heart in flames); words of romanticism and its evanescent body that, as the pages are turned, come up against the Chilean history of the former sanatorium now converted into a mental hospital, and against the modern decision to exclude and enclose the unproductive bodies that disturb the circulation of capital with their refusal to be useful *for* something—to fulfill the unique finality of economic gain.

The text travels from nonsense (madness) to the hyperbolic surcharge of meaning (literary poetics) in order to create a nexus of solidarity between two forms of breaking loose from the constrictive normality of common sense and from losing one's mind in the sinuousities of nonreason. As dazzling compensation for the poverty of their lives, the writing of D. Eltit touches up the fissures of sense that tear at the insides of the insane, employing the preciosity of style of a bookish cult of the word crafted from medieval and romantic tradition and imbued with the baroque surplus of a sumptuary value. The graphic design of *El infarto del alma* and its visuals make the hyperliterariness of this kind of writing depend on a typographic body (machine typeset) that imitates the layout of medical reports. Scientific composition and literary textuality, in a state of tension generated by the graphical-editorial conceptualization of the book, perform the difference that separates the neutrality of diagnostics professed by medicine and the ardent subjectivity of a literary poetics that lets its words fly around the signs of madness so that they acquire the figurative density and the expressive volume that are systematically denied them by the technologies of knowledge of the psychiatric institution. The poetic and political gesture of *El infarto del alma* consists of offering an overabundance of metaphors and double meanings to these subjects, who are almost entirely deprived of the capacity to account for themselves, and compensates for their deprivations with the expensive luxury of a mise-en-scène that multiplies around them symbolic resources analogous to their disorders and irregularities.

Flights and Surpluses

In *A Lover's Discourse: Fragments*, Roland Barthes writes: "Every lover is mad, we are told. But can we imagine a madman in love? Never."[19] This unimaginable "never" is what *El infarto del alma* puts into images though its texts and photographs. The lover appears crazy because he is governed by the irrationality of a passion that drives him mad and makes him into someone possessed, into someone invaded by an-other. But why did Barthes say that the insane, when in love, cannot be conceived as literary figures? Might it be because the asocial mark of madness that dissolves all social connection impedes the mentally ill from forging the communicative relationship that brings every "one" to desire the human completeness from the "other"? Could it be because the depersonifying vertigo of madness invalidates the attempt to believe that two separate, distinguishable, and recognizable human beings are "made for one another"? Or might it be because the distinguishing characteristics of the mentally ill—the mind without control of its will and the body without control over its appearance—are no longer capable of elaborating the laborious stratagems of seduction? In any case, *El infarto del alma* gives a visual geometry and an idiomatic contour to the question of the sense of nonsense that leads the insane to love each other without the constitutive (identifying) reference of knowing who one is and who the other is, without the existential problem of one being faced with the other without the narcissistic consolation of being someone special for the other.

It is no accident that it is two women who became passionately involved with these images. Women and madness have a special relation, which is already classically incorporated into our archaeology of reason. It is not only because of the historical debt of psychoanalysis to the hysteric's body as a revelation of knowledge and its foundation as a discipline: a discipline born from the encounter between the simulating body and the theory that became fascinated with unraveling the enigma of what the symptom dissimulated. The relationship between women and madness can also be attributed to the cultural symbolization of the feminine that has traditionally been assimilated to the capricious and extravagant (with the disturbance of conduct and the aberrations of judgment with which dementia is associated) and that has also been demonized by the figure of the witch and her occult powers, mysteriously possessed by the irrational forces that obscure the horizon of the Logos. This horizon reveals the constitution of the norm that separates the luminous from the tenebrous, the normal from the abnormal, the familiar from the strange, and is hegemonically under the custody of masculine rationality that decrees that "women" and "madness" represent the same two types of incongruencies in the systematic logic of sense.[20]

Women, art, passion, and madness: these are the motifs that *El infarto del alma* interweaves with its delirious symbols and its feverish metaphors that allude to the mental breakdowns and mental failures of catastrophic subjectivities that nevertheless employ the poetics of love to escape from the bonds of repressive normality by means of the soft parentheses of the embrace and the caress. These motifs are unleashed in the writing of D. Eltit, by the compulsive rhythm of lack and desire. A hollowed-out lack, but also a thirst for the absolute. Utopian tension that leans toward the most extreme limits of *to want* (*querer*), reinforced by the passion of love and of writing that crazily overflow the restricted framework of everyday passivity ("and between the reiterated kisses the sign of love appears in me. After all I traveled in order to live my own love story. I am in the asylum because of my love of words, because of the passion that words continue to provoke in me").[21] At the same time, P. Errázuriz takes her camera to ignite her "love of images" and convert "her eye into a gift for the inmates."[22] Love and desire, *passion of art*. The itinerary of the authors appears very similar to the deviation of the characters in the book who flee from productive categorizations (health, normality, integration, etc.), since both routes sustain themselves in the same love: "a love that spends and wears away and therefore is pure squandering" (ibid.). The couples-in-love would have nothing to do but wait, except for this desperate surrender to the ultimate realm of a love that is imprisoned and apparently terminal, without further denouements, because in this book the couple has no way of prolonging its "we" into the future of a shared life that awaits them. All that remains for them is "to love the other with the same intensity as that of their illness" in a furtive and total abandon to the conditionless of the moment. As for the photographer and the writer, they only want "the charge of an absolute desire" with an aesthetic precision that is unfolding "very far away, very distant from the investors" (ibid.); this is also an unconditional desire, one that does not compromise with the reception criteria of democratic pluralism that is invoked to reconfirm the typologies of dominant taste. Instead the authors attempt to fracture the cultural market's uniformity of vision—its law of numbers and quantity—with the provocation of aesthetic residues furiously opposed to the banality of the series.

The flash of desire that causes anarchy in the rules of social taste here comes from the aesthetic shock: "today my dazzling desire will be art" (ibid.): an aesthetic shock that disintegrates the "self" normalized by the identity closures of reason and exposes the public gaze to turbulent encounters in the most clandestine regions of the social map. *El infarto del alma* attracts and condenses these critical ruptures of the aesthetic shock in the name of art, in other words, in the name of a wish "to lose your head" (like insane people) over a photographic shot or a grammatical twist. The precision of the shot or the grammatical twist turns the potency of affect and effect transmitted by the oscillations of sense in these borderline subjectivities.

Certain "minor" poetics,[23] hatched on the edges of major institutional disintegration, shake up the control of hegemonic thought by raising voices intended to reinforce this potency of affect and effect that "hurls forth a desperate, reactive negation" as the "ultimate gesture of resistance,"[24] by opposition to the antiutopian closure of a turn-of-the-century milieu that also impels the postdictatorship in its leveling of value and potency of meaning making. This minor literature creates a general movement unleashed by a posthistoric series of semantic emptiness that draws on the artificiality of codes and superficiality of content, the abstraction and reification of the world, the commercial fetishization of products in a time bereft of proper or quality experience where what "reigns is the pure intensity of the enjoyment of surplus value."[25] The commercial banality of this type of productive and communicative exchange, whose logic of economic gratification demands that sign and behavior subject themselves to the sole principle of making money, gives the statement that runs through *El infarto del alma* ("I desire nothing as much as my own desire") the symbolic value of a countergeneralization whose aesthetic and critical criteria are opposed to the devaluing flows of the market, which attempts to strip all forms and productions of any autonomy of conscience and desire. *El*

infarto del alma would affirm the *gratuitousness* of the desire for an aesthetic gesture that mixes conceptual rigor and expressive brilliance in order
to provoke emotions for no good reason: for the love of art.

Let us pause for a moment in the twists and turns of this "for no good
reason" that can sound sly, headstrong, or recalcitrant in relation to the
logic of cultural coordination and subordination that conceives of art as
an answer to questions already formed by social discourse and not as a
questioning force in itself.[26] But let us pause first in the vulnerable circumstances of a *querer* (to want, to love) so difficult to formulate and to inscribe
in postdictatorship Chile, where it would effectively appear that the libidinal weariness and the affective withdrawal caused by the "mourning"
characteristic of the postdictatorial climate produce a melancholic state
that inhibits desire, curbs the will, and suppresses or represses desires.[27]
When desire reemerges, it can misleadingly take the form that the new
system of political-institutional rearticulation of the Transition deceitfully
projects as desirable images: "the hysterical desire" that "desires the social
space that has been reassigned inside liberalized cultural industry" and the
"schizoid desire" that "desires to maintain itself in a position that is liminal, sacrificial, by radicalizing tactics of . . . neodissidence that incorporate
a leftover symbolism of protest. This latter motivates the functionalizing
and instrumentalizing force of the state apparatus because it gives this force
a limit inside of which, or from which, to orient its assimilative practice."[28] Both desires, outlined thus, would be captives of a predesigned map
of spatial distribution with its assigned areas—be these areas called "center"
(the metaoperation that controls the networks of sign exchange) or "periphery" (the most distant borders of the hegemonic points of condensation of
the universal value of signs). The periphery, thus territorialized by the logic
of the center, proves its functionality for the organization of the cultural
system that distributes roles and areas according to the hierarchy of powers that allow it to keep watch over subject positions and the behavioral
modes of its discourses. The desire to occupy the periphery of the system,
in order to represent it or to represent oneself in it, would only indulge
the topology of the dominant that regulates and administers the tension
between centrality and borders, limit and excess, through recognizable categories. To disorganize this topology, to break its overly functional symmetries and inversions, it would be necessary to appeal to a politics of
space that uses localization neither as fixed point nor as known territory,
but instead as a mobile site of tactical articulations between different sit-
uational contexts, mediations of codes, and positionalities of discourses. It

would be necessary to free a *fugitive desire* that would know how to put in movement a plurality of unexpected convergences and divergences.

"Today my dazzling desire will be art": desire to love, and aesthetic passion for creating art. *El infarto del alma* brings together this triple flight of significations that rebel against the rules of order responsible for normalizing patterns of speech and conduct in order to make the unclassifiable again become an object of classification and to make the unsituated end up residing in some fixed place. A triple flight that mocks both the delimitations of genre and the sedentary categorizations with a gesture-limit (product of "a hunger for love that seems interminable") whose force of alterity and alteration escapes from the discursive rationality that attempts to restrict its movements and codify its symbols.[29]

Some say that "otherness, like everything else, has fallen under the law of the market, of supply and demand," and that "the discourse of difference" only fabricates simulacra of alterity as circulating parts of a system of "regulated exchange,"[30] and that nothing—neither excess nor residue—could manage to disrupt, because the capitalist machine has become expert in incorporating transgressions and disequilibriums into the production of multiplicity and heterogeneity reactivated by the logic of market diversification. According to this thesis, the generalization of the "commodity-form" and of the "sign-form" totalized by the market will lead us fatally to the reign of nonvalue and its paroxysm of indifference, a reign where already no disturbing other would fit because the system of capitalist appropriation would finally reduce and translate any differentiation to its laws of passive uniformity, equalizing all the differences between them. An apocalyptic thesis for the end of the century that describes a sole law of the system (be it market, posthistory, neoliberalism, globalization, or multinational capitalism) seen as a totality closed by the redundancy of the achievements of power that reproduce themselves inexorably, without any critical dislocation or emancipating flight that manages to exit from the sealed-off perimeter. According to this theoretical "overconstruction,"[31] the market would necessarily take the conspiratorial form of the "total," since it is its own model of abstract conceptualization that internalizes the rule of indivisibility of power and thus contributes to the hermetic closure of a system that is apparently without perforations or exits through which the alternative, the divergent, the minoritarian can open a pathway from within.[32] There is something monstrously paralyzing in this infinity of the system described by the infallible logic of a knowledge that anticipates everything (effects and countereffects) without considering anything, either lapsus or errata, susceptible to distorting the predetermined logic of this unbreakable totality; a totality whose systematic nature would be so perfect that it would not allow itself to be changed by any unbalancing of planes, breaks in surfaces, or holes in the flowcharts.[33] In opposition to the image of a system unshakeable in its law (a law that would never fail to know how to reunite the metamorphic diversity of capitalist fragmentation), certain artistic practices prefer to place their bets on the unknown—on the hypothetical, the conjectural—of a difference perhaps destined for defeat, without any certainty, one that mobilizes the critical imagination around the risks of a wager on the belief that not all modes of experiencing subjectivity can be anticipated by the market, nor can they be converted to its form of serial production. Countering the monotony of the thesis that only conceives itself in verifying the indifferent law of a neutral nondifferentiation of value is the arbitrariness of "desiring" passionately enveloped in the *for no good reason* of amorous, aesthetic, and cultural dislocation. This desire multiplies the small utopian-desiring flights with which art and its artillery of incertitude open up codified reality with imaginary leaps that exceed the calculations (determination, predictability) of the already known.

Notes

1. Cites/Sites of Violence

1. Reflection on the effects of the indifferentiation of difference that leads to market pluralism's "relativism of values" runs through various chapters of Beatriz Sarlo, *Scenes From Postmodern Life*, trans. Jon Beasley-Murray (Minneapolis: University of Minnesota Press, 2001).

2. See Carlos Ruiz, "Concepciones de la democracia en la transición chilena," in *Seis ensayos sobre la teoría de la democracia* (Santiago: Andrés Bello, 1993).

3. Ernesto Laclau, *New Reflections on Revolution in Our Time* (London: Verso, 1990). Laclau says: "all objectivity is a threatened objectivity. If despite all of this objectivity is able to partially affirm itself as objectivity, this can only happen on the basis of what represses it. Therefore, to study the existential conditions of a certain social identity is equivalent to studying the mechanisms of power that make it possible."

4. Tomás Moulian, *Chile actual: Anatomía de un mito* (Santiago: Arcis/Lom, 1997), 37.

5. Ibid., 39.

6. Villalobos says the following: "in Chile the problem is not so much memory, but its performative construction within the institutional rhetoric that makes it up. . . . Faced with oft-repeated reconstructive efforts, it is necessary to let oneself be helped abruptly by *that which continues to happen*, before conforming to juridical actions that tend to exorcize the ghosts that haunt the present. One of those operations is the Rettig Report, a true network of memory, which, as a confining document, as prolific artifact of the justice of the times, gives back to the present a basis of relative tranquillity. At the same time, conventional and mass opinion says it is a "human rights violation"; but it is not enough with the report displayed as public spectacle (an evasive way to apportion blame, where *all of us would be responsible*).

Since before its release it was necessary to have languages that could name 'what happened.'" Sergio Villalobos-Ruminott, "Crítica de la operación efectiva del derecho," unpublished document from the Cultural Criticism Seminar of Arcis University, December 1997.

7. "These painless workings of the word" are the zone where nowadays the catastrophic is consumed: "no longer in the drama, in the ill-fated heavens of what happened politically, but in the ruins of words that now inhabit symbolic rituals of recovery, of repentance, of demonization or the routines of the already spoken." Nicolás Casullo, "Una temporada en las palabras," *Confines* (La Marca, Buenos Aires), no. 3:17.

8. The documentary by filmmaker Patricio Guzman *La memoria obstinada* (1996) unleashes this network of emotions: the video shows the work of remembrance in a dialogic memory (made of communicative exchanges and transfers) that leads the characters to performatively live the shock of remembering through memories filled with biographical details. For a commentary on Guzman's video, see Nelly Richard, "Con motivo del 11 de septiembre: Notas de lectura sobre *La memoria obstinada* de Patricio Guzman," *Revista de Crítica Cultural* (Santiago, Chile), no. 15 (November 1997).

9. For example, Martín Hopenhayn says: "bereft of the Grand Project, daily life becomes what it is: life lived each day, and every day. A sane minimalism? Perhaps: everyone has their small projects capable of filling up and justifying the day, the week, the month, at most a whole year. . . . The Mission is disseminated in programs, initiatives that are born and die, local proposals. . . . Minimalism has come to be seen as valuable for everyday actions. Every great project is labeled pretentious or unrealistic, and there is a resurgence of appreciating the finely shaded, the detail, the conjuncture. This minimalism is embodied in the logic of software, which everyone creates or exchanges according to preference, situation, or objective, and where no other horizon exists than what needs to be done in the moment." Martín Hopenhayn, *Ni apocalípticos ni integrados* (Santiago, Chile: Fondo de Cultura Económica, 1994), 22–26.

10. "It is sad and reflects a terrible mediocrity," according to the Association of the Families of the Detained-Disappeared, "to renounce these absolute values for others that are relative." *Recuento de Actividades 1992*, Association of the Families of the Detained-Disappeared, 148.

11. For a rigorous and subtle analysis of the postdictatorial climate, see Alberto Moreiras, "Postdictadura y reforma del pensamiento," *Revista de Crítica Cultural*, no. 7 (November 1993).

12. Ibid., 27.

13. Julia Kristeva, *Soleil noir: Depression et melancolie* (Paris: Gallimard, 1987), 19. Translated as *Black Sun: Depression and Melancholia* (New York: Columbia University Press, 1989). In this book Kristeva reconsiders—with extreme delicacy—the Freudian figure of grief that projects the symptoms of melancholy and depression onto the scenario of aesthetic transfiguration of art and literature.

14. T. Moulian says: "for many of the converted who race along the tracks laid out by the system, forgetting represents the dark symptom of repentance of a life denied. This forgetting is a protective device faced with lacerating memories, seen in flashes as nightmares, phantasmatic reminiscences of the lived. It is a forgetting that is enmeshed with a guilt about forgetting. A shame, unnamed and unspeakable, because it is unfaithful to others and toward life itself, the shame of connivance and conviviality" (*Chile actual*, 32).

15. It seems to me that the unheard-of success of Moulian's book is in part due to the fact that the book tells a hi(story), that it narrates the memory of history, that memory goes back and forth in history, mobilizing a subject of "remembrance" positionally marked.

16. This line of argument is widely displayed in Moulian, *Chile actual*.

17. Hugo Vezetti says: "if memory is an active dimension of experience, if memory is less a faculty and more a practice, . . . the work of remembrance requires that people (politicians, but above all, intellectuals, artists, institutions and collective spaces of production) be capable of sustaining a complex and permanent construction; actualizing the past depends on a certain *choice*, a certain freedom in the present, so that the past does not impose its weight but instead is recuperated by a horizon that opens onto the future." Hugo Vezetti, "Variaciones sobre la memoria social," *Punto de Vista* (Buenos Aires, Argentina), no. 56 (December 1996).

18. Hernán Vidal, *Dar la vida por la vida* (Santiago, Chile: Mosquito Editores, 1996), 90.

19. Ibid.

20. Germán Bravo, *4 ensayos y un poema* (Santiago, Chile: Intemperie Ediciones, 1996).

21. According to W. Thayer: "probably the mistrust that the word 'transition' evokes in us comes from our—not innocent—usage, when we refer to a state of affairs that we know is not transitioning nor on the way to doing so; a state of affairs that we feel will not move in a positive direction, or that it already moved, and from there, its last transit, won't move anymore, threatening us with a definitive presence. . . . The actual transition is not what goes (away), it is a conservative state that remains without anything happening to it." Willy Thayer, *La crisis no moderna de la universidad moderna* (*Epílogo del conflicto de las facultades*) (Santiago, Chile: Editorial Cuarto Propio, 1996), 169.

22. "De imagen y verdad," *Contagio* (Comisión Intercongregacional de Justicia y Paz, Bogotá, Colombia), no. 4:3.

23. Bravo, *4 ensayos y un poema*, 25.

24. *Recuento de actividades año 1991*, Agrupación de Familiares de Detenidos-Desaparecidos, 45.

25. I. Avelar says the following: "the object of grief is always useless—there is no usefulness for the reminiscence of the bereaved, its object is beyond the useful—and, at the same time, nonexchangeable, nontransferable because grief, by definition,

rejects any kind of transaction or negotiation, any substitution. Grief, contrary to the market, would not allow for metaphor. Grief would flow outside the well-known Marxist distinction between use value and exchange value, and create a third value not foreseen by Marx: the value of memory, the value of pure emotion: without a doubt an antivalue, since what would define grief is its being withdrawn from any circuit of exchange." Idelbar Avelar, "Alegoría y postdictadura: Notas sobre la memoria del mercado," *Revista de Crítica Cultural*, no. 14 (June 1997): 25.

26. Pablo Oyarzún writes in his prologue to *La dialéctica en suspenso: Fragmentos sobre una historia*, by Walter Benjamin (Santiago: Arcis/Lom, 1996), 15: "being unique, unanticipated, and testimonial, these are a possible catalog of the determinant traits of the concept inherited from experience."

27. The work of artist Carlos Altamirano (*Retratos*, December 1996, National Museum of Fine Arts, Santiago) stages that critical tension between the sensitivity of memory and the insensitivity of the mass media: a strip of mural made of public and private photographic images—worked on by a computerized professional design aesthetic—the mural incorporates a line of portraits of the detained-disappeared (framed in the gold frames used by the museum), whose eroded imprint struggles to stay afloat in the middle of the mediating current that tries to align them—as equivalent signifiers—with the rest of the images that fall under the light of advertising's extroverted shrillness. For a critical reading of the Carlos Altamirano exhibition, see *Retratos de Carlos Altamirano*, with texts by Fernando Balcells, Rita Ferrer, Justo P. Mellado, Roberto Merino, and Matías Rivas (Santiago: Ocho Libros Editores, 1995).

28. Bravo, *4 ensayos y un poema*, 33.

29. Ibid., 28.

30. Moulian, *Chile actual*, 7.

31. For a critical analysis of the tensions between these discourses, see the chapter titled "En torno a las ciencias sociales: Líneas de fuerza y punto de fuga," in *La insubordinación de los signos (cambio político, transformaciones culturales y poéticas de la crisis)*, by Nelly Richard (Santiago: Editorial Cuarto Propio, 1994); and the response by J. J. Brunner, "Las tribus rebeldes y los modernos," in *Bienvenidos a la modernidad*, by José Joaquín Brunner (Santiago: Planeta, 1994).

32. S. Villalobos writes in reference to the tension of thinking as critical maladjustment, as nonclosured present by way of a consolatory "politics of naming" that are practiced by "the discourses of Transition" and its "reconstructive mechanisms": sociology hadn't thought of the transition as such but had offered the correct language to name it. Villalobos, "Crítica de la operación."

33. Casullo, "Una temporada," 13.

34. About this knowledge of the precarious and of historical discontinuities (which permeate such powerful works as Diamela Eltit's in literature and Eugenio Dittborn's in the visual arts), one could say that it is a "constructive knowing in the Benjaminian sense"; a knowing that "comprises a mosaic of fragments . . . which the crisis has placed before us shattering the great names of the language of truth." Franco

Rella, *El silencio y las palabras: El pensamiento en tiempo de crisis* (Barcelona: Paidós, 1992), 70.

2. Torments and Obscenities

1. Luz Arce, *El infierno* (Santiago: Planeta, 1993); Marcia Alejandra Merino, *Mi verdad* (Santiago: ACT, 1994).

2. That was the title of an article published about these testimonies in *Hoy* magazine, no. 762 (March 1992): "Confessions of Six Agents of the DINA: Women Don't Know How to Shut Up." The excessive loquaciousness that is normally attributed to women would be, in the case of the informers-accusers, infringing on the rule of silence with which the Transition keeps its secrets hidden.

3. Merino, *Mi verdad*, 6.

4. Ibid., 8.

5. According to F. Lombardo, "Bodies. The body always has its reasons, it makes metaphors out of the unnameable, it forms cysts, oozes, goes mad in the silent multiplication of cells that were once life itself unfolding, but now are an insane proliferation of what life has made, done to itself and done to others." Francesca Lombardo, "Cuerpo, violencia, traición," *Revista de Crítica Cultural*, no. 11 (June 1996): 36.

6. Diamela Eltit says: "when the stage of informing finished, Luz Arce and Marcia Alejandra Merino had already entered into a new vital stage. Their energies resurged with the absorbing goal of becoming part of the corps of military intelligence and become officers of that service. To achieve that goal, they sought the protection of seasoned officers who, from their commanding heights of power, kept them alive, appealing to that most classical of terrains that define male-female encounters: sexuality. When the narratives enter that stage, the parameters have already changed. A close reading lets us see that they are truly compromised by the networks of military intelligence; they become participants, both intellectually and emotionally, of the conflicts and internal struggles. Each one of their respective partners-captors-lovers starts anew with a 'political' career." Diamela Eltit, "Cuerpos nómades," *Feminaria* (Buenos Aires), nos. 17–18 (November 1996): 57.

7. "We are surrounded by political, state, governmental, and institutional secrets, invoked in 'the higher interest of society.' We could see the proliferation of these secrets of the Transition in opposition to the secrets of the circuits of survival that existed under the dictatorship, those of political clandestineness. The strongest current secrets that go from ear to ear and eye to eye on the other side of the benign face of politics belong to those networks of survival mounted on the degrading profits of cocaine, and of the sophisticated business of its white dusts, as well as those who enjoy and suffer from its properties." Olga Grau, "Calles y veredas," *Revista de Crítica Cultural*, no. 14 (June 1997): 19.

8. Arce, *El infierno*, 339.

9. Ibid.

10. Luz Arce asks herself: "and . . . am I not a woman? He gave me hundreds of reasons. He didn't convince me, but in those days it was the highest praise to be a militant above all else" (51).

11. Ibid., 56.

12. For an analysis of the meanings of torture, in particular the relationship between power, body, and voice, see Elaine Scarry, *The Body in Pain: The Making and the Unmaking of the World* (New York: Oxford University Press, 1985).

13. Michel de Certeau says: "torture is situated in a triangular relationship between the individual body, the social body, and the word, which establishes a contract between the two. The executioner's gesture engraves the order incarnate on the flesh by obtaining a primordial confession: to ensure that he, the agent of power, is normative and legitimate." Michel de Certeau, "Corps torturés, paroles capturées," quoted in Maren Viñar and Marcelo Viñar, eds., *Fracturas de la memoria* (Montevideo, Uruguay: Ediciones Trilce, 1993), 104.

14. "Being kidnapped and jailed form part of a double process in which first one must break the silence of the prisoner in order to extract a confession and later reinstall in him (her) a silence through physical threats and social restraints after their liberation so that he or she not reveal what happened. The testimonial narrative of the secret or imprisonment is the product of two different but connected verbal acts: to speak (or not to speak) *during* the interrogation and torture, and to speak (or not) *about* what happened. Where before there was silence, now there is speech; where before words were extracted out of fear of torture, there now exists a significant silence. In this way, if by surviving the prisoner was first obligated to produce a convincing text (a confession, be it real or half true), now, in another 'anticonfessional text,' he or she must contradict that first word and convince the reader (and him- or herself?) of [the prisoner's] innocence." Fernando Reati, "De falsas culpas y confesiones: Avatares de la memoria en los testimonios carcelarios de la guerra sucia," in *Memoria colectiva y políticas de olvido* (Buenos Aires: Beatriz Verbo Editora, 1997), 213.

15. Arce, *El infierno*, 78.

16. It would be worthwhile to read these autobiographies and confront them with the questions that speak to the tensions within the genre: "For whom am I an 'I'?"; or better yet, "For whom do 'I' write?" since "the evocation of the past is conditioned by the autofiguration of the subject in the present: the image that the autobiographer has of herself, the one she wants to project or the one demanded by the public." Sylvia Molloy, *Acto de presencia: La escritura autobiográfica en Hispanoamérica* (Mexico City: Fondo de Cultura Económica, 1996), 14–19. Translated as *At Face Value: Autobiographical Writing in Spanish America* (Cambridge: Cambridge University Press, 1991).

17. Arce, *El infierno*, 352.

18. Diamela Eltit, "Perder el sentido," *La Epoca* (Santiago), Literature and Books Supplement, 1995.

19. Idelber Avelar, "Alegoría y postdictadura," *Revista de Crítica Cultural*, no. 14 (June 1997): 22.

3. Neobaroque Debris

1. Federico Galende, "La insurrección de las sobras," *Revista de Crítica Cultural,* no. 10 (May 1995): 24.

2. In the text on "literatura y experiencia en tiempos sombríos" [literature in dark times], I. Avelar lucidly asks the following: "in analyzing the problematics of experience in postdictatorial literature, it might be worthwhile to revisit two questions posed by Walter Benjamin in the thirties: (1) What are the conditions of transmissibility of personal experience in a society dominated by automation and commodities? Who will be interested in a narrative of experience when stories have been replaced by information? And (2) What role could literature play after its links to collective memory have been severed? For the aesthetic subject born, let's say, with Baudelaire, what is left of experience that can be narrated?" Idelber Avelar, "Bares desiertos y calles sin nombres," *Revista de Crítica Cultural,* no. 9 (November 1994): 37.

3. Idelber Avelar, "Alegoría y postdictadura: Notas sobre la memoria del Mercado," *Revista de Crítica Cultural,* no. 14 (June 1997): 23.

4. Diamela Eltit, *El padre mío* (Santiago, Chile: Francisco Zegers Editor, 1989).

5. Taking into account the huge number of critical articles on the work of Diamela Eltit, the secondary attention given to *El padre mío* is noteworthy. The book has not been excerpted in anthologies of Chilean testimonial literature, thereby maintaining a relative "marginality" to both literary and testimonial genres.

6. Eltit, *El padre mío,* 13.

7. John Beverley and George Yúdice would be the most emphatic exponents of this view of testimony. See Beverley, "The Margin at the Center," and Yúdice, "Testimonio and Postmodernism," in *The Real Thing: Testimonial Discourse and Latin America,* ed. George M. Gugelberger (Durham: Duke University Press, 1996). In another text, Beverley speaks, for example, of how "testimony models a possibility of a democratizing politics of alliances based on a 'united front' formed by a segment of intellectuals . . . with popular classes and groups, a united front that does not subordinate its components to a representative instantiation (party, state, text, etc.)." John Beverley, introduction to the magazine *Crítica Literaria Latinoamericana* (Lima, Peru), no. 9 (1992): 9. Yúdice, on his part, says that "testimony can be understood as a representation of struggle, but that its most important function is to be a link of solidarity between diverse communities. Thus, its cultural politics crosses established borders and identities in favor of a democratizing transformation." George Yúdice, "Testimonio y concientización," in the same publication, p. 226.

8. Eltit, *El padre mío,* 57.

9. There are various forms in which D. Eltit underlines this baroque dimension of exteriority, decorativeness, and surface in her presentation text. She says, for example, regarding urban vagabonds: "their presences composed in pure appearance, following a complex and harrowing cosmetic order, allow a glimpse of multiple meanings,

from the multiplicity of additives that compose the violent exteriority to which they have been reduced" (12).

10. Juan Armando Epple, *El arte de recordar* (Santiago: Mosquito Editores, 1994), 50.

11. Ivette Malverde, "Esquizofrenia y literatura," in *Una poética de literatura menor: La narrativa de Diamela Eltit*, ed. Juan Carlos Lértora (Santiago: Editorial Cuarto Propio, 1993), 158.

12. George Yúdice, "Testimonio y concientización," 207.

13. Malverde, "Esquizofrenia y literatura," 164.

14. Eltit, *El padre mío*, 15.

15. Malverde underlines the fact that it "is significant that a figure that positions herself as a daughter be the one who rescues the memory and words of the father. Let us remember that in a patriarchal order, it is the father who upholds order and the logos. By violating that order, and having the father be a schizoid subject, a marginal figure emptied of meaning as defined from the dominant center, the daughter offers an account of him and of an overturned order, filling the void from the standpoint of a new possible order that can arise from a woman's consciousness. It is no longer a matter of a social-verbal structure in which the linguistic system makes order out of chaos, reestablishing the meaning of the referent, but a restructuring of that order through a multiplying fragmentation of possible meanings that can arise from the signifiers of the father's three types of speech. It is a new mobile order, multi-faceted, which accounts for, especially through silence, the ominous names of power, that, albeit in constant displacement, are always omnipresent" (Esquizofrenia y literatura," 163.)

16. Eltit, *El padre mío*, 16.

17. Ibid.

18. By detailing the modality of her gesture, Eltit writes in the presentation (preface): "By availing myself of the advantages and disadvantages of being in these zones but not from the viewpoint of a sociologist or anthropologist, I was able to open a speculative swathe in the margin, confiding in the narrative, which allowed me to creatively weave and join distant elements, liberating the analogical flow and the aesthetic burden encrusted in bodies, gestures, behavior, and fragments of a way of life. Relying on creativity and in particular on the use of narrative montages, I was able to bring out the dramatic nature that these figures had within them" (12).

19. Ibid., 16.

20. In a beautiful and to date unpublished piece, Julio Ramos speaks of how "metaphor only adds another effect of offering, another linkage point in the chain of transfers, of exchange of gifts and faculties between the diverse and distant places along the way": between the places of literature and the "circuits of responsibility and solidarity." The articulation of these places would be thanks to the "spatial condensation that metaphor performs between the unequal points of an analogy" (Julio Ramos, "Dispositivos del amor y locura").

4. The Congealment of the Pose and Urban Velocities

1. This kind of photographic archival work as visual sequence was first put together by Eugenio Dittborn, to be shown at an event that accompanied the presentation of my book *Margins and Institutions: Art in Chile since 1975* (Melbourne: Francisco Zegers Editor / Art and Text, 1986), at the University of Sydney, Australia, in 1987.

2. Eugenio Dittborn "Bye Bye Love," interview, *Revista de Crítica Cultural*, no. 13 (November 1996): 51.

3. For a complete overview of Dittborn's oeuvre, see his *Remota* (Santiago: Pública Editores, 1997), which includes his artistic itinerary with a collection of critical pieces on his work.

4. Ibid., 26.

5. This quote is from a key text by R. Kay on Dittborn's work. See Ronald Kay, *Del espacio de acá* (Santiago: Visual, 1980), 44.

6. Susan Sontag, *Sobre la fotografía* [On Photography] (Buenos Aires: Edhasa, 1980), 135.

7. Pierre Bourdieu, *La fotografía: Un arte intermedio* (Mexico: Nueva Imagen, 1979), 39. Translated as *Photography: A Middle-Brow Art* (1990).

8. Eugenio Dittborn, *Fallo fotográfico* (Santiago, 1981).

9. This is the title of the second novel of writer Guadalupe Santa Cruz, published by Editorial Cuarto Propio in 1992.

10. Dittborn, *Fallo fotográfico*.

11. Ibid.

12. Beatriz Sarlo, *Escenas de la vida postmoderna* (Buenos Aires: Ariel, 1994), 14.

13. "To truly 'know' a city, we need to walk its streets, but to 'see' it, we should remain removed, so that we can perceive the whole. At a distance the contours 'represent' the city. Its massive density is the clash of knowledges, its silhouette is perishable, marked by recognition." Daniel Bell, "El eclipse de la distancia," in *La mirada oblicua: Estudios culturales y democracia*, ed. Silvia Delfino (Buenos Aires: La Marca, 1994), 40.

14. For two Latin American readings / interpretations of the city that deal with the new urban problematics at the crossroads of globalization and the local, see Nestor García Canclini, *Consumidores y ciudadanos* (Mexico: Grijalbo, 1995). Of particular interest is the section called "Cities under Globalization"; and Jesús Martín Barbero, "La ciudad virtual: Transformaciones de la sensibilidad y nuevos scenarios de comunicación," *Universidad del Valle* (Cali, Colombia), no. 14 (August 1996): 4–21.

15. "Now the dominant attitude is visual. First, the modern world is an urban world. Life in the great city and the way in which stimuli and sociability are defined give birth to a welter of occasions so that people *can see* and *want to see* things." Bell, "Eclipse," 39.

16. Kay, *Del espacio de acá*, 33.

17. José Bengoa, *La comunidad perdida* (Santiago: Ediciones Sur, 1996), 66.

5. Dismantlings of Identity, Perversions of Codes

1. Marshall Berman, *Todo lo sólido se desvanece en el aire* (Mexico: Siglo XXI Editores, 1988), 90. Translation of *All That Is Solid Melts into Air: The Experience of Modernity* (1983).

2. In a newspaper article titled "Ropa usada: Un ahorro para todos" (Used Clothing: A Savings for All), which served as a guide for this text, we read the following: "the clothing sold is usually from the previous season. If you consider that in Europe summer ends in August, then the clothes are almost new, since it would not be more than a year old." From the newspaper *La Epoca* (Santiago), January 23, 1994.

3. Jean Baudrillard, "La mode ou la féerie du code," *Revue Traverses* (Centre Georges Pompidou), no. 3 (1984): 8.

4. "It is no secret to anyone that in modern malls clients are offered great service and comfort. However, there are many people who have often complained that their budgets don't allow them access to such luxuries" (*La Epoca*, January 23, 1994).

5. John Fiske, *Understanding Popular Culture* (London: Routledge, 1989), 5.

6. "If it's true that most people who can afford it shop at the malls, where the costs are much higher, there is a good percentage of consumers who prefer to buy used clothes. It's a matter of getting the most out of your budget, of acquiring more items of clothing for the same amount of money" (*La Epoca*, January 23, 1994).

7. "Those women who went downtown and said they were clothes shopping for the au pair, but were truly buying them for their own family, and when asked said they had personally brought them from their last trip to Europe," nowadays admit they go downtown to shop. Conversely, various used-clothing stores have moved toward Providencia in order to seduce a new clientele, recodifying social inequality in a different way ("people from other sectors [classes] have the preconceived idea that the stores are similar to the ones downtown, and, as a result, when they appear closer to home, they feel out of place and leave" [Ibid.]).

8. See Roland Barthes, *Sisteme de la mode* (Paris: Editions du Seuil, 1967). Translated as *The Fashion System* (New York: Farar, Straus, Giroux, 1983).

9. See Beatriz Sarlo, "Abundancia y pobreza," in *Escenas de la vida postmoderna* (Buenos Aires: Ariel, 1994), 17.

10. "In/Out: Four Projects by Chilean Artists (CADA, Dittborn, Downey, Jaar)," Washington Project for the Arts, curated by Alfredo Jaar, Washington, D.C., 1983.

11. This description is from the previously mentioned exhibition catalog.

12. *La Epoca*, January 23, 1994.

13. Néstor Perlongher, "Deseo y derivas urbanas," *Fahrenheit 458* (Buenos Aires), no. 4 (1988).

14. Michel de Certeau, *L'invention du quotidien* (Paris: 10/18, 1980), 12; Spanish translation by Nelly Richard.

15. See Celeste Olalquiaga, "Cultura buitresca: Reciclaje de imágenes" *Revista de Crítica Cultural*, no. 6 (May 1993): 10.

6. The Academic Citation and Its Others

1. Michel Foucault, "Curso del 7 enero de 1976," in *Microfísica del poder* (Madrid: Las Ediciones de la Piquette, 1979), 129.

2. The publication of the *Anales de la Universidad de Chile*, 6th ser., no. 1 (September 1995), was prepared by an editorial committee that consisted of Francisco Brugnoli, Braulio Fernández, Fernando Lolas, Jorge Martínez, and Darío Oses. This first issue included texts by Fernando Lolas, Iñigo Díaz, Humberto Giannini, Nelly Richard, Darío Oses, Ennio Vivaldi, José Ricardo Morales, Jaime Lavado, Pablo Oyarzún, José Joaquin Brunner, and Hector Croxatto.

3. "La condición de la universidad: Pensamiento y crítica," introduction to the "Estudios" section, ibid., 35.

4. Ibid.

5. The invitation stated the desire to "cover the maximum heterogeneity (of authors) including the generational, and also to invite academics or cultural personalities foreign to the University of Chile" (36).

6. Willy Thayer, *La crisis no moderna de la universidad moderna (Epílogo del conflicto de las facultades)* (Santiago: Editorial Cuarto Propio, 1996), 187; italics mine.

7. Federico Galende, prologue to *Crisis de los saberes y espacio universitario en el debate contemporáneo* (Santiago: Arcis/Lom, 1995), 11.

8. Patricio Marchant, "Discurso contra los ingleses," *Revista de Crítica Cultural*, no. 2 (November 1991): 4.

9. Patricio Marchant, *Sobre árboles y madres* (Santiago: Ediciones Gato Mur, 1984).

10. F. Rella said that "in the time of crisis and of transformation, . . . the lacunas of discourse, its 'poverty,' the fact that the language of knowledge does not tell everything, are the principal paths of the speech full of truth. The truth speaks in error and in lack." Franco Rella, *El silencio y las palabras* (Buenos Aires: Paidós, 1992), 71.

11. Pablo Oyarzún, "Traición, tu nombre es mujer," in *Ver desde la mujer*, ed. Olga Grau (Santiago: Editorial Cuarto Propio, 1992), 151.

12. I refer the reader to the text "¿Una autobiografía fantástica?" by Miguel Vicuña, in the journal *El espíritu del valle* (Santiago), no. 1 (December 1986): 71.

13. For a critical analysis of the assembly of practices associated with the "avant-garde scene" or "new scene" of the 1980s in Chile, consult Eugenio Brito, *Campos minados (Literatura post-golpe en Chile)* (Santiago: Editorial Cuarto Propio, 1990): and Nelly Richard, *Margins and Institutions: Art in Chile since 1975* (Melbourne: Art and Text, 1987).

14. Gonzalo Muñoz, "Escritura de una escena," photocopied document from his intervention at the seminar of the Arcis Institute, Santiago, 1986.

15. Ibid.

16. Pablo Oyarzún, "Universidad y creatividad," *Anales de la Universidad de Chile*, 152.

17. Document titled "Anales de la Universidad de Chile, VI, Serie Normas Editoriales," attached to the letter of invitation sent to the authors.

18. One of the "commonplaces" that dominates in university work mostly oriented toward professorial endeavors would have to do with the fiction of "maintaining that research is reported but not written: here the researcher is essentially a prospector of raw materials, and it is on this level that his problems are raised; once he has communicated his 'results,' everything is solved; 'formulation' is nothing more than a vague final operation, rapidly performed according to a few techniques of 'expression' learned in secondary school and whose only constraint is submission to the code of the genre ('clarity,' suppression of images, respect for the laws of argument)." Roland Barthes, *The Rustle of Language* (New York: Hill and Wang, 1986), 70.

19. Thayer, *La crisis,* 349. The fact that the text that I wrote (an earlier version of this one) for the aforementioned issue of the *Anales* had required the accompaniment of an explicative epilogue (Francisco Brugnoli: "A propósito del artículo de Nelly Richard") says enough about the unpresentability of certain participations in the pre-established framework of a convocation as formal as this one and about the "untranslatability of the citation" (for lack of context) to which I refer here.

20. M. Foucault asks himself, "What else is a system of instruction, after all, but a ritualization of speech; but a qualification and a fixing of the functions for the subjects that speak; but the constitution of a doctrinal group at the moment of least imprecision; but a distribution and an adaptation of the discourse with its powers and knowledges?" Michel Foucault, *El orden del discurso* (Barcelona: Tusquets, 1973), 38.

21. This is the title of one of the chapters of the book of P. Marchant cited earlier in which he polemically argues with the "university philosophical discourse."

22. F. Brugnoli states, referring to the operations of language of the artisitic-cultural scene of the eighties: "the doubt established itself in the referential value of the name and of all systems of signification; from there the necessity to open the borders of the named and give preeminence to the exercises of displacement and metaphor, in the process of successive negativity that permitted new forms of speech. By questioning the value of the representation, the signifier was valued above all. One could speak of a work that forced the redesignation and that, for the same reason, operated critically with the concept of institutionality of language" (Brugnoli, "A propósito," 86).

23. According to F. Galende: "pedagogy is the immediate distribution of ideas toward the specific fields of their social yield (that are) training grounds ready to add obedient cognitive soldiers to the sphere of circulating knowledges" (Galende, prologue, 11).

24. Pablo Oyarzún, "Fragmentos de una conversación en torno a la universidad," a conversation between P. Oyarzún and A. Valdés, in the journal *Lo* (Santiago), no. 1 (November 1992).

7. Antidiscipline, Transdiscipline, and the Redisciplining of Knowledge

1. As an example, I would like to mention the Gender and Culture in Latin America program of the College of Philosophy and Humanities of the University of Chile, and the Diploma in Cultural Criticism of the Arcis University, as two spaces

interested in disobeying the systems of disciplinary fidelity and in articulating a tension—political and theoretical—between the borders of academia and heterodox bodies of knowledge that come from elsewhere.

2. Kemy Oyarzún, "Introducción," *Nomadías* (Santiago: Cuarto Propio/PGAL), no. 1 (December 1996): 7.

3. Along with insisting on the temporary and tentative character of the term "cultural criticism" that designates a multiform assembly of texts that are imprecise in their contours, I prefer to leave to the imagination of the reader the responsibility of electing, in the readings that make up every bibliography, the texts that would happily share some of the traits here described.

4. Carlos Pérez V., "Introduction to the Seminar of Cultural Criticism," Arcis University, April 1997.

5. M. Foucault, *The Order of Things: An Archeology of Human Sciences* (New York: Random House, 1970); *El orden del discurso* (Barcelona: Tusquets, 1973), 27.

6. Willy Thayer, "Introduction to the Seminar of Cultural Criticism," Arcis University, April 1997.

7. P. Bové states: "the critical action can not only disclose and undermine the discourse of oppression, but it can open space to help others form their own subjectivities in opposition to the discursive and institutional discourses generated and affixed by dominant structures and their agents." Paul Bové, *In the Wake of Theory* (Middletown, Conn.: Wesleyan University Press, 1992), 45.

8. There are many and diverse definitions that can be proposed for this new model of academic reorganization of knowledge called "cultural studies": a model already amply formalized in the international (principally Anglo–North American) academy and in growing implementation in various Latin American universities. For reference, I offer two descriptions that define the project of cultural studies from two different latitudes. J. Beverly speaks of cultural studies as a "program tied more or less directly to the political activism of the sixties, the New Left, Althusserian Marxism or Neogramscian, feminist theory and the women's movement, the civil rights movement, the resistance to the colonial and imperial wars, deconstructionism." John Beverly, "Estudios culturales y vocación política," *Revista de Crítica Cultural,* no. 12 (July 1996): 46. S. Delfino refers to cultural studies in light of the problems that the field allows us to analyze: problems relating to "daily life and information, audiovisual genres and consumption of symbolic goods, urban journeys as perceptive transformations, the passage from a mass democracy to a political use of the visibility of minorities or the proliferation of demands for localized concrete rights." Silvia Delfino, "Prólogo," in *La mirada oblicua: Estudios culturales y democracia* (Buenos Aires: La Marca, 1993), 5.

9. Vincent Leitch, *Critical Criticism, Literary Theory, Poststructuralism* (New York: Columbia University Press), 9.

10. "I ask myself if, in the final analysis, theory and writing could not identify themselves. Writing, in the current sense of the word, is a theory. It has a theoretical

dimension, and no theory ought to refuse writing, no theory should move about uniquely inside of a simple 'written-ness,' that is, from a perspective that is purely instrumental regarding language. . . . Theory would be a language that . . . observes itself in a kind of permanent self-criticism." Roland Barthes, in *La Teoría* (Barcelona: Anagrama, 1971), 9.

11. Reflecting on the changes that occurred in the design that associated the project of the humanities in Latin America with the models of citizen identification, Julio Ramos states: "at this end of the twentieth century, marked by the distinctive globalization of the media-drenched societies, perhaps social formations don't require any more legitimating intervention from these modeling tales of national integration, to the extent that the state withdraws from the republican contracts of the representation of the 'common well-being' and that the mass media and consumption interweave other parameters for citizen identification and its multiple exclusions." Julio Ramos, "El proceso de Alberto Mendoza: Poesía y subjetivación," *Revista de Crítica Cultural*, no. 13 (November 1996): 34.

12. Jean Baudrillard, *La transparencia del mal* (Barcelona: Anagrama, 1991), 14.

13. Beatriz Sarlo, "Los estudios culturales y la crítica literaria en la encrucijada valorativa," *Revista de Crítica Cultural*, no. 15 (November 1997): 36. Along the lines of Adorno, for whom "a value-neutral aesthetic is a contradiction in terms," B. Sarlo argues in favor of values, stating the following: "if cultural sociology manages to dislodge a silly idea of impartiality and aesthetic priesthood, at the same time it rapidly evacuates the analysis of the properly aesthetic resistances that produce the semantic and formal density of art. The problem of values is liquidated together with the myths of the absolute liberty of creation. The sociological perspective dissolves the self-justifying good conscience, but it also corrodes the density of the reasons for creating art." Beatriz Sarlo, *Escenas de la vida posmoderna* (Buenos Aires: Ariel, 1994), 156.

14. Theodor W. Adorno, *Teoría estética* (Madrid: Taurus, 1992), 367.

15. John Beverly, "¿Hay vida más allá de la literatura?" *Estudios* (Caracas), no. 6 (1995): 39.

16. N. Casullo posits that in order for cultural studies to be something more than mere "accessories to eventual administrations" of the real in its most restrictedly adaptive dimension, it is necessary to reflect on "the dissolution of the critical paradigm" that linked "the threat, the drama, and the weapons of criticism" and whose memory is necessary "as a cultural problematics . . . that does not reconcile itself with technical-instrumental logics, languages, and horizons of a cultural dominant . . . where everything appears as vacuously easy to be said, to be made transparent: pseudocriticism. And where the institutional, 'progressed,' and victorious culture offers affirmatively, at every junction, *all* the words in order to explain 'the world.'" Nicolás Casullo, "Investigaciones culturales y pensamiento crítico," *Sociedad* (Faculty of Social Sciences of the University of Buenos Aires), no. 5 (October 1994): 83.

17. J. Ramos argues in favor of the critical potential of cultural studies in the following terms: "to the extent that they cut diagonally across the epistemic framework of

the disciplines, cultural studies imagine the at times radical questioning of the principle of autonomy—the principle of immanence that regulates the validation of principles produced by the rationalized fields of modern knowledge—with effects as much in the strategies for the framing of new objects of investigation and curricular design, as in the conceptions of the complex relation between knowledge and power that overdetermine the investigations themselves" (Ramos, "El proceso," 36).

18. P. Bové speaks of how the academic professionalization of critical work makes the "so-called oppositional critics operate 'professionally' with little significant 'oppositional' value or function at all and 'transform the intellectual values into economic and social capital' in accordance with the high indices of 'commercialization and fetishism inside of the professions' that affect the contentious value of critical discourse" (Bové, *In the Wake of Theory*, xvi).

19. Roland Barthes, *The Rustle of Language* (New York: Hill and Wang, 1986), 56.

20. Ibid.

21. John Beverley, "Writing in Reverse: On the Project of the Latin American Subaltern Group," in *Disposition XIX* (Ann Arbor: University of Michigan Press, 1994), 285.

22. Beverley, "Estudios culturales y vocación politica."

23. The commentary of Beatriz Sarlo, referring to this functionality of cultural studies, states the following: "in the last ten or fifteen years, cultural studies appeared as an appropriate solution for the traits of a new scene. Without wishing to overdo the characterization, I would say that social movements and cultural studies were fellow travelers extremely useful to the democratic transition, on the one hand, and to the ruin of modern totalizations, on the other" (Sarlo, "Los estudios culturales," 33).

24. Beverley, "Estudios culturales y vocación politica," 48.

25. Please see the reply of the author that criticizes Beverley's notion of cultural studies: Federico Galende, "Un desmemoriado espíritu de época: Tribulaciones y desdichas en torno a los estudios culturales," *Revista de Crítica Cultural*, no. 13 (November 1996): 52.

26. Ibid.

27. Ibid.

28. M. de Certeau stated, concerning the dangers for any specialist of "the irruption of the unforeseen: some agitated tacit element invalidates the mental tools elaborated that depend on stability. But the instruments also formed part of what had become agitated." Michel de Certeau, *La toma de la palabra, y otro escritos politicos* (Mexico: Universidad Iberoamericana, 1995), 30.

29. P. Bové states: "as Gramsci sees it, counterhegemonic forces always need an institutional structure to direct resistance and to reorganize the cultural possibilities" in new directions; the critical challenge would consist of *connecting* the dynamic of the changes with said structure without letting what is already instituted in them take hold and immobilize them. (Bové, *In the Wake of Theory*, 39).

30. While clarifying the distinction between "institutionalization" and "codification,"

S. Hall makes the distinction: "I am in favor of institutionalization because one must pass through the organizational moment—the long route through the institutions in order to . . . construct some form of intellectual collective project." Stuart Hall, *Critical Dialogues in Cultural Studies,* ed. David Morley and Kuan-Hsing Chen (London: Routledge, 1996), 149.

31. Jacques Derrida, "Les antinomies de la discipline philosophique-Lettre préface," in *La grève des philosophes* (École et philosophie) (Paris: Editions Osiris, 1986), 15.

32. I agree with P. Bové when he insists that "one should never write in the abstract about the nature of 'oppositional criticism.' 'Criticism' of any sort must always be concrete and specific no matter how theoretically informed. 'Oppositional criticism' particularly cannot be defined or theorized so much as it must be enacted . . . To catch something of the force of an 'oppositional critical' act, one must first of all see it as an act and in action; one must see it engaged critically with some element of the empowered structure of the society and culture against which it takes up its stance. . . . It cannot exist as a series of generalities, of prescriptive statements laying out a program, method, or set of values'" (Bové, *In the Wake of Theory,* 48–49).

8. The Graphic Model of an Advertising Identity

1. I refer the reader to the complete review made by J. Pinedo of this controversy in "Una metáfora de país: La discusión en torno a la presencia de Chile en el pabellón Sevilla 1992." Javier Pinedo, *Ensayismo y modernidad in América Latina* (Santiago: Ediciones Arcis/Lom, 1996), 87–113.

2. *El pabellón de Chile, huracanes y maravillas en un exposición universal* (Santiago: La Máquina del Arte), 1992.

3. Ibid., 13.

4. Ibid.

5. Roberto Durán, comisario general adjunto of Chile-Expo '92, interview in *El Diario* (Santiago), June 3, 1991.

6. T. Moulian calls this metamorphosis "evolution": "I call 'evolution' the long process of preparation, during the dictatorship, for an exit from the dictatorship, destined to permit the continuity of its basic structures in other political trappings, in democratic clothing. The objective is a 'chameleonism' to the operations that in present-day Chile realize themselves in order to secure the reproduction of the 'infrastructure' created during the dictatorship, stripped of the troublesome forms, of the brutal and bare 'superstructures' of the past." Tomás Moulian, *Chile actual: Anatomía de un mito* (Santiago: Arcis/Lom, 1997), 145.

7. José Joaquín Brunner, "Entre la cultura autoritaria y la cultura democrática," in *América Latina: Cultura y modernidad* (Mexico: Grijalbo, 1992), 374.

8. "Obviously, what they had in mind was to create an organism where managerial power would also be represented, so that if Chile decided to participate in the Expo, this participation would be the reflection of a project of the whole country, and

not just a state or unilateral vision of Chile," states Fernando Léniz in *El pabellón de Chile*, 28.

9. Moulian, *Chile actual*, 28.

10. Nevenka Marsic, *El pabellón de Chile*, 58.

11. Ibid., 56–57.

12. Moulian, *Chile actual*, 31.

13. "Chile was summed up in 'six basic themes' ('Chile, living land,' 'Chile, land of tasty dishes,' 'Chile, country of generous riches,' 'Chile, function,' 'Chile, enterprise of ideas,' 'Chile, the remotest place on earth,' and 'Chile, solid people') that would each have its own section, and each section would have a color, its own signs and would be made up of a series of shelves with metallic trays. In them one would abundantly encounter the cases corresponding to each one of the elements. . . . The products that our country offers will be represented in these cases of different forms, in accordance with each one of the six general themes. . . . Every one of the cases will contain general information, a postcard, a handkerchief with a map, and a container with a piece of lapis lazuli." "Un hito en nuestra historia," *El Mercurio* (Santiago), February 1992.

14. Guillermo Tejeda, "Hielos mentales en la cultura chilena," *La Época* (Santiago), September 8, 1991.

15. Bernardo Subercaseaux, *Chile, ¿un país moderno?* (Santiago: Ediciones B, 1996), 62–64.

16. Ana Pizarro, "Todos los Chile: Chile," *La Época*, October 13, 1991.

17. *El pabellón de Chile*, 18.

18. Guillermo Tejeda, "Un hito en nuestra historia," *El Mercurio*, February 1992.

19. Ibid.

20. Cited by Paul Virilio in *El arte del motor* (Buenos Aires: Manantial, 1996), 14.

21. Tejeda, "Un hito."

22. Ibid.

23. This culture of amusement is a culture that defines itself more and more "by the technology of packaging than by the content, and where the way things are combined becomes more important than the *content,* effect more sought after than the substance . . . and the recognition of diversity is more and more like a 'chromatic-commercial' optimization of the circulation of information." Martín Hopenhayn, *Ni apocalípticos ni integrados* (Santiago: Fondo de Cultura Económica, 1994), 41.

24. "We don't want to be confused with our neighbors," states G. Tejeda in the article "Hielos mentales en la cultura chilena," *La Época*, September 1991.

25. Gabriel García Márquez, *Cien años de soledad* (Buenos Aires: Editorial Sudamericana, 1967), 23.

26. Ibid.

27. Juan Carlos Castillo, in *El pabellón de Chile*.

28. Subercaseaux, *Chile*, 61.

29. Tejeda, *La Época*.

30. Ibid.

31. Subercaseaux, *Chile,* 84.

32. Gerard Imbert, *Los discursos del cambio: Imágenes e imaginarios sociales en la España de la transición (1976–1982)* (Madrid: Akal/Comunicación, 1990), 140.

33. I derive these observations from the reading of G. Imbert, *Los discursos del cambio.*

9. Turbulence, Anachronism, and Degenerations

1. The Santiago School, circumstantially formed as a collective for the project of the postcards presented to Fondart (Fondo de Desarrollo de las Artes de la Cultura), brought together four of the most important figures of the Chilean artistic scene: Juan Dávila, Gonzalo Díaz, Eugenio Dittborn, and Arturo Duclos.

2. For a review of the polemic generated around the *Simón Bolívar* case, see *Revista de Crítica Cultural,* no. 9 (November 1994): 25–36.

3. The project of the Santiago School consisted of four mailings of four different postcards (one by each artist), sent at twenty-day intervals: "The Decade of the Eighties," "The Decade of the Nineties," "The Worktable," and "The City of Santiago."

4. Referring to the production of the Avanzada scene, A. Valdés speaks of "a kind of impulsivity that passes through any kind of barrier between the arts and the genres, and that corresponds to a particular form of experimenting and processing in the works and the situation that Chile lived through during this period. In a moment of insufficiency of the representation of social phenomena that appeared to occur beyond and on this side of the discourses made to analyze them and explain them, these artists proposed images that demanded second and third readings; they proposed inscriptions that were occasionally cryptic, with something of the writings of the catacombs in them. They wanted to traverse a space that did not respond to preconceived designs, and create an active exploration in meaning, a perception of the experience of authoritarianism by other means than those then offered by ideological discourse." Adriana Valdés, *Composición de lugar: Escritos sobre cultura* (Santiago: Editorial Universitaria, 1995), 70.

5. Justo Pastor Mellado, "La escena de avanzada ha muerto, viva la Escuela de Santiago," *La Nación* (Santiago), July 29, 1994.

6. As it was published in the daily *El Mercurio,* August 14, 1994: "The president of the Senate, Gabriel Valdés, labeled as 'detestable' the controversial portrait that the Chilean painter Juan Domingo Dávila made of the Liberator Simón Bolívar. He said that, without any intention of censoring the aforementioned work, 'this should never have been painted.' . . . Valdés declared that art has a limit, which is good taste and decorum." In another declaration, the pianist Roberto Bravo stated that the "painting of Simón Bolívar is a *monstrosity*" and that "it is an embarrassment that it was made in Chile," in the daily *El Mercurio,* August 1994.

7. "I see from the viewpoint of my own aesthetic tastes. They themselves are a personal biographical construction, emerging from the social-cultural topics and strategies

that were at my disposal and continue to be. Taste and its social markings; taste, the theories, fashion: aesthetic opinion circulates through these zones and their limits." Beatriz Sarlo, "Una mirada política: Defensa del partidismo en el arte," *Punto de Vista* (Buenos Aires), no. 27 (August 1985): 3.

8. Justo Pastor Mellado, "De los mitos privados a las ostentaciones públicas," *La Nación*, August 19, 1994.

9. Needless to say, the conditions for discussing the critical strategies of artistic productions like that of Dávila would imply an articulation of the aesthetic debate completely nonexistent in the culture of the democratic market of the years of the Transition. Only such an aesthetic-critical debate could give place to the construction of that which B. Sarlo calls "a political gaze" over art; a gaze that permits one "to resolve the forms of coexistence and the crisscrossing of definitions, their sociointellectual conditions and formal rules: a political gaze that attends to the figures of the new . . . that prepares to dispute the hegemony of the great cultural paradigms, to question the legitimacy of their imposition, although perhaps it does not manage ever to complete this symbolic battle. . . . The political gaze would fix its attention precisely on those discourses, practices, actors, and accounts that affirm the right to intervene against the unification, exhibiting, in the face of such unification, the scandal of other perspectives" (Sarlo, "Una mirada política," 3).

10. These statements were from the press released by the Venezuelan Embassy and published in the Santiago daily *La Época*, August 11, 1994.

11. Mabel Moraña, *Políticas en la escritura en América Latina* (Caracas: Excultura, 1997), 78.

12. "The *mestizaje* of Bolivar's facial traits is the effect of a retouching with paint, as if the original were a polychrome wooden statuette. This is the importance of the retouching as analytical figure: that is to say, it always conjures the most dreadful possibility, the phantasm of skin whitening. This fear covers, probably, a rite of initiation where rape is at the core of the problem." Justo Pastor Mellado, "Pintura e indeferenciación de los sexos," *La Nación*, August 12, 1994.

13. Francine Masiello, "Género, vestido, y mercado: El comercio de la ciudadanía en América Latina," *Estudios* (Caracas), no. 9 (1997): 92.

14. Excerpt from the *Declaración de la Escuela de Santiago,* signed "Dávila-Díaz-Dittborn-Duclos," *La Época*, August 21, 1994.

15. Ibid.

16. Mellado, "Pintura e indeferenciación."

17. Jorge Mario Eastman, ambassador of Colombia in Chile, expressed himself in the following manner: "Bolívar was adored by women; Dávila, on the other hand, attempts to make him deviate toward hermaphroditism, which constitutes not only a historical blasphemy but also artistic rubbish." In the newspaper *La Tercera* (Santiago), August 26, 1994.

18. This declaration was made by Aniceto Rodríguez, ambassador of Chile in Venezuela, published in *La Época*, August 13, 1994.

19. States Carlos Pérez V.: "Parodic citation and fragmentation, hybrid montage and simulation . . . all critical operations invented by the vanguards against the cultural institution (which the institution ended up incorporating in its corpus), recited, sexualized, carnivalized by Dávila, adopt that ominous, nonfamiliar character that Freud referred to as the phantasmatic manifestation of the repressed. Through the ironic manipulation of such operations . . . Dávila has managed to irritate the cultural body, introducing into it the externals of a body stripped of all social protocol and sexual prototype, absorbed in the inertia of its degradation and perverted by the markings of its marginality. The work of Dávila can be defined as a revulsive (an exterior substance that congests and inflames the exterior of a body) that works over the applicable institutions of identity and their agonizing dogmas of inwardness and purity." Carlos Pérez V., "Identidad y escatología," in *Rota* (Santiago: Galería Gabriela Mistral, November 1996).

20. Excerpt from the *Declaration de la Escuela de Santiago.*

21. Raquel Olea, "Libertad de arte y otro imaginarios," *La Época,* August 19, 1994.

22. Editorial in *El Mercurio,* August 23, 1994.

23. This is how Darío Paya, representative of the UDI, expresses himself in the newspaper *La Segunda* (Santiago), August 23, 1994.

24. Following a reading suggested by D. Eltit, we could think, for example, that perhaps it was a question of ridiculing the homosexual carnival in order to exorcize "the anguish provoked by the forgetting of other bodies—disappeared, tortured, humiliated"; or that perhaps one sought to camouflage other references to the press that showed "the antiheroic figure of a homosexual former ambassador implicated in crimes of corruption." According to J. P. Mellado, "the photo of Dávila attempted to turn away the attention from another cover photo that reproduced the image of another notable figure: that of General Pinochet, smiling, looking through the sights of a weapon" (dossier of the *Revista de Crítica Cultural,* no. 9).

25. It is not superfluous to point out that in spite of being a space dependent on the Ministry of Education and therefore officially involved with its institutional politics, the Gabriela Mistral Gallery has developed in recent years an artistic management engaged with works of critical experimentation that do not easily fit within the traditional commercial or museum circuit.

26. Concerning the polemic about the *Simón Bolívar,* J. P. Mellado affirmed that "the problem is not the work of Dávila. What is on the horizon is the criminalization of Fondart. I have information that makes me imagine the following scenario: a Christian Democratic sector, which has never been hegemonic in the governmental management of culture, tries a strategy of socialist displacement. The work of Dávila is an excuse to initiate an attack against the directors of the Fondo and the Cultural Division, as part of a wider campaign that takes into account the Christian Democratic takeover of structures that could originate by having the project undertaken based on a new cultural institutionality" (*Revista de Crítica Cultural,* no. 9).

27. In an unpublished essay entitled "Pinturas, monumentos, museos conmemorativos: Cuatro imágenes vaciadas de representación de la historía," Sandra Accatino

again takes up the opposition of O. Calabrese between "limit" and "excess" in order to defend this thesis. For Calabrese, "the limit entails pushing to the most extreme consequences the elasticity of the contour without destroying it. The excess is the exit from the contour after having broken it." "The ecstatic realm . . . cancels out the possibility of leaving from the confines blocking the border of the system," while "the dynamic . . . works in the periphery of the system." Omar Calabrese, *La era neobarroca* (Madrid: Cátedra, 1989), 82.

28. Pérez, "Identidad y escatología."

29. Ibid.

30. *El Mercurio,* December 22, 1996. The justifications of the prize given by the conservative Circle of Art Critics greatly insisted on this aestheticizing recuperation of the work of Dávila, arguing that "the work possesses a technique that is unsurpassable," that "it was delimited by the space"; and they celebrated "its intense colors, the sharp impact to the retina, caused by the power given off by the pigment."

10. Gender, Values, and Difference(s)

1. This degree deals with the Gender and Culture Program in Latin America (PGAL) coordinated by Kemy Oyarzún, inaugurated in August 1995. Before the creation of the program, the College of Social Sciences of the University of Chile had an Interdisciplinary Program of Gender Studies directed by Sonia Montecino. For an evaluation of the situation of gender programs in Chilean universities, see *Revista de Crítica Cultural,* no. 12, (July 1995).

2. Olga Grau, "Familia: Un grito de fin de siglo," in *Discurso, género y poder: Discurso públicos, Chile, 1978–1993* (Santiago: Arcis/Lom/La Morada, 1997), 134.

3. Sonia Montecino, *Madres y huachos: Alegorías del mestizaje chileno* (Santiago: Editorial Cuarto Propio/Cedem, 1993), 115.

4. Julieta Kirkwood is, without a doubt, the person who has developed the most rigorous and creative reflection, from the perspective of the social sciences, on the feminism of those years: see Julieta Kirkwood, *Ser política en Chile: Los nudos de sabiduría feminista* (Santiago: Editorial Cuarto Propio, 1990).

5. J. Kirkwood stated: "political realization is something more than a reference to the power of the state, to the institutional organizations, to the organization of the economy and to the dialectic of the use of power. It means rethinking the organization of the daily life of women and men; it means questioning, in order to deny—or at least, to begin to doubt—the affirmation of two areas experientially incisively cut through, the public (political) and the private (domestic), that stereotypically consecrates exclusionary and rigid realms of action for men and women" (ibid., 181).

6. I refer the reader to Raquel Olea, "Feminism, política y redemocratización," *Revista de Crítica Cultural,* no. 5 (July 1992).

7. Referring to the "hyperrepresentation of the family sign" in today's Chile, O. Grau signals that "it is interesting to observe that, to the extent in which the modern

state as unifying element of political life and as authority of maximum power is weakened, the gazes of governmental policies move toward the family as a possible representative sign of unification and as socially performative sign. In this way the desire
for a sort of alliance or complicity between family and state, reinforced by the religious
discourse, is established" ("Familia," 129).

   8. M. Hopenhayn comments on this hegemony of voice in the following: "but it
is not only the fundamentalism of the Right that redoubles its public presence and its
pretensions for exercising cultural hegemony. Even in the center of political life we
bear witness to a phenomenon that twenty years ago would have appeared alarming
and that today we accept almost as a given: the strong influence of the church and of
its values in the discourse of the state and of the parties. Not only because the government appears led by a party that declares its Christian roots; but above all because
it is taboo for any political force that aspires to possess a public presence to put forth
a discourse that is openly antireligious or marginal to the values of the church. The
secular state, an ideal incarnated in the preceding decades, loses its contours. The pastoral and the encyclicals would appear to be more than opinions of the ecclesiastical
institution and aspire to a normativity that government and citizenship should take up
and interiorize." Martín Hopenhayn, "Moral y secularización en el Chile finisecular:
Especulaciones para el debate," *CIEPLAM* (Santiago), no. 38 (December 1993).

   9. For an analysis of the Pastoral Letter, see Eugenia Brito, "El discurso sobre la
'crisis moral,'" in *Discurso, género y poder* (Santiago: Arcis/Lom/La Morada, 1997).

   10. This definition was given by the Christian Democratic senator Adolfo Zaldívar,
who intervened actively in the polemic, in *El Mercurio,* August 20, 1995.

   11. Such was the opinion of lawyer Marcela Achurra, from the Jaime Guzmán
Foundation, in "¿En qué está la discusión chilena sobre Beijing?" *La Época,* August
20, 1995.

   12. This quotation is taken from the editorial "Permisividad y delicuencia" of the
newspaper *La Época,* used in the chapter "El discurso sobre la 'crisis moral,'" in *Discurso, género y poder,* 55.

   13. Teresa de Lauretis, "La tecnología del género," *Mora* (Facultad de Filosofía y
Letras de la Universidad de Buenos Aires), no. 2 (November 1996): 8.

   14. Adolfo Zaldívar, in *El Mercurio,* August 1995.

   15. Sara Navas, cited in *Discurso, género y poder,* 121.

   16. Ibid.

   17. Anthony Giddens comments: "In a moment of minute rupture from tradition,
the people who anchor themselves to tradition should ask themselves and respond to
others as to why they do it. The universalization is crossed by active struggles and confrontations. . . . The profound effect of the influences counter to tradition explains why
the concept and the existence of fundamentalism have acquired such importance. . . .
The 'insistence' of fundamentalism on the tradition and its emphasis on 'purity' can
only be understood in these terms. . . . The defense of the tradition can only adopt
the strident tone that it possesses today in the context of a rupture with tradition,

universalization, and diasporic cultural exchanges." Anthony Giddens, *Más allá de la izquierda y la derecha* (Beyond Left and Right) (Madrid: Cátedra, 1996), 91–92.

18. These citations from newspapers are used by Kemy Oyarzún in his very lucid article "Sabers críticos y estudios de género," *Nomadías* (Santiago), no. 1 (December 1996).

19. J. Franco signals how the minister Josefina Bilbao "carefully removes the dangerous meanings" and "goes back to the Royal Academy's Dictionary to define this concept." Jean Franco, "Género y sexo en la transición hacia la modernidad," *Nomadías*, no. 1 (December 1996): 36.

20. Oyarzún, "Sabers críticos," 22.

21. "The key questioning for the moment in Chile is reflecting sharply, critically, and self-critically around a process of 'institutionalization' of the studies of gender that places a scholar in the context of the turn-of-the-century and postdictatorial academy. In this sense, it is urgent to revise the type of relation envisioned by gender studies faced with disciplines that . . . have not developed in all their richness in the interior of the academy, but instead precisely at the core of social movements, inside of which the social women's movement stands out. One of the most stirring problems around the installation of gender studies in Chilean universities continues to affect not only the 'nature' of disciplines that until now appear abandoned faced with the legitimacy and authorization of the academy, but in addition, and perhaps more disturbingly, it was clear that precisely the 'apocryphal' nature of the critical disciplines of gender obliged us (and still oblige us) to question the academy itself and to rethink the processes of 'institutionalization' of the critical disciplines" (Oyarzún, "Sabers críticos," 11–12).

22. Willy Thayer, *La crisis no moderna de la universidad moderna* (Santiago: Editorial Cuarto Propio, 1996), 223.

23. "But just as capitalism in general . . . lacks prohibited acts—although in every case it always installs peremptory although eventual and variable requirements and cosmetics—seemingly the university also lacks gradually prohibited discourses. The ease with which the discourses of women, as well as those of cultural studies and of minorities, became part of the curriculum of university study and bibliography greatly resembles the liberality of the supermarket" (ibid., 223).

24. Words spoken by Bishop Francisco Javier Errázurriz, quoted in *La Época*, August 11, 1995.

25. Las Yeguas de Apocalipsis is a homosexual two-person collective made up by the artist Francisco Casas and the writer Pedro Lemebel, who have worked with performances, videos, installations, poetry, and literature since the end of the eighties. *The Two Fridas* parodied the original of Frida Kahlo by dividing into two the "I" of the self-portrait, multiplying the identity of its doubles through a transsexual cosmetic that redramatizes the femininity (already made up) of Frida.

26. "There are many ways," states J. Franco, "to read the representation of Las Yeguas del Apocalipsis; in the AIDS years the double portrait signals a difference

between the 'original' (Kahlo laments the separation from Diego, cutting an artery of her heart), and the copy that appropriates and transforms the sentiments and affections, supposedly specialities of the feminine. The postcard calls into question the 'she' and ' he' of *the* woman and *the* man as stable and polarized identities. . . . In the case of the postcard-pastiche of the painting of Kahlo, the Chilean artist had created a living copy that questioned the patheticism that surrounds the myth of Kahlo as victim-woman" ("Género y sexo en la transición hacia la modernidad," 33).

    27. Ibid., 33.

    28. Oyarzún, "Sabers críticos," 20.

    29. According to F. Collin: "the difficulty for every movement of political liberation, to not confuse the struggle against subjection with the myth of the subject, that is to say, to not reduce the unknown to the known, is shown in its relation to the work of art. It is necessary to point out that such movements (whether Marxism or feminism, to take just two examples) rarely give rise to new artistic forms and tend to reduce the interpretation produced in works of art to expressions, illustrations, or confirmations of a truth already formally acquired. In the social itself, the political reductionism manages paradoxically to not give credit except to those whose lives take a militant form or to that which in their life takes this form. The collectivity sets its own a priori limits: it only functions under conditions. It controls ferociously the entrances and exits of what can be claimed to be a collective we." Francoise Collin, "Praxis de la diferencia," *Mora*, no. 1 (August 1995): 12.

    30. Pedro Lemebel, coauthor of the performance *The Two Fridas*, speaks precisely about this subversive potential of art that disorders genders, while commenting on his own trajectory as artist and writer (a trajectory that goes from short story to performance to the urban chronicle): "the rest came with the Mares of the Apocalypse, a political-cultural experience that we carried out with Francisco Casas in the eighties, when Chile was under protective custody. . . . It is possible that this corporal exposition in a political framework was evaporating the generic recipe for a story. . . . I don't know, the whole thing, the mares, the disrespect, the invitation to mix genres and 'poor' arts with militant pamphlets, the temptation to illuminate the raw successes and to throw off the switch on ontological truth. I always hated the philosophy professors, in reality, all the professors. I was annoyed by their doctrinarian posture about knowledge, about street people, the Indians, the poor, queers. A world to which we were foreign." Pedro Lemebel, "El desliz que desafía otros recorridos: Entrevista con P. Lemebel," interview by Fernando Blanco and Juan Gelpí, *Nómada* (Puerto Rico), no. 3 (June 1997): 94.

11. Take the Sky by Assault

    1. Olga Grau, "Calles y veredas," *Revista de Crítica Cultural*, no. 14 (June 1997): 21.

    2. Jacques Rancière, *En los bordes de lo político* (Santiago: Editorial Universitaria, 1994), 15.

3. Willy Thayer, *La crisis no moderna de la universidad moderna* (Santiago: Editorial Cuarto Propio, 1996), 170.

4. *El Rodriguista* (Santiago), no. 70 (April–May 1997).

5. For an analysis of the political discourse of the MRPF, I refer the reader to Hernán Vidal, *FPMR: El tabú del conflicto armado en Chile* (Santiago: Mosquito Editores, 1995). According to the author, "It was the assassination of Senator Jaime Guzmán that brought about the distancing of the great majority of the officials that still belong to the MRPF. The operation of 'bringing to justice' was carried out during the period of discussions anticipated in the National Consultation initiated by the National Directorate of the MRPF toward the end of 1990, in which opinions were gathered among its militants about the need for reorganizing its political strategy to confront the process of redemocratization. A moratorium on major operations was expected until a unitary consensus had been reached. In this context of reflection, the 'bringing to justice' proved to be a lack of prudence by those elements desirous of forcing the organization to maintain a military line without deviations" (237).

6. *El Rodriguista,* 19.

7. Beyond the spectacular nature of the event, the sympathy with which the news was received can also be explained by the fact that (1) for many, the "flight of justice" that liberated those who had struggled against the military dictatorship accomplished a function of symbolic compensation while making amends for a double injustice, that of the imprisonment of the heroes of the antidictatorial struggle, and of not sanctioning the cases of violation of human rights by the representatives of the dictatorship; and (2) it was an extremely "clean" operation that was executed without violence so as not to cause deaths or injuries.

8. Alejandro Foxley, in *El Mercurio,* December 31, 1996.

9. "The absence of exterior negation deprives the internal order of much of its brilliance. The signs of imperfection of this order stand out with greater force if no symbolic enemy covers them up." Harry Pross, *Estructura simbólica del poder* (Barcelona: Editorial Gustavo Gili, 1980), 87.

10. Jean Baudrillard, *La transparencia del mal* (Barcelona: Editorial Anagrama, 1991), 115. Close to this quote by Baudrillard is the phrase that figures on the back cover of the book *El gran rescate,* written by one of the fugitives, saying that "the event shook the country, demonstrating, among other things, that under the apparent post-Pinochet calm, forces existed that boiled over from deep within." Ricardo Palma Salamanca, *El gran rescate* (Santiago: Lom, 1997).

11. Among other readings about the symbolic nature of terrorism, I refer the reader to Baudrillard, *La transparencia del mal,* in particular to the chapter "The Mirror of Terrorism."

12. José Antonio Viera-Gallo, "El terrorismo en Chile," *La Segunda* (Santiago), December 31, 1996, 13.

13. "It was incredible, like in the movies," or indeed "it was such an exceptional thing that in a certain way it gives prestige to the cleverness of the Chilean to do things

with a cinematic flair," are two among many of the phrases taken up in the press that commented on the escape, qualifying it as "spectacular."

14. Michel Foucault, *Discipline and Punish* (New York: Pantheon Books, 1977), 171.

15. *El Rodriguista*, 11.

16. "We decided on an aerial route, especially when there was a proven vulnerability in the system's control and defense of the country, which had already been mocked though a simple operation of army intelligence with the transfer of Manuel Contreras in an official helicopter before the presence and anticipation of hundreds of journalists and government authorities" (ibid., 8).

17. *La Segunda,* December 31, 1996, 3.

18. While telling of the preparation for the escape, part of R. Palma's book comments on how the plan was going to contradict the expectations of the guards: "the hypothesis that they maintain is that from here everyone has to escape in an old-fashioned way, no matter what, by blowing up bars and leaving corpses strewn all around, and whoever can escape, escapes." An additional allusion is made to the fact that, according to the government, the front would not have been "in the position to undertake something successful, but instead only something desperate. . . . Therefore, the hypothesis of the old-fashioned escape becomes more feasible for them" (Palma Salamanca, *El gran rescate,* 46–47).

19. "In spite of the whole campaign against the so-called 'terrorists,' people did not condemn the event. In spite of all the efforts to give it 'seriousness,' people saw it good-naturedly, laughed about the situation and applauded," states Rodrigo Roco in *El Rodriguista,* 125.

20. M. Bakhtin states: "*Seriousness* is official and authoritarian, and is associated with violence, with prohibitions and restrictions. Seriousness instills fear and intimidation. . . . Laughter, on the other hand, implies overcoming fear. It imposes no prohibitions. The language of laughter is never employed by violence or authority." Mikhail Bakhtin, *La cultura popular en la edad media y en el renacimiento: El contexto de Francois Rabelais* (Madrid: Alianza, 1990), 85–86.

21. *El Rodriguista,* 3.

22. These are the expressions cited from *El gran rescate.*

23. Thus states the *Carta Abierta,* published in *El Rodriguista,* signed by Pablo-Mauricio-Ricardo-Patricio.

24. "That was how the Maximum Security Prison was built. . . . The presence of technology for good performance was an additional element that was not lacking. Cameras everywhere, eavesdropping microphones and a hundred more nasty things that made it efficient and feared. Its example was a model to spread over all terrains, swallowing up the miserable" (*El gran rescate,* 49).

25. This is the sense that M. de Certeau gives the word "symbolic." Michel de Certeau, *The Capture of Speech, and Other Political Writings* (Minneapolis: University of Minnesota Press, 1997), 5.

26. Roco, in *El Rodriguista,* 24.

27. De Certeau, *The Capture of Speech*, 8.

28. *El Rodriguista*, 25.

29. *El gran rescate*, 141.

30. The message sent by the "Commander Salvador," which was read on the day the book was launched, insists that the presentation wishes not only to demonstrate that "the Manuel Rodríguez Patriotic Front lives" but also to represent "a new style of presenting things." *La Segunda*, December 31, 1997.

31. *La Segunda*, March 26, 1997, 4.

32. In the inset of *La Segunda* on March 26, there appeared the following editorial headlines and subheadings: "Writers pulverize the literary content of the letter of the assassin of Jaime Guzmán: Three writers (Rosa Cruchaga, José Luis Rosasco, and Enrique Lafourcade) analyzed for *La Segunda* the supposed letter that Ricardo Salamanca, a terrorist who escaped from the Maximum Security Prison, sent to his mother. They discovered in it some literary influences by underlining the following: among others, images about 'life is illusion,' 'the air is ashen,' 'the telluric intensity of my footsteps,' 'your submarine coral eyes,' 'your winged cetacean skin.'"

33. This is the self-definition of hybrid gender that figures on the back cover of *El gran rescate*.

34. Fragment of the letter published in *La Segunda*.

35. The recurrence of the maternal figure ripples through not only the texts but also the situations, tying together "mother" and "writing" in several ways throughout the story and its presentation: the story in the book that deals with the crafting of the basket that—hanging from the helicopter—becomes for the fugitives the instrument of their freedom states that "it started to give life and gestation to the baby that would finally have to transform itself into the maternal womb, taking in the rescued fugitives" (135); and on the day of the presentation of the book, it is the mother who takes the place of the son-writer (clandestine) in order to read the letter sent by him and to autograph the book, after we have been told that "being in prison the author formed with other prisoners a literary magazine called *Incest*" (from the newpaper *La Hora*, December 30, 1997).

36. Palma, *El gran rescate*, 21

37. Ibid., 31.

38. Ibid., 32.

39. Thus spoke Germán Marín, in his text presenting the book *El gran rescate*, at the SECH, adding: "of course, this man, as he warns throughout the book, is not the familiar one dimensional reader, stuck on Marxist-Leninist manuals, nor the type who nourishes himself on Foquista guerrilla, Marcusian or Third-World theories, etc. There are other elements at play here, and from that premise, as it is understood, this book is not destined to shed light on these theories."

40. Although following a diagram very different from that sketched by J. Ramos in his analysis of the trial of Alberto Mendoza, in the case of the Chilean fugitives, a relationship is articulated as well (by way of the letters and the book) between poetry,

illegality, and the search for knowledge: see Julio Ramos, "El proceso de Alberto Mendoza: Poesía y subjetivación," *Revista de Crítica Cultural,* no. 16 (November 1996): 40.

41. "The potential for dialogue and liberation of the metaphoric translation resides in its effectiveness in expanding the spaces of dissent and negotiation, thereby allowing a certain incorporation of the difference in the established order, and, as well, a more attenuated presence for the control and normalization mechanisms. . . . The displacement effect produced through the metaphoric substitutions opens the possibility of dissent and transformation of the existing meanings from inside the system." Benjamín Arditi, *Conceptos, ensayos sobre teoría política, democracia y filosofía* (Asunción: CDE/RP Ediciones, 1991), 187.

42. R. Palma states: "Is not art just this? Art not as a simple technique but instead an impertinent form of rebellion faced with what seems already given, already determined by others. In our case it is the same, our art also springs from boredom and the unbearable nature of what lies before us. A revolution is also this, or the attempt to do this" (22).

12. For Love of Art

1. F. Guattari distinguishes between "'the struggles of interest': the economic struggles, the social struggles, the union struggles in the classical sense," and "the struggles of desire" as "struggles relative to freedoms" that go through diverse questionings of daily life and pertain to what is called "molecular revolution," which exhibits an intensification of multiple vectors of subjective mutation. Félix Guattari, *Cartografías del deseo* (Santiago: Francisco Zegers Editor, 1989), 48.

2. According to B. Sarlo, it would be a matter not only of questioning the dominant commercialization of cultural production but also, more tactically, and in localized fashion, of "attending to what is less visible, less audible: discourses and practices that, through the fissures, already escape from the determinations of the market, or from its habitual circuits. But also it is a question of differentiating what, in the market, works against its rules, asks unpredictable questions, imagines new models of response." Beatriz Sarlo, "Una mirada política: Defensa del partidismo en el arte," *Punto de Vista,* no. 27 (August 1986): 3.

3. Diamela Eltit and Paz Errázuriz, *El infarto del alma* (Santiago: Francisco Zegers Editor), 1994.

4. J. Ramos speaks of these operations of "spending and of excess . . . that operate on the flip side of instrumental logic and of the economics of accumulation . . . as an alternative practice of exchanges" that go through "a logic of supplementarity, something that searches within itself to fill a lack, that therefore implies a very basic economic form, which, without a doubt, goes against the grain of neoliberal consumption and speculation." Julio Ramos, "Dispositivos del amor y la locura" (manuscript).

5. Ibid.

6. "Although I don't move, I don't travel, I make, like everyone, my immobile

trips that I can only measure with my emotions, expressing them in the most oblique and deviant manner of my writings." Gilles Deleuze, *Conversaciones* (Valencia: Pre-Textos, 1996), 21.

7. In "Diario de viaje," one of the texts of *El infarto del alma,* D. Eltit writes: "Now we journey with Paz Errázuriz toward the psychiatric hospital of the town of Putaendo, a hospital built in the forties to help those sick from tuberculosis and that, after the development of the widely available preventative vaccine, is converted into a mental hospital receiving patients from different psychiatric centers of the country. These are the overly sick, in their majority indigent, some of them without formal identification papers, cataloged as N. N."

8. Ibid.

9. Ibid.

10. Speaking of the black margin that marks each of P. Errázuriz's photos printed in the book, S. Biancha states: "This black line also establishes margins and could appear as a border with which those in power institute differences, like the separation that society erects between the 'sane' and the 'sick,' between the rich and the poor, between us and *the others*." Soledad Bianchi, *¿La insoportable levedad? (Imágenes y textos, postdictadura y modernidad en Chile)*, Working Document of the Centro de Investigaciones Sociales, no. 21 (Santiago: Universidad Arcis, 1997), 41.

11. This is how Willy Thayer reflects on the symbolic nature of the family album in "Pathética de la reunión familiar," *Piel de Leopardo* (Santiago), no. 5 (October 1994): 9.

12. Sandra Lorenzano, "Cicatrices de la fuga," *Debate Feminista* (Mexico), no. 13 (April 1996): 227.

13. Gilles Deleuze and Félix Guattari, "Año cero-rostridad," in *Mil mesetas: Capitalismo y esquizofrenia* (Valencia: Pre-Textos, 1996), 192.

14. S. Lorenzano says: "in order to speak of a world of exasperated subjectivity like that of madness, the text is constructed also with voices in the first person" (233).

15. Eltit, *Infarto del alma.*

16. According to Julia Kristeva: "the work's imaginary is the most extraordinary and disturbing copy of the mother-son dependency. Its substitution and its displacement toward a limit are fascinating because of its inhumanity. . . . The work of art cuts off natural filiation; it is parricide and matricide, proudly solitary. But look behind the scenes, as the analyst does: you will encounter a dependency, a secret mother over which sublimation is constructed." Julia Kristeva, "Sobre el amor: Conversación con Julia Kristeva," interview by Francoise Collin, *Debate Feminista* (Mexico), no. 4 (1991): 154.

17. "El otro, mi otro," in *El infarto del alma.*

18. S. Lorenzano proposes, as a means of organizing the reading of *El infarto del alma,* two lines that interweave and are in dialogue: "starting from the nucleus of love-desire there is a first line that seeks to textualize the internal, intimate experience, of this state of lovesick madness, playing at speaking from within the psychotic discourse; it is made up of the fragments that are entitled *El Infarto del alma* (that are a hodgepodge discourse about desire, written by a woman distanced from, or perhaps

abandoned by, her lover) and the disturbing paragraphs called in Lacanian fashion 'The Lack,' in which desire is unsatisfied hunger. . . . . The second line that organizes the book explores the world of the lovers from a gaze that is situated at the limits; exterior, but not alien, to this madness that inhabits Putaendo, conscious of the fragility of its supposed equilibrium" (Lorenzano, "Cicatrices de la fuga," 234).

19. Roland Barthes, *A Lover's Discourse: Fragments* (New York: Hill and Wang, 1978), 120.

20. States Luce Irigaray: "Each sex is related to madness. All desire is related to madness. But, apparently, one type of desire has raised itself to the level of wisdom, measure and truth, leaving to the other sex the burden of a madness that it itself did not want to see or endure. This relation of desire with madness has a position of privilege in the relationship with the mother, and is true as much for men as it is for women. But, too often, men abdicate it and unload it on women." Luce Irigaray, "El cuerpo a cuerpo con la madre," *Cuadernos Inacabados* (Barcelona), no. 5 (1985): 6.

21. "Diario de viaje," in *El infarto del alma.*

22. States D. Eltit in her "Diario de viaje": "I am witness to a moving photographic session when Paz Errázuriz, with extreme delicacy, goes from group to group, responds to the most diverse demands, permits the flow of the multiple unforeseen poses, as if she had been contracted for a wedding in which all the guests were best men or the newlyweds, or the child protagonist of a popular baptism. Paz Errázuriz converts her eye into a gift for the psychiatric inmates. She gives them her photographic look, the surety of her images. When she captures their poses, she confirms the relevance of their figures; when she smiles at them, she recognizes in them all that is exalted in their corporeal conduct. When she bends her body, searching for an angle, she gives them all her professionalism."

23. I employ this term in the sense that is given to it by Deleuze and Guattari: "a minor literature is not that of a minor language, but instead that of a minority population in a major language. Anyhow its primary character is that the language is affected by a strong coefficient of deterritorialization. . . . The secondary character of the minor literatures is that everything in them is political. . . . The third character is that everything achieves a collective value. . . . Literature is what produces an active solidarity, in spite of skepticism; and if the writer is on the margins of his fragile community, this situation places him even more in the condition to express another potential community, to force the means of another conscience and of another sensibility," Gilles Deleuze and Félix Guattari, *Kafka: Pour une littérature mineure* (Paris: Les Editions de Minuit, 1975), 29. J. C. Lértora selects the keyword "minor literature" to analyze the literary work of D. Eltit in "Diamela Eltit: Hacia una poética de literatura menor," in *Una poética de literatura menor: La narrativa de Diamela Eltit,* ed. Juan Carlos Lértora (Santiago: Editorial Cuarto Propio, 1993).

24. This is the way that I. Avelar interprets the narrative gesture of Eltit in the postdictatorial horizon. See Idelber Avelar, "Alegoría y postdictatura: Notas sobre la memoria del mercado," *Revista de Crítica Cultural,* no. 14 (June 1997): 25.

25. Alberto Moreiras, "Postdictatura y reforma del pensamiento," *Revista de Crítica Cultural,* no. 14 (June 1997): 25.

26. As stated by P. Oyarzún, it could be, in any case, that "to say 'it doesn't appear so to me' or 'I don't wish to see it that way' or other similar things" would be "an inscription of the political and an inscription of the subject in politics." P. Oyarzún insists in affirming, in the "Conversación" that follows the text by Willy Thayer in *La crisis no moderna de la universidad moderna*: "it appears to me that effectively it is like this, that desire, spirit, and disposition have to do essentially with the political. Nietzsche uncovered this in the sense that the political has to do with affective states and not simply with the ideological principles or the organic interests that determine them" (227).

27. I refer the reader to A. Moreiras, "Postdictatura y reforma."

28. Ibid., 33.

29. *El infarto del alma.*

30. Jean Baudrillard, *La transparencia del mal* (Barcelona: Editorial Anagrama, 1991), 138.

31. The "theoretical overconstruction" here would have to do with the act of superimposing and confusing the totality as a figure, with totalization as operation.

32. The slippages between model, totalization, and experience, in the case of the "total system" of the market and of its apparatus, justify the following commentary by Fredric Jameson: "there is a *difference* between the concept and the thing, between the global and the abstract model and our own individual social experience, from which it is meant to afford some explanatory distance but which it is scarcely designated to 'replace.'" It would be these breaches between model and practice that allow the deployment of heterogeneous forces that contradict, in each circumstance and according to their play of contradictions, the hegemonic project. Frederic Jameson, *Postmodernism, or The Cultural Logic of Late Capitalism* (Durham, N.C.: Duke University Press, 1991), 406.

33. While referring to the relation between "abstract machine" and "concrete procurements," G. Deleuze insists that "there is no diagram that does not imply, aside from the points that connect, points relatively free or liberated, points of creativity, of mutation, of resistance" through which to trace the lines of flight that impede the system from being homogeneous. Gilles Deleuze, *Foucault* (Mexico: Paidos, 1987), 70.

Select Bibliography

Bengoa, José. *La comunidad perdida*. Santiago: Ediciones Sur, 1996.

Bianchi, Soledad. *¿La insoportable levedad? (Imágenes y textos, postdictadura y modernidad en Chile)*. Documento de Trabajo del Centro de Investigaciones Sociales, no. 21. Santiago: Universidad Arcis, 1997.

Bravo, Germán. *Cuatro ensayos y un poema*. Santiago: Intemperie Ediciones, 1996.

Brito, Eugenia, Riet Delsing, Alejandra Farías, and Olga Grau. *Discurso, género, y poder: Discursos públicos; Chile, 1978–1993*. Santiago: Ediciones Arcis/Lom, 1997.

Brunner, José Joaquín. *Bienvenidos a la modernidad*. Santiago: Planeta, 1994.

———. *Cartografías de la modernidad*. Santiago: Dolmen, 1993.

Cánovas, Rodrigo. *Novela chilena: Nuevas generaciones*. Santiago: Editorial Universidad Católica de Chile, 1997.

De La Parra, Marco Antonio. *La mala memoria: Historia personal de Chile contemporáneo*. Santiago: Planeta, 1997.

División de Cultura–Ministerio de Educación. *Utopías(s)*. Santiago, 1993.

Epple, Juan Armando. *El arte de recordar*. Santiago: Mosquito Editores, 1994.

Foxley, Ana María, and Eugenio Tironi, eds. *La cultura chilena en Transición, 1990–1994*. Santiago: Secretaría Comunicación y Cultura–Ministerio Secretaría General del Gobierno, 1994.

Garretón, Manuel Antonio. *Hacia una nueva era política: Estudio sobre las democratizaciones*. Santiago: Fondo de Cultura Económica, 1995.

———. *La faz sumergida del iceberg: Estudios sobre la transformación cultural*. Santiago: Cesoc/Lom, 1993.

Garretón, M. A., S. Sosnowski, and B. Subercaseaux, eds. *Cultura, autoritarismo, y redemocratización en Chile*. Santiago: Fondo de Cultura Económica, 1993.

Hopenhayn, Martín. *Ni apocalípticos ni integrados.* Santiago: Fondo de Cultura Económica, 1994.

Jocelyn-Holt, Alfredo. *El peso de la noche: Nuestra frágil fortaleza histórica.* Santiago, Ariel, 1997.

Lechner, Norbert. *Los patios interiores de la democracia: Política y subjetividad.* Santiago: Fondo de Cultura Económica, 1988.

Lizama, Jaime. *Los nuevos espacios de la política.* Santiago: Documentas / Estudios, 1991.

Montecino, Sonia. *Madres y huachos: Alegorías del mestizaje chileno.* Santiago: Editorial Cuarto Propio / Cedem, 1993.

Moulian, Tomás. *Chile actual: Anatomía de un mito.* Santiago: Ediciones Lom / Arcis, 1997.

Parrini, Vicente, ed. *Matar al Minotauro: Chile, ¿crisis moral o moral en crisis?* Santiago: Planeta, 1993.

Richard, Nelly. *La insubordinación de los signos (cambio politico, transformaciones culturales y poéticas de la crisis).* Santiago: Editorial Cuarto Propio, 1994.

Ruiz, Carlos. *Seis ensayos sobre teoría de la democracia.* Santiago: Editorial Andrés Bello, 1993.

Subercaseaux, Bernardo. *Chile, ¿un país moderno?* Santiago: Ediciones B, 1996.

Thayer, Willy. *La crisis no moderna de la universidad moderna (epílogo del conflicto de las facultades).* Santiago: Editorial Cuarto Propio, 1996.

Valdés, Adriana. *Composición de lugar: Escritos sobre cultura.* Santiago: Editorial Universitaria, 1995.

Nelly Richard is a critic, essayist, and author of several books on aesthetics and culture, including *Márgenes e instituciones*, *Masculino/femenino*, and *La insubordinación de los signos*. Her work has been collected in various periodicals and anthologies, signaling her as one of the outstanding figures of Latin American cultural criticism. Since 1990 she has directed *Revista de Crítica Cultural*, an important venue for reflection and intellectual debate, and she is the director of the cultural criticism program and of the Rockefeller Foundation program on postdictatorship and democratic transition at Universidad Arcis in Santiago de Chile.

Alan West-Durán is a poet, translator, and professor of modern languages at Northeastern University. He also translated Alejo Carpentier's *Music in Cuba* (Minnesota, 2001).

Theodore Quester is a professional translator based in Texas.

Jean Franco is professor emerita of English and comparative literature at Columbia University.